D1295432

GREAT
SCIEN
TISTS

Astronomers and
Cosmologists

Cavendish
Square

New York

Published in 2014 by Cavendish Square Publishing, LLC
303 Park Avenue South, Suite 1247, New York, NY 10010

CPSIA Compliance Information: Batch #WW14CSQ

All websites were available and accurate when this book was sent to press.

Library of Congress Cataloging-in-Publication Data
King, Firman D.
Astronomers and cosmologists / by Firman D. King, et. al.
p. cm. — (Great scientists)
Includes index.
ISBN 978-1-62712-548-2 (hardcover) ISBN 978-1-62712-549-9 (paperback) ISBN 978-1-62712-550-5 (ebook)
1. Astronomers — Biography — Juvenile literature. 2. Physicists — Biography — Juvenile literature. 3. Astronomy — Juvenile literature. 4. Cosmology — Juvenile literature.I. Title.
QB35.K55 2014
520—d23

Editorial Director: Dean Miller; Editorial Assistant: Amy Hayes; Art Director: Jeffrey Talbot; Designer: Joseph Macri; Production Manager: Jennifer Ryder-Talbot; Production Editor: Andrew Coddington; Photo Researchers: Laurie Platt Winfrey, Carousel Research, Inc.; Joseph Marci; Amy Greenan; and Julie Alissi, J8 Media

Printed in the United States of America

Contents

Introduction   5

Alhazen   8
Spherical and Parabolic Mirrors   9

Anaximander   11
The Origin of the Universe   12

Aristarchus of Samos   13
The Size of and Distance to the Sun   14

Walter Baade   15
Stellar Populations   16

Edward Emerson Barnard   18
Interstellar Matter   19

Dame Jocelyn Bell Burnell   20
Pulsars   22

Friedrich Wilhelm Bessel   23
The Distance to 61 Cygni   25

Tycho Brahe   26
Precise Measurements in Astronomy   27

E. Margaret Burbidge   28
Nucleosynthesis   30

Annie Jump Cannon   32
Spectral Classification of Stars   33

George R. Carruthers   34
Far-Ultraviolet Astronomy
from Space   36

Gian Domenico Cassini   37
The Scale of the Solar System   39

Subrahmanyan Chandrasekhar   41
The Chandrasekhar Limit   42

Nicolaus Copernicus   44
The Heliocentric System   46

Sir Arthur Stanley Eddington   47
Verifying the General
Theory of Relativity   49
The Mass-Luminosity Relation   50

Sandra Faber   51
Dark Matter   52

Hippolyte Fizeau   54
Measuring the Speed of Light   55

Léon Foucault   57
The Rotation of the Earth   59

Herbert Friedman   61
Rocket Astronomy   62

Galileo   64
Principles on the Mechanics
of Motion   66
Galileo's Use of the Telescope   67

Margaret Geller   69
The Large-Scale Distribution
of Galaxies   70

Alan H. Guth   72
The Inflationary Universe   73

George Ellery Hale   75
Magnetic Fields in the Sun   76

Edmond Halley   78
Solving the Mystery of Comets   79

Stephen Hawking   80
Evolution of the Universe   82
Black Holes   83

Sir John Herschel   84
Mapping the Stars   86

Sir William Herschel   87
Sidereal Astronomy   88

Ejnar Hertzsprung   90
The Measurement of
Cosmic Distances   92

Antony Hewish   93
What Causes a Pulsar?   95

Sir Fred Hoyle   96
Steady State Cosmology   98
Nucleosynthesis of Elements   99

Edwin Powell Hubble   100
Hubble's Law of the
Expanding Universe   102

Sir William Huggins   104
Spectrum Analysis of Stars   105

Christiaan Huygens   106
The Principle of Secondary
Wave Fronts   108

Jacobus Cornelius Kapteyn   109
Spectrum Analysis of Stars   111

Johannes Kepler   112
Kepler's Three Laws of
Planetary Motion   114

Gerard Peter Kuiper   115
The Origin of the Solar System   117

Henrietta Swan Leavitt   118
The Period-Luminosity Law
for Cepheid Variable Stars   119

Georges Lemaître   120
The Primeval Atom   122

Jane X. Luu   123
The Kuiper Belt   125

Antonia Maury   127
Classification of Stellar Spectra   128

Albert Abraham Michelson   129
The Michelson-Morley Experiment   131

Maria Mitchell   133
What the Stars Reveal   134

Wilhelm Olbers   136
Comets and a Paradox   137

Jan Hendrik Oort   138
The Structure of the Galaxy   139

Cecilia Payne-Gaposchkin   141
The Composition of Stars   142

Ptolemy   143
Ptolemy's Epicycles: A Model
for Planetary Motion   145

Vera C. Rubin   146
Dark Matter   148

Henry Norris Russell   149
The Hertzsprung-Russell Diagram   151

Carl Sagan   152
Exploration of the Planet Mars   154

Allan Rex Sandage   155
The Big Bang   157

Maarten Schmidt   159
Quasars   160

Harlow Shapley   161
Finding the Size of the Milky Way   162

Vesto Melvin Slipher   164
The Doppler Shift of the
Andromeda Nebula   165

Fritz Zwicky   166
Neutron Stars and Dark Matter   168

Glossary   169

Index   171

An Introduction to Great Scientists: *Astronomers and Cosmologists*

Science offers an ever-expanding and seemingly ever-changing array of facts and theories to explain the workings of life and the universe. Behind its doors, we can explore fascinating worlds ranging from the tiny—the spiral ladder of DNA in every human cell and the particle zoo of quarks and mesons in every atom—to the unimaginably vast—the gradual, often catastrophic shifting of continents over the globe and the immense gravitational fields surrounding black holes in space. Unfortunately, the doors of science often remain shut to students and the general public, who worry they are unable to understand the work done in these technical fields.

Great Scientists seeks to serve as a key. Its goal is to introduce many notable people and concepts, sparking interest and providing jumping-off points for gaining further knowledge. To this end, these books offer a select survey of scientists and their accomplishments across disciplines, throughout history, and around the world. The life stories of these individuals and the descriptions of their research and advancements will prove both informational and inspirational to budding scientists and to all those with inquisitive minds. For some, learning the paths of these scientists' lives will enable ambitious young students to follow in their footsteps.

Science disciplines are foundational by nature. The work done by the earliest pioneers in a specific field often leads to inspire and inform the next generation of minds, who take the findings and discoveries of their heroes and mentors and further the body of knowledge in a certain area. This progress of scientific inquiry and discovery increases the world's understanding of existing theories and tenants, blazing trails into new directions of study. Perhaps by reading this work, the next great astronomers or cosmologists will discover their spark of creativity. Whether interested in the theoretical sciences, mathematics, or the applied fields of engineering and invention, students will find these life stories proof that individuals from almost any background can be responsible for key discoveries and paradigm-shifting thoughts and experiments.

The Organization of *Astronomers and Cosmologists*

This volume profiles more than fifty representative figures in the history of astronomy and cosmology. Entries are usually 800 to 1,700 words in length, with some longer essays covering individuals who made numerous significant contributions to the development of the fields, such as Galileo, George Carruthers, Stephen Hawking, Sir Fred Hoyle, Johannes Kepler, Maria Mitchell, and Carl Sagan. In addition to celebrating famous names that made great strides in scientific inquiry and paved the way for others to follow, the book gives credit to individuals and groups who have gone largely unrecognized, such as women and minorities, as well as many contemporary scientists who are making the newest advances.

The profile of each scientist begins with a list of the scientist's areas of achievement, as many of these individuals had impact in more than one discipline. The first person covered in this book, Alhazan, made significant contributions in the fields of mathematics and physics, as well as astronomy and cosmology. Many more like him had such an influence in multiple sciences that inclusion in several different books would be logical, but selections were made to place each scientist in the field most emblematic of his or her work. After a brief statement of that individual's contribution to science, a timeline covers major life events, including birth and death dates, major awards and honors, and milestones in the scientist's education, research, employment, and private life. The entry then details the struggles and triumphs that characterize the lives of many who pursue knowledge as a career.

The Science Behind the Scientist

An important goal of the Great Scientist series is to expand the reader's understanding of science, not just cover the biographical data of specific scientists. To that end, each profile contains one or more sidebars within the article that provide a simple snapshot introduction to a key topic within the featured scientist's achievements, including theories, research, inventions, or discoveries.

While the scientific subjects are not covered in painstaking detail, there is enough information for readers to gain a working knowledge of topics important to the fields of astronomy and cosmology.

Illustrating the Science

Several of the sidebars in this book are accompanied by diagrams that help to reinforce the information covered through graphical representation of complex theories and discoveries. In addition, wherever possible, a photograph, painting, or sculpture of the profiled scientist is provided, although there are no likenesses for some of history's earliest contributors.

Additional Resources

Each profile ends with a two-part bibliography, pointing readers to some of the most significant books and papers written by the particular scientist, as well as other content written about the subject and field of study. It's worth noting that these bibliographies are selected works and by no means a complete listing—many of these scientists have contributed dozens of works. The book concludes with a glossary that offers clear definitions of selected terms and concepts, and a comprehensive index that allows readers to locate information about the people, concepts, organizations, and topics covered throughout the book.

Skill Development for Students

Great Scientists: Astronomers and Cosmologists can serve as a basic biographical text on a specific individual or as a source of enrichment for students looking to know more about an entire scientific field. It's an excellent reference for reading and writing assignments, and it can be a foundational beginning of major research and term papers. The bibliographies at the end of the profiles and sidebars are invaluable for students looking to learn more and delve deeper yet into these fascinating subjects.

Alhazen

Disciplines: Astronomy, cosmology, mathematics, medicine, and physics

Contribution: Alhazen revolutionized the study of optics with important new ideas and experiments on reflection and refraction, leading to later advancement of the telescope.

965	Born in Basra (now Al Basra, Iraq)
c. 1000	Travels to Cairo, Egypt, to the court of the Fatimid caliph al-Hakim
c. 1005	Forced to feign madness in order to escape the wrath of the caliph
1021	Emerges from obscurity upon the death of al-Hakim
1039	Dies in Cairo
1270	His major work, *Kitab al-Manazir* (Optics), is translated into Latin as *Opticae Thesaurus Alhazeni libri vii* and becomes an important influence on European thought

An image from Alhazen's work *Thesaurus opticus.*

Early Life

Abu Ali al-Hasan ibn al-Haytham, known in the West as Alhazen (pronounced "al-ha-ZEHN"), was born in Basra, in what is now Iraq, in 965. Basra was a major center for the brilliantly thriving Islamic intellectual culture of the time and Alhazen was educated there. He soon acquired a reputation as a mathematician and engineer.

A Colorful Career

Having boasted that he could design a scheme to control the flooding of the Nile, Alhazen was summoned to Cairo by the caliph al-Hakim. The caliph received him graciously and treated him generously. When Alhazen realized that his flood control plan was impracticable and that al-Hakim was a tyrant and perhaps insane, he found it necessary to feign madness himself in order to avoid the caliph's wrath. Maintaining this pretense, he sank into deliberate obscurity for a number of years.

During these years he continued his research supporting himself by jobs, such as copying mathematical manuscripts. When al-Hakim died in 1021, Alhazen was able to drop his counterfeit madness. He lived quietly in Cairo until his death in 1039.

A Great Scholar

Despite the perils of his later career, Alhazen maintained a large and diverse scholarly output. He is known to have produced more than 200 works on subjects as varied as optics, astronomy, mathematics, mechanics, and medicine, as well as commentaries on classical philosophers.

In astronomy, he proposed a physical mechanism

for the (erroneous) Earth-centered cosmology of Ptolemy. In mathematics, he studied geometry, particularly the conics. In mechanics, his ideas on inertia partially anticipated those of Galileo Galilei by five centuries. In medicine, he wrote about the function and diseases of the eye. The great work for which he is primarily remembered, however, is in optics.

A New Optics

Alhazen was the first important student of optics since the ancient Greeks, and he would be the last for several centuries. Ancient writers such as Euclid, Hero, and Ptolemy described vision in terms of rays from the eye to the object perceived. Alhazen realized that this was backward.

Spherical and Parabolic Mirrors

Mirrors with curved surfaces can be used to bring light rays together at a point, thereby concentrating their energy. Light rays striking the mirror from slightly different directions are brought together (focused) at slightly different points, forming images of extended sources.

The most common mirror shapes used for these purposes are spherical, where the mirror's surface is a part of a sphere, and parabolic, where the surface has the shape of a paraboloid formed by rotating a parabola around its axis. Both cases were studied and described by Alhazen.

It is a property of a spherical mirror that when parallel rays of light are incident on it, they are concentrated on the axis of the mirror. This axis points in the direction from which the rays came and intersects the mirror's surface at the point where the rays strike it perpendicularly. When a source of light is distant—compared to the radius of curvature of the mirror, the distance from the center of the sphere to its surface—the rays arrive at the mirror almost parallel to one another.

Although all rays are concentrated on the axis of a spherical mirror, they are not all concentrated at the same point on the axis. Those rays that strike the surface close to the axis are concentrated at a point that is half the radius of curvature from the surface; this point is called the focus of the mirror. Rays that strike the surface farther from the axis are brought together

farther out along the axis. This inability to form a true focus of all incident rays is called spherical aberration and is an important factor in reflecting telescope design.

Spherical aberration can be minimized by using a mirror that has a diameter much smaller than its radius of curvature—in other words, a mirror that is only slightly curved. In this case, all rays striking the mirror are near the axis (paraxial) to a good approximation and are brought to a good focus.

Alhazen found another solution to this problem. For a parabolic mirror, all rays incident parallel to the axis are brought together at the focus of the parabola. Although aberration again occurs for rays not parallel to the axis, unlike a sphere, a paraboloid does not appear the same from all directions. The optical performance of a parabolic mirror is excellent for many purposes.

It is difficult, however, to form a precise parabolic surface, so most optical instruments built before the 1980s used spherical mirrors. Today, advanced manufacturing techniques have made parabolic mirrors practical even for large astronomical telescopes.

Bibliography

Nussbaum, A. *Geometric Optics: An Introduction.* Reading, Mass.: Addison-Wesley 1968.

Malacara, D. ed. *Geometrical and Instrumental Optics.* Boston: Academic Press, 1988.

Mouroulis, P. *Geometrical Optics and Optical Design.* New York: Oxford University Press, 1996.

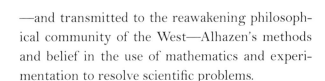

When an object is illuminated, rays are reflected from every point of the object in all directions. Some of these rays enter the eye, which permits vision. He went further with this new idea, producing the text that became the foundation of modern optics.

In contrast to most scholars of his era, Alhazen was an active experimenter. He had a lathe on which he made mirrors and lenses for his experiments and he conducted quantitative experiments on refraction by immersing graduated cylinders in water.

In addition, he applied the methods of geometry to optics, analyzing spherical and parabolic mirrors. By calculation and geometric construction, he was able to discover and prove the important properties of these mirrors, which enable the later development of reflecting telescopes. He worked out approximations for refraction at small angles of incidence (when the rays of light are almost perpendicular to the surface) that are correct and that can be used to understand thin lenses, such as those used in simple telescopes and microscopes. Alhazen also analyzed the optical phenomena of sunrise and sunset.

An Enduring Influence

After Alhazen's death, the study of optics declined in the Islamic world, not to recover for several centuries. His most important work, *Kitab al-Manazir* (Optics), however, proved to be a lasting and critical influence in the revival of science in the West. This text was perhaps the most modern scientific work in terms of method and thought to be published in the Middle Ages. It was translated into Latin in 1270 and in this form became widely known to scholars in Western Europe.

The thirteenth century English scholastic philosopher Roger Bacon incorporated many of Alhazen's ideas into his scientific writings; indeed, many of Alhazen's discoveries are often incorrectly ascribed to Bacon. Bacon also embraced

—and transmitted to the reawakening philosophical community of the West—Alhazen's methods and belief in the use of mathematics and experimentation to resolve scientific problems.

In this way, Alhazen not only left to the world his own substantial discoveries but also sowed one of the most critical seeds of the Renaissance, thus opening the way for modern scientific thought.

Bibliography

By Alhazen
Kitab al-Manazir, tenth or eleventh century (commonly known as *Optics*; Latin trans. as *Opticae Thesaurus Alhazeni libri vii*, 1270, and partial English trans. as *The Optics of Ibn al-Haytham: Books I-III*, on Direct Vision, 1989).
Al-Maqaalah fai Tamaam Kitaab al-Makhrauotaaot, tenth or eleventh century (Completion of the Conics, 1983).
Maqaalah fai Hay'at al-'Aalam, tenth or eleventh century (On the Configuration of the World, 1990).

About Alhazen
Said, H. M. ed. *Ibn al-Haitham: Proceedings of the Celebrations of the Thousandth Anniversary Held Under the Auspices of Hamdard National Foundation, Pakistan*. Karachi, Pakistan: Hamdard Academy, 1970.
Omar S. B. *Ibn al-Haytham's Optics: A Study of the Origins of Experimental Science*. Minneapolis: Bibliotheca Islamica, 1977.
Sabra. A. I. *Optics, Astronomy, and Logic: Studies in Arabic Science and Philosophy*. Brookfield, Vt.: Variorum, 1994.

(Firman D. King)

Anaximander

Disciplines: Astronomy, physics, and science (general)

Contribution: Anaximander was the first Greek to make a world map and a star map.

| c. 610 BC | Born in Miletus, western Asia Minor (now Turkey) |
| c. 547 BC | Dies, probably in Miletus |

Life

Anaximander (pronounced "a-NAK-sih-mandur") was born of Greek heritage in or about the year 610 BC in a place now known as Turkey. Although he is called the first Greek scientist, he is more accurately categorized as a philosopher of nature. His theories on the workings of nature classify him as the second of the philosophers whose ideas propelled and established the culture of Western civilization.

His teacher was a man named Thales, who is universally considered to be the first Greek philosopher of nature.

Only Known Work

The only book that is known to have been written by Anaximander has been given the title *On the Nature of Things*. Throughout this work, he describes the origin and functioning of the natural world, which includes all the celestial spheres.

Anaximander confirms the concept of geocentrism the almost universally held theory of the ancient world. This theory stipulates that Earth is the center of the universe and that the stars, the sun and moon, and the planets revolve around Earth in circular patterns. Anaximander also proposed that Earth is shaped like a cylinder with dimensions in a ratio of 3:1, with the width three times the height.

Mapping the Universe

Mapmaking was an important and daunting task in the ancient world, and Anaximander excelled in this area. In addition to creating a map of the then-known world, he made an even greater contribution to science by devising a star map of the celestial spheres.

As a result, Anaximander is credited with being the originator of the first geometrical model of the universe. He introduced a visual schematic of the universe that featured mathematical proportionality and symmetry which, to this point, had been lacking in previous attempts at this task.

Drawing on his resourcefulness as a skilled mapmaker, Anaximander adapted his mathematical proportions toward determining the hours of the day. He accomplished this by aligning the annual movement of the sun with the pointer on the already established sundial.

Insight into Evolution

Anaximander proposed that the origin of living beings was derived from the sea, arguing that both animal and human life were first contained in moisture.

He postulated a process of separation to explain the existence of distinct entities in their individual structures. From the original, chaotic moisture came the sea, and from the sea came aquatic life, which separated and branched off into life on dry land.

In fact, Anaximander speculated that the first human beings could not have survived as infants by their own power. Rather, he thought that they must have been nurtured from living beings of another kind that were already complete and established.

Bibliography

By Anaximander

On the Nature of Things, c. 6th century BC (not an extant text).

About Anaximander

Kahn, Charles H. *Anaximander and the Origins of Greek Cosmology*. New York: Columbia University Press, 1960.
Seligman, Paul. *The "Apeiron" of Anaximander*. Westport, Conn.: Greenwood Press, 1974.
Guthrie, W. K. C. *A History of Greek Philosophy*. Vol. 1. Cambridge, England: Cambridge University Press, 1962.

(Joseph R. Lafaro)

The Origin of the Universe

The most distinctive feature of Anaximander's worldview is his theory of Apeiron, which is a Greek word that is variously translated as "Boundless," "Limitless," or "Infinite." He maintained that the Boundless is the material source out of which is derived all material, as well as immaterial, reality.

The *Apeiron* is the originating principle that itself is unlimited, yet it is solely responsible for the creation of the universe. Anaximander explains that the *Apeiron* surrounds and directs all things that exist. It is that substratum from which all things, both nonliving and living begin. It is that which sustains all things in their existence, and it is that which endures forever even though all things change and corrupt.

This boundless mass is eternal, in that it never had a beginning, and it is ageless, meaning that it will last forever. Although all other things come to be and pass away, the Apeiron itself remains imperishable and ungenerated. It alone is the underived, material source that provides the vital energy to account for the movement and regularity of nature. It accomplishes this task by a process of separating from itself the forces of hot and cold, dry and moist, from which are derived such qualities as hardness, softness, liquid, and vapor.

Anaximander's theory of *Apeiron* anticipates the modern scientific notions of energy and space. Many modern thinkers have marveled at the insight and wisdom of this great pioneer.

Bibliography

Copleston, Frederick. *A History of Philosophy*. Vol. 1. New York: Image Books, 1960.
Burtt, E. A. *The Metaphysical Foundations of Modern Physical Science*. New York: Harcourt, Brace, 1925.
Butterfield, H. *Origins of Modern Science*. New York: Collier Books, 1962.

Aristarchus of Samos

Discipline: Astronomy and mathematics

Contribution: Aristarchus was the first person to attempt to determine the size of the sun and its distance from Earth and to propose a heliocentric theory of the universe.

c. 310 BC	Born on Samos
c. 280 BC	According to Ptolemy, makes observations of the summer solstice
c. 250 BC	Completes the work known as *On the Sizes and Distances of the Sun and Moon*
c. 250 BC	Proposes the first heliocentric theory of the universe
c. 230 BC	Dies in Alexandria

Life

Very little is known about the life of Aristarchus (pronounced "ar-uh-STAHR-kus"). He was born in about 310 BC, and his native island, Samos, is in the Aegean Sea off the coast of Turkey. He studied with Strato of Lampsacos, probably in Alexandria before going to Athens to head Aristotle's Lyceum.

Although he was known as "the mathematician," Aristarchus clearly had a practical bent. The Roman writer Vitruvius credited him with inventing a type of sundial, and Ptolemy refers to his observations of the summer solstice of 280 BC. He died in Alexandria in about 230 BC.

Calculations Regarding the Sun and Moon

The only surviving work of Aristarchus is the manuscript commonly known as *On the Sizes and Distances of the Sun and Moon* (written c. 250 BC;

English translation, 1913). Reminiscent of an exercise in Euclidean geometry, the work poses the problem of finding the size of and distance to the sun relative to the moon and Earth.

Aristarchus found that the sun is between eighteen and twenty times farther away than the moon and between 7.1666 and 6.333 times bigger than Earth. Although these results are much too low, they were the first hints of the immense size of the universe.

A Heliocentric Universe

Possibly impressed by the great size of the sun, Aristarchus entertained the possibility that Earth might circle the sun, rather than the other way around. It probably made sense to him to assume that the heavenly body that was thought to be the largest in the universe would dominate the motions of the other bodies. In all likelihood, Aristarchus assumed that all the planets circled the sun.

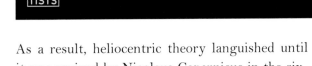

The early Pythagoreans had believed in a similar scheme with ten bodies circling a "central fire" that was definitely not the sun. Thus, the Pythagorean system was not heliocentric.

The heliocentric idea brought ridicule to Aristarchus. The Stoic poet Cleathes charged him with impiety for daring to put in motion "the hearth of the heavens." From a scientific perspective, the daily motions of the sun and other heavenly bodies in a heliocentric system can be explained only by requiring Earth to rotate. At the time, there was no reason to believe in a rotating Earth. Furthermore, any motion of Earth around the sun should produce an apparent change in the position of the stars (parallax), which was not observed.

Aristarchus explained this lack of parallax by assuming that the stars were very far away and, in so doing, he made the universe unacceptably large.

As a result, heliocentric theory languished until it was revived by Nicolaus Copernicus in the sixteenth century and extended by Johannes Kepler and Sir Isaac Newton.

Bibliography

By Aristarchus
On the Sizes and Distances of the Sun and Moon, c. 250 BC (English translation, 1913).

About Aristarchus
"Aristarchus of Samos." *The Dictionary of Scientific Biography*. New York: Charles Scribner's Sons, 1970.

Heath, Sir Thomas. *Aristarchus of Samos*. Oxford, England: Oxford University Press, 1913.

Africa, Thomas W. "Copernicus' Relation to Aristarchus and Pythagoras." *Isis* 52 (1961).

(John A. Cramer)

The Size of and Distance to the Sun

Aristarchus observed that the sun is much farther from Earth than the moon and, consequently, much bigger than Earth.

Aristarchus' *On the Sizes and Distances of the Sun and Moon* begins in accepted mathematical style, listing assumptions. He notes three assumptions: first, that the sun illuminates the moon; second, that Earth's shadow at the moon is twice the diameter of the moon; and, third, that the moon appears half full when the moon-earth-sun angle is 87 degrees. He also tacitly assumes, fourth, that the moon's orbit is a perfect circle around Earth and, fifth, that the sun's rays are parallel at Earth and moon.

From the third and fifth assumptions, Aristarchus calculated that the sun is nineteen times farther from Earth than the moon; the correct figure is more than 400 times. His third assumption is wrong: the angle is not 87 degrees but 89.87 degrees. With the correct value, his method provides reliable results.

Since the moon is the same visual (angular) size as the sun, using the second assumption Aristarchus then calculated that the sun is about seven times bigger than Earth; the correct figure is about 109.

Despite the shortcomings of Aristarchus' results, his work led to important improvements. In the next century, his methods were used and improved by Hipparchus of Rhodes to obtain excellent values of the size and distance of the moon.

Bibliography

Neugebauer, Otto. "Archimedes and Aristarchus." *Isis* 39 (1942).

Dreyer, John L. E. *A History of Planetary Systems from Thales to Kepler*. Cambridge, England: Cambridge University Press, 1953.

Crowe, Michael J. *Theories of the World from Antiquity to the Copernican Revolution*. New York: Dover, 1990.

Walter Baade

Discipline: Astronomy and physics

Contribution: Baade revolutionized stellar astrophysics with his finding that there appear to be two major categories of stars. He was also influential in demonstrating that Earth is located in a spiral galaxy and in measuring the size of the universe.

Mar. 24, 1893	Born in Schröttinghausen, Westphalia, Germany
1919	Earns a Ph.D. from the University of Göttingen
1919	Joins the staff of the University of Hamburg's Bergedorf Observatory
1920	Discovers the asteroid designated 944 Hidalgo
1922	Discovers Comet 1922c (Comet Baade)
1926-1927	Travels to California on a Rockefeller Fellowship
1928	Journeys to the Philippines to witness a solar eclipse
1931	Accepts a staff position at Mount Wilson Observatory in California
1944	Presents his findings of two stellar populations
1948	Discovers the asteroid designated 1566 Icarus
1954	Awarded the Gold Medal of the Royal Astronomical Society
1958	Retires from Mount Wilson Observatory
1959	Returns to the University of Göttingen as Gauss Professor
Jun. 25, 1960	Dies in Bad Salzuflen, Westphalia, Germany

Early Life

Wilhelm Heinrich Walter Baade (pronounced "BAH-duh") was born in 1893 to Konrad and Charlotte Baade in Schröttinghausen, Germany, where his father was the director of schools. Baade's parents planned a career in the clergy for their son, but his interests in school clearly leaned toward mathematics and science, especially astronomy.

In 1913, Baade began studies in science at the University of Göttingen, where he stayed until he received his Ph.D. in astronomy in 1919. He was able to continue his studies through World War I because he was exempted from military service as a result of a birth defect in his hip.

After receiving his Ph.D., Baade worked as an assistant at the Bergedorf Observatory, operated by the University of Hamburg.

Travels Abroad

Baade was awarded a Rockefeller fellowship for the year 1926-1927, which allowed him to travel to California to use the new large telescopes there. His careful and meticulous work impressed the U.S. astronomers. This trip taught Baade that he would need larger telescopes to conduct his research than were available to him in Germany.

Upon his return to Germany, he became good friends with astronomer and optician Bernhard Voldemar Schmidt. Together, they traveled to the Philippines to observe a solar eclipse in 1928. With Baade's encouragement, Schmidt later constructed a new type of telescope that has been an important tool for astronomers.

The California Years

In 1931, Baade accepted a position at the Mount Wilson Observatory in California. Collaborating on work with the Swiss astronomer Fritz Zwicky, Baade coined the term "supernova" to explain exploding stars. He was the first to suggest that neutron stars may be associated with supernovas, and he discovered the neutron star remnant of the supernova that formed the Crab nebula. Zwicky was unable to accept Baade's German heritage after the rise of Nazism in Germany, and so their friendship ended with the advent of World War II.

When the United States entered World War II, Baade was classified as an enemy agent because he was a German citizen. He was required to remain in the immediate area of Mount Wilson for the duration of the war. During this time, Baade discovered that stars can be classified into two different populations.

After the war, Baade turned his attention to galaxies. He was instrumental in showing that the Milky Way is a spiral galaxy. He also revised the scale whereby distances to other galaxies are measured. In 1952, Baade discovered a galaxy that was the optical counterpart to the strange celestial radio signal called Cygnus A.

Upon his retirement in 1958, Baade spent time traveling and giving lectures. He then returned to Germany and died shortly thereafter.

Stellar Populations

Stars can be classified based on their spectral characteristics into two different populations of stars.

During World War II, Los Angeles was under blackout conditions, which permitted Baade to use the equipment at the Mount Wilson Observatory to its fullest extent in order to study the heavens.

A long puzzle for astronomers had been why it was so difficult to photograph the central portions of the Andromeda galaxy and its two satellite galaxies, Messier 32 and NGC205. Ordinary photographic techniques at the time were more sensitive to blue light. Baade tried using a special photographic emulsion that was sensitive to red light, which resolved the images of the core of the Andromeda galaxy and its satellite galaxies.

Baade realized that this discovery meant that not all stars are alike. He called these two types of stars Population I and Population II. The sun is a Population I star. Further analysis indicated that Population II stars do not have as many metals in their spectra as do Population I stars. (To an astronomer, anything other than hydrogen or helium is called a metal.) Astronomers interpreted this information to mean that Population II stars formed at about the time that the galaxy formed and that Population I stars formed as a later generation.

Bibliography

Whitney, Charles A. *The Discovery of Our Galaxy*. New York: Alfred A. Knopf, 1971.

Abell, George O., David Morrison, and Sidney C. Wolff. *Exploration of the Universe*. 6th ed. Philadelphia: W. B. Saunders, 1993.

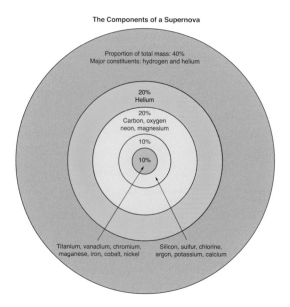

The Components of a Supernova

Proportion of total mass: 40%
Major constituents: hydrogen and helium

20%
Helium

20%
Carbon, oxygen
neon, magnesium

10%

10%

Titanium, vanadium, chromium,
maganese, iron, cobalt, nickel

Silicon, sulfur, chlorine,
argon, potassium, calcium

Baade coined the term "supernova" to describe the stage in a star's life when it suddenly releases large amounts of energy.

Legacy

Baade had an extraordinary impact on astronomy. Most of his work was unpublished, but almost everything that was published had far-reaching consequences. Nevertheless, he was given few honors during his lifetime. He did receive awards from the Royal Astronomical Society and the Astronomical Society of the Pacific, both shortly before his retirement.

Bibliography

By Baade

"On Supernovae," *Proceedings of the National Academy of Sciences*, 1934 (with Fritz Zwicky).
"The New Stellar Systems in Sculptor and Fornax," *Publications of the Astronomical Society of the Pacific*, 1938 (with Edwin Powell Hubble).
"Photographic Light Curves of the Two Supernovae in IC4182 and NGC1003," *Astrophysical Journal*, 1938 (with Zwicky).
"The Crab Nebula," *Astrophysical Journal*, 1942
"Identification of the Radio Sources in Cassiopeia, Cygnus A, and Puppis A," *Astrophysical Journal*, 1954 (with Rudolph Minkowski).
"On the Identification of Radio Sources," *Astrophysical Journal*, 1954 (with Minkowski).
"Polarization in the Jet of Messier 87," *Astrophysical Journal*, 1956.

About Baade

Gingerich, Owen. *The Great Copernicus Chase and Other Adventures in Astronomical History.* Cambridge, Mass.: Sky Publishing, 1992.
North, John. *The Norton History of Astronomy and Cosmology.* New York: W. W. Norton, 1995.
Richardson, Robert S. *The Star Lovers.* New York: Macmillan, 1967.

(Raymond D. Benge, Jr.)

Edward Emerson Barnard

Discipline: Astronomy
Contribution: Barnard discovered numerous comets and the fifth satellite of Jupiter. His observations and photographs helped prove that space includes vast clouds of dust.

Dec. 16, 1857	Born in Nashville, Tennessee
1866	Becomes a photographer's assistant
1881	Discovers his first comet
1883-1887	Appointed an astronomer at Vanderbilt University
1888	Joins the staff at Lick Observatory in California
1889	Begins to photograph the Milky Way
1892	Wins the gold medal of the French Académie des Sciences
1892	Discovers Amalthea, the fifth satellite of Jupiter
1894	Makes detailed observations of the planet Mars
1895	Joins the staff of the University of Chicago and Yerkes Observatory in Wisconsin
1897	Wins the Gold Medal of the Royal Astronomical Society
1898	Named vice president of the American Association for the Advancement of Science
1913-1916	Concludes that "dark nebulas" are interstellar clouds
1916	Discovers the star with the fastest known apparent motion
Feb. 6, 1923	Dies in Williams Bay, Wisconsin

Early Life

Edward Emerson Barnard was born in Nashville in 1857 after his father's death, and his impoverished mother struggled to support her two sons through the Civil War. Edward attended school for only two months, but he learned astronomy from a popular book. In 1866 he became a photographer's assistant, a job that acquainted him with film and lenses.

In 1877, young Barnard met the famed astronomer Simon Newcomb, who was visiting Nashville. Newcomb brusquely told the boy that he must learn mathematics to become an astronomer, unless he intended to discover comets.

Astronomical Discoveries

In 1881, using a 5-inch telescope, Barnard found a new comet and received a $200 award. In 1883, he was appointed astronomer at the Vanderbilt

Throughout his career, Holmes would discover more than a dozen comets.

University observatory in Nashville, where he found seven more comets by 1887. During his life, he would discover at least sixteen comets.

Barnard joined the staff of the new Lick Observatory near San Jose, California, in 1888.There, he discovered the fifth satellite of Jupiter, later named Amalthea. Barnard used a telescopic camera to photograph the rich details of the Milky Way, including its "dark nebulas." Initially he suspected that these were "holes" or areas without stars.

The planet Mars was in the news at that time. The Boston astronomer Percival Lowell incorrectly claimed to see long, thin lines on its surface that he believed were canals built by Martians. In 1894 Barnard made detailed observations of Mars through the 36-inch Lick telescope and saw no such lines.

Yerkes Observatory

In 1895 Barnard accepted a post as an astronomer at the University of Chicago, which was erecting Yerkes Observatory in Wisconsin. He would spend the rest of his career at Yerkes. Between 1913 and 1916 he gradually changed his mind about the dark nebulas. He decided that they were not holes after all. Rather, they were clouds of matter obscuring distant stars. In 1916 Barnard discovered a star crossing the sky at ten seconds of arc per year, the fastest "proper motion" known at that time. It was later named Barnard's Star.

Honors

In 1897 Barnard won the prestigious gold medal of the Royal Astronomical Society. One year later in 1898, he served as vice president of the American Association for the Advancement of

Interstellar Matter

Barnard's observations and photographs of the Milky Way helped to persuade astronomers that the vast spaces between stars are not entirely empty and that huge clouds of matter exist between them.

When Barnard began his observations in the 1890s, astronomers were puzzled by nebulas, fuzzy patches of light in the sky. Some thought they were distant galaxies of stars. Others suggested that they were clouds of matter condensing into new planetary systems.

Barnard photographed the Milky Way in great detail and found it to be covered with dark blotches. At first, he assumed that the blotches were "holes" in space where stars were absent. In the summer of 1913 however, as he was photographing the southern Milky Way, small cumulus clouds passed over the galaxy. Against the brilliant band of stars, the clouds appeared ink-black. In fact, they resembled the dark markings that he had photographed previously. He concluded that the galactic blotches are

huge interstellar clouds that appear dark against the Milky Way. It was subsequently determined that some nebulas are, indeed, independent galaxies of stars far from the Milky Way. Others, however, including the dark blotches on the Milky Way, are vast clouds of dust, as other astronomers established after Barnard's death. Later theorists would explain how these enormous dust clouds condense under gravitational pull into new stars and planetary systems.

Bibliography

Fisher, David E. *The Birth of the Earth*. New York: Columbia University Press, 1987.

Cohen, Martin. *In Darkness Born: The Story of Star Formation*. Cambridge, England: Cambridge University Press, 1988.

Ross Taylor, Stuart. *Solar System Evolution: A New Perspective*. Cambridge, England: Cambridge University Press, 1992.

Science. From 1900 to 1917, he received other major prizes from the French Académie des Sciences, the French Astronomical Society, and the Astronomical Society of the Pacific.

Barnard married Rhoda Calvert in 1881; they had no children. His wife died in 1921, and Barnard became ill the next year. A few weeks before his death in 1923, he was still making astronomical observations from his bed.

Bibliography

By Barnard

"Observations of Jupiter with a Five-Inch Refractor, During the Years 1879-1886," *Publications of the Astronomical Society of the Pacific*, 1889.

"Visual Observations of Halley's Comet in 1910," *Astrophysical Journal*, 1914.

"A Small Star with the Largest Known Proper Motion," *Astronomical Journal*, 1916.

"On the Dark Markings of the Sky, with a Catalogue of 182 Such Objects," *Astrophysical Journal*, 1919.

About Barnard

Frost, Edwin B. *Biographical Memoir: Edward Emerson Barnard, 1857-1923*. Washington, D.C.: National Academy of Sciences, 1924.

Sheehan, William. *The Immortal Fire Within: The Life and Work of Edward Emerson Barnard*. Cambridge, England: Cambridge University Press, 1995.

Verschuur, Gerrit L. *Interstellar Matters: Essays on Curiosity and Astronomical Discovery*. New York: Springer-Verlag, 1989.

(Keay Davidson)

Dame Jocelyn Bell Burnell

Discipline: Astronomy

Contribution: Bell Burnell was the first astronomer to note the anomaly that resulted in the discovery of pulsars. She also worked in X-ray infrared, and optical astronomy.

Jul. 15, 1943	Born in Belfast, Northern Ireland
1956-1961	Attends Mount School in York, England
1965	Receives a B.S. degree from the University of Glasgow, Scotland
1965	Begins work for a Ph.D. at the University of Cambridge
1967	Discovers pulsars using a powerful radio telescope
1968	Studies X-ray astronomy at the University of Southampton, England
1974-1982	Works at the Mullard Space Science Laboratory
1982	Named a senior research fellow at the Royal Observatory in Edinburgh
1991	Appointed a professor of physics at Open University in Milton Keynes, England
2001-2004	Appointed dean of science at the University of Bath, England
2002-2004	Becomes president of the Royal Astronomical Society
2007	Elevated to Dame Commander of the Order of the British Empire
2008-2010	Becomes the first female president of the Institute of Physics

Early Life

Susan Jocelyn Bell was born in Belfast, Northern Ireland, on July 15, 1943. From her teenage years, Bell wanted to become an astronomer. She became interested in the subject through reading the books of her father, the architect of Armagh Observatory in Northern Ireland.

Bell attended a Quaker girls' boarding school in England. Between the ages of fifteen and eighteen, she had a good physics teacher, an elderly man who had come out of retirement for a second time to teach. There was little equipment in the school, but Bell recalled that her teacher showed her "how easy physics was."

After completing secondary school, she went to Scotland to study science at the University of Glasgow. Upon receiving her baccalaureate in science from Glasgow in 1965, Bell began studies for a Ph.D. at the University of Cambridge in England.

Discovering Pulsars

Bell spent her first two years at Cambridge building a large radio telescope—a high-resolution dipole array—that her supervisor, Anthony Hewish, had designed. It was nearly 4.5 acres in area and so was very sensitive. It was able to record rapid variations in signals. When construction was completed and the telescope was operational in July, 1967, a sky survey began.

Bell was given the task of analyzing the signals received, which involved inspecting 400 feet of chart paper from a chart recorder every four days. In October, Bell noticed "a bit of scruff" occupying about half an inch of chart. She brought the anomaly to Hewish's attention, but he initially regarded it as insignificant. This reading could have been caused by an equipment problem, interference, or satellites in orbit. All these possibilities had to be checked out.

Further observations indicated that the position of the strange signals stayed fixed with respect to the stars, which implied that the source was neither terrestrial nor solar in origin. In late December, Bell found another such source. Bell, under the direction of Hewish, had discovered pulsars, but their discovery was merely an appendix to her dissertation on twinkling quasars.

In 1974, Hewish shared the Nobel Prize in Physics with Martin Ryle, a radio astrophysicist. Hewish's award was given "for his pioneering research in radio astrophysics, particularly the discovery of pulsars." Bell's contribution was not mentioned in the Nobel citation.

Career

On finishing her Ph.D. thesis, Bell moved from Cambridge to the south coast of England to be near her fiancè, and she began to study gamma-ray astronomy at the University of Southampton.

She married Martin Burnell in 1968 and thereafter was known as Jocelyn Bell Burnell.

When her husband moved, she did too and worked in X-ray astronomy at University College, London. She worked part-time for eighteen years running a satellite called Ariel V.

Working part-time and carrying the load of domestic responsibilities and child rearing meant less time for research. Following her husband around the country did not help Bell Burnell receive promotions. Only after they divorced in 1989 was she able to apply for a job solely on the basis of what it was, rather than where it was. From 1991 to 2001 she was a professor of physics at the Open University, where she began work on neutron stars. She then became dean of science at the University of Bath, after which she accepted a visiting professor post at Oxford.

In more recent years Bell has branched out beyond the laboratory. She has pursued her passion for poetry and has given lectures on the portrayal of astronomy in poetry. Bell Burnell has also worked hard to make sure women have greater opportunities for research in the sciences, lecturing on the importance of women in science and chairing a working group for the Royal Society of Edinburgh to promote women exploring the fields of science, technology, math, and engineering in Scotland.

Bibliography

By Bell Burnell

"Little Green Men, White Dwarfs, or What?," *Sky & Telescope*, 1978.

"Simultaneous Millimetre and Radio Observations of Cygnus X-3 in Quiescent Radio State," *Monthly Notices of Royal Astronomical Society* 274: 633, (with R. P. Fender, G. G Pooley, S. T. Garrington, and R. E. Spencer), 1995.

Pulsars

A pulsar is a spinning neutron star of very small diameter and incredibly dense.

Pulsars are so named because the radio radiation that is received from them is pulsed. An ordinary star shines in every direction. Pulsars are more like lighthouses, as only a small part of the pulsar radiates and the radiation is strongly beamed into a cone of diameter between 5 and 50 degrees in size. As the pulsar rotates, if the beam points in the direction of Earth, a pulse is received. Information about the pulsar and its environment must be extracted by analyzing this pulse.

Pulsars are strongly magnetized neutron stars that contain huge amounts of energy. They have a shell, analogous to that of an egg, but pulsars are the most perfectly round thing ever found, made up of iron that is ten times more dense than iron found on Earth. Inside this shell is a superfluid, a liquid state of matter characterized by apparently frictionless flow.

These power sources emit radio waves that have periods of milliseconds to several seconds. Pulsars spin incredibly fast—so fast in fact that the energy produced from this revolution can produce a thousand million volts. They are so dense that a teaspoonful of material from a neutron star would weigh 100 million tons. It is now evident that these objects must be very compact because they pulse rapidly. They also must be very massive because they are such good time-keepers. They have large reserves of energy and can send out signal after signal after signal, with no sign of diminution. Since the initial discovery, pulsars that pulse several hundred times a second have been found, as have planets around pulsars, even though there are theoretical reasons why such a thing should not be possible.

Bibliography

Pulsar Astronomy. A. G. Lyne and F. Graham-Smith. Cambridge, England: Cambridge University Press, 1990.

"Flaring and Quiescent Infrared Behavior of Cygnus X-3," *Monthly Notices of Royal Astronomical Society* 283: 798 (with R. P. Fender, P. M. Williams, and A. S. Webster), 1996.

"Comments on the Superluminal Motion in Cygnus X-3," *Monthly Notices of Royal Astronomical Society* 285: 187 (with R. N. Ogley and S. J. Newell), 1997.

About Bell Burnell

Broad, William and Nicholas Wade. *Betrayers of the Truth: Fraud and Deceit in the Halls of Science.* New York: Simon & Schuster, 1982.

Porter, Roy ed. 2d ed. *The Biographical Dictionary of Scientists.* New York: Oxford University Press, 1994.

Wade, Nicholas. "Discovery of Pulsars: A Graduate Student's Story." *Science* 189, 1975.

Nobel Prize Women in Science: Their Lives, Struggles, and Momentous Discoveries. Sharon Bertsch McGrayne. New York: Carol, 1993.

Encyclopaedia Britannica Online, s.v. "Bell Burnell, Jocelyn." Accessed August 9, 2013, http://www.britannica.com/EBchecked/topic/59610/Jocelyn-Bell-Burnell.

"Honorary fellows: Professor Jocelyn Bell Burnell—University of Oxford" Institute of Physics, http://www.iop.org/about/awards/hon_fellowship/hon_fellows/page_56412.html

Lee, Jane J. "Six Women Scientists Who Were Snubbed Due to Sexism," *National Geographic,* May 19, 2013.

(Maureen H. O'Rafferty)

Friedrich Wilhelm Bessel

Disciplines: Astronomy, earth science, mathematics, and technology

Contribution: Bessel founded modern precision astronomy. He measured the first stellar parallax enabling the calculation of the distance between Earth and a star.

Jul. 22, 1784	Born in Minden, Brandenburg (now Germany)
1799	Leaves the *gymnasium* to become a bookkeeper for a trading company in Bremen
1805	Works as an assistant at the observatory in Lilienthal
1810	Supervises the construction of a new observatory at Königsberg for King Frederick William III of Prussia
1818	Publishes *Fundamenta Astronomiae*
1823	Develops the method of the personal equation
1826	Determines the length of the seconds pendulum
1838	Makes the first definite parallax measurement of a fixed star
1841	Deduces a value for the ellipticity of Earth
1844	Discovers the binary (double) character of the stars Sirius and Procyon from their disturbed proper motion
Mar. 17, 1846	Dies in Königsberg, Prussia (now Kaliningrad, Russia)

Early Life

Friedrich Wilhelm Bessel was born in 1784 in Minden, near Hannover. At the age of fifteen, he left the *gymnasium* (high school) and became an apprentice to a merchant in Bremen. He would later put the skills that he acquired there as a calculator and bookkeeper to good use.

Bessel was self-taught in the sciences. In his spare time, he studied how to determine the position of a ship at sea using planetary observations. This led him to study mathematics, astronomy, and the principles of astronomical instruments, and to practice observing astronomical events. His recalculation of the orbit of Halley's comet attracted the attention of Wilhelm Ölbers, a Bremen astronomer. He recommended Bessel for an assistant position at an observatory in 1806.

Star Catalog

In 1810, Bessel became director of the new Prussian observatory in Königsberg. While the observatory was being built, he worked on the reductions of stellar observations made in the mid-eighteenth century by the English astronomer James Bradley. This work, published in 1818, brought him international recognition and honors. It provided a reference system for the measurement of the positions of the sun, moon, planets, and the stars, and established him as the founder of modern precision astronomy. The Prussian king ordered Bessel to make a triangulation of East Prussia.

Bessel's careful comparison of astronomical observations led to the discovery of unavoidable systematic differences among trained observers.

This discovery kindled interest in the nature of vision itself. The random variation between observations led Bessel to apply the probabilistic theory of errors in his work.

Parallax

The accomplishment that spoke most to the imagination of Bessel's contemporaries was the first accurate determination of the distance to a star. In his time, the radius of Earth's orbit was known, but astronomers had not been able to measure stellar distances. In principle, stellar distances can be derived from the change in angular direction from which the star is viewed as Earth circles the sun. This change is extremely small, however, and thus hard to detect.

The annual parallax of a star is the difference in position of the star as seen from Earth and from the sun. Bessel calculated the parallax of 61 Cygni as 0.314 inches, with a mean error of +/-0.020 inches. This measurement placed the star at a distance of about 10.4 light-years from Earth.

Instrumental Rigor

In order to determine the parallax, Bessel used a heliometer (a telescope in which the objective glass is cut along the diameter). As in his other projects, he subjected this instrument, and his entire measuring procedure, to a painstaking analysis in order to estimate systematic errors. He took account of these errors in his calculations. Such precise habits were soon adopted by German physicists and are now common throughout scientific studies.

Bessel died in 1846 at the age of sixty-one.

Bibliography

By Bessel

"Fundamentu astronomiae pro anno MDCCLV deducta ex observationibus viri incomparabilis" in *Specula Astronomica Grenovicensi per annos 1750-1762 institutis*, 1818.

"Persönliche Gleichung bei Durchgangsbeobachtungen," *Königsberger Beobachtungen*, 1823.

"Bestimmung der Entfernung des 61. Sterns des Schwans," *Astronomische Nachrichten*, 1838.

Gradmessung in Ostpreussen und ihre Verbindung mit Preussischen und Russischen Dreieckketten, (with J. J. Baeyer), 1838.

"Untersuchungen über die Wahrscheinlichkeit der Beobachtungsfehler," *Astronomische Nachrichten*, 1838.

About Bessel

Fricke, Walter. "Bessel, Friedrich Wilhelm." *Dictionary of Scientific Biography*, Vol. 2. New York: Charles Scribner's Sons, 1970.

Pannekoek, Anton. *A History of Astronomy*. London: G. Allen & Unwin, 1961.

The Distance to 61 Cygni

As Earth revolves around the sun, the angle at which one sees a star varies slightly. Using this phenomenon, in 1838 Bessel made the first trustworthy estimate of an interstellar distance.

Bessel realized that the angular distance between two stars can be determined accurately. If one of these stars is close to Earth and the other is much farther away, the variation of angular distance is a sound basis for a determination of the distance to the nearby star.

In order to measure the angle between target star 61 Cygni and a comparison star, Bessel used a heliometer. Directed at a star, both parts will contribute to the image formed of the star. When the two parts are shifted along the cutting line, however, two images appear.

Pointing the heliometer at two stars, Bessel shifted the two parts along the cutting line until the image of one star formed by half of the lens coincided with the image of the other star produced by the second half. He measured this displacement and calculated the angle between the two stars, correcting for temperature fluctuations in his instrument. In order to calculate the distance, Bessel had to eliminate many other factors, such as the relative aberration of 61 Cygni in relation to the comparison star.

Bibliography

Clason, Clyde B. *Exploring the Distant Stars: Thrilling Adventures in Our Galaxy and Beyond*. New York: G. P. Putnam's Sons, 1958.

North, John. *The Norton History of Astronomy and Cosmology*. New York: W. W. Norton, 1995.

Herschel, John. "Stellar Parallax." *Essays in Astronomy*, edited by Edward Singleton Holden. New York: D. Appleton, 1990.

Motz, Lloyd and Jefferson Hane Weaver. *The Story of Astronomy*. New York: Plenum Press, 1995.

Ley, Willy. *Watchers of the Skies: An Informal History of Astronomy from Babylon to the Space Age*. New York: Viking Press, 1963.

Tycho Brahe

Disciplines: Astronomy and invention

Contribution: The accurate astronomical instruments that Tycho developed to measure the positions of stars and motions of planets, provided the data that enabled Johannes Kepler to deduce the laws of planetary orbits. Tycho's celestial measurements were the most accurate prior to the invention of the telescope.

Dec. 14, 1546	Born in Knudstrup Castle, Scania, Denmark (now Sweden)
1559-1562	Studies law at the University of Copenhagen
1562-1565	Attends the University of Leipzig
1563	Observes the conjunction of Jupiter and Saturn
1571	Constructs a small observatory in Denmark
1572	Precisely measures a supernova's position, proving that it was a star
1573	Publishes his first book, *De Nova Stella*
1576	Granted Hveen Island to construct a large observatory
1577	Proves that a comet in this year was well beyond the moon's orbit
1577-1597	Accurate measurements of star positions and planetary motions
1599-1601	Appointed Imperial Mathematicus to the Holy Roman emperor
1600	Appoints Kepler as his assistant
Oct. 24, 1601	Dies in Prague, Bohemia (now Czech Republic)

Early Life

Born to a wealthy Danish family, the infant Tyge Brahe Ottosøn—who is generally known by the name Tycho (pronounced "TI-koh)—was abducted, then reared as an heir by his childless uncle. At the age of thirteen, Tycho was sent to the University of Copenhagen to study law. During his first year, an accurately predicted eclipse of the sun seemed so miraculous to Tycho that he began neglecting his legal studies in favor of astronomy.

After three years at Copenhagen, Tycho was sent to the University of Leipzig with a tutor instructed to cure him of his perverse preoccupation with astronomy. While his tutor slept, however, Tycho measured stellar positions. On August 17, 1563, he observed a conjunction of Saturn and Jupiter. Although the almanacs had predicted this event, they were grossly inaccurate, missing the event by as much as a month. Tycho, then and there, devoted his life to accumulating precise observations so that accurate tables could be published.

After Leipzig, Tycho spent five years traveling, studying, and designing better instruments for celestial measurements. In 1570, he returned to his family estate in Denmark, where he used his inheritance to build a small observatory.

On November 11, 1572, Tycho saw a very bright star where no star had been before. According to the established science, fixed stars never changed appearance or position: only planets or comets moved through the fixed stars. Although many astronomers observed the new object, only Tycho was able to measure its position accurately.

Using his newly constructed instruments, he determined, unequivocally, that the new object (today called a supernova) was indeed a star. The following year, he published his observations, and descriptions of the instruments used, in his first book, *De Nova Stella* (The New Star). Tycho's fame was thus established in a single stroke.

The Island Observatory

Having acquired some measure of renown, Tycho now wished to establish a large observatory. In 1576, Frederick II, king of Denmark, gave Tycho title to the Island of Hveen and generous financial support to realize this dream. For the next twenty years, Tycho collected observations and substantially corrected nearly every known astronomical record.

One of his first observations proved that the great comet of 1577 was not an atmospheric phenomenon of Earth, as had previously been believed, but located out among the planets. Under Tycho's direction, the observatory at Hveen became the astronomical center of northern Europe and scholars and nobles flocked to see the impressive array of large and extremely accurate instruments.

After the death of King Frederick in 1588, Tycho's income was greatly reduced. Nevertheless,

Precise Measurements in Astronomy

Tycho's sole discovery and greatest contribution was that, to be a science, astronomy requires precise and continuous observational data.

According to Ptolemy's Earth-centered theory of the universe, the stars, planets, sun, and moon all revolved around Earth in circular orbits. During the sixteenth century Nicolaus Copernicus proposed a sun-centered model in which Earth and other planets revolved in circular orbits around the sun. Computations based on either model were used to predict planetary motions among the fixed stars. Tycho's extensive and extremely accurate data showed, however, that both theories were in error.

Before Tycho, the most accurate measurements were reliable to no more than ten minutes of arc (there are sixty minutes in a degree). Tycho's data were accurate to about one minute of arc. If a 12-foot pointer were used to sight a star, a shift of the end of the pointer by 1/25 of an inch would give an angular error of one minute of arc.

Previous observers were content to observe planetary positions at certain key points in their orbits. Tycho tracked them through their entire orbits by daily observation. His observations were made without benefit of the telescope (invented seven years after his death) but with various sighting tubes and pointers. Tycho, an unusually keen and meticulous observer, took great care to stabilize and calibrate his instruments carefully to ensure maximum accuracy.

Bibliography

Sagan, Carl. "The Harmony of Worlds." *Cosmos*. New York: Random House, 1980.

Ferris, T. "The Sun Worshipers." *Coming of Age in the Milky Way*. New York: Anchor Books, 1988.

he remained at Hveen, meticulously recording positions of stars and planets, until the 1,000 brightest stars had been accurately pinpointed. Tycho left the island in 1597, traveling extensively until receiving an appointment by Emperor Rudolph II. In 1599, Tycho joined the emperor in Prague and began to construct another observatory.

Tycho and Kepler

On February 4, 1600 Johannes Kepler, a young mathematician searching for accurate data on planetary motions, joined Tycho's staff. Tycho had an impressive array of accurate data but did not have the genius to use it to construct a coherent model of the universe. Kepler had the genius but lacked the precise data to check his models. Each needed the other and each was afraid of being preempted.

Thus, a stalemate developed. Tycho tried to pick Kepler's brain while releasing the data in small dribbles, while Kepler, frustrated by this, did not share his insights. The situation was resolved on October 13, 1601, when Tycho became seriously ill, dying eleven days later. Kepler, appointed his successor, inherited the data, which he used to obtain the correct laws of planetary motion.

Bibliography

By Tycho

De nova et nullius aevi memoria prius visa Stella, 1573 (De Nova Stella; partially trans. in *A Source Book of Astronomy*, 1929).
Tychonis Brahe Dani Opera Omnia, 1913-1929.

About Tycho

Gade, John Allyne. *The Life and Times of Tycho Brahe*. New York: Greenwood Press, 1969.
Koestler, A. "Tycho de Brahe." *The Sleepwalkers*. Middlesex, England: Penguin Books, 1989.

(*George R. Plitnik*)

E. Margaret Burbidge

Disciplines: Astronomy and physics
Contribution: Burbidge increased astronomers' understanding of the synthesis of elements within stars, the rotation of galaxies, and the nature of quasars.

Aug. 12, 1919	Born in Davenport, England
1943	Earns a Ph.D. in astronomy from the University of London
1948-1951	Works at the University of London Observatory
1951-1953	Receives a fellowship to Yerkes Observatory
1955-1957	Receives fellowship to Caltech
1957-1959	Receives Shirley Farr Fellowship to Yerkes Observatory
1959	Shares the Warner Prize with Geoffrey Burbidge
1959-1962	Associate professor at Yerkes Observatory
1964	Elected a fellow of the Royal Society of London
1976-1978	President of the American Astronomical Society
1978	Elected to the National Academy of Sciences
1979-1988	Directs the Center for Astrophysics and Space Science at UCSD
1984	Receives the National Medal of Science
1988	Receives the Albert Einstein Medal
2005	Receives the Royal Astronomical Society Gold Medal

Early Life

Margaret Burbidge was born Eleanor Margaret Peachey in Davenport, England, on August 12, 1919. Her parents were Stanley John Peachey, a chemistry teacher and Marjorie Stott Peachey. In 1921, the family moved to London, where her father set up a laboratory to work on the chemistry of rubber. Burbidge was encouraged to study science from an early age and became interested in astronomy as a child.

She received a bachelor's degree with first-class honors from the University of London in 1939. During World War II, Burbidge was able to continue her studies while most of her male colleagues served in the military. She was awarded a Ph.D. for her study of astrophysics in 1943. In 1948, she married fellow astronomer Geoffrey Burbidge and became known as Margaret Burdidge. From 1948 to 1950, Margaret Burbidge worked as the assistant director of the University of London Observatory and from 1950 to 1951,

she was the acting director. During this period, she was also the editor of *Observatory* magazine.

Fellowships in the United States

In 1951, Burbidge received a fellowship from the International Astronomical Union to work at Yerkes Observatory. This observatory, located in Williams Bay, Wisconsin, and owned and operated by the Department of Astronomy and Astrophysics at the University of Chicago, contained the largest refracting telescope ever built. In 1953, Burbidge returned to the United Kingdom.

A fellowship to the California Institute of Technology (Caltech), located in Pasadena, California, brought Burbidge back to the United States in 1955. In 1957, she was awarded a Shirley Farr Fellowship and returned to Yerkes Observatory. In 1959, she was made an associate professor at the observatory.

Nucleosynthesis, Galaxies, and Quasars

During the 1950's, Burbidge and her husband worked with the British astronomer Fred Hoyle and the U.S. physicist William A. Fowler studying the evolution of stars. They studied the elements present within stars and concluded that these elements must have been created within the stars themselves. This process, known as nucleosynthesis, explains the existence of heavier elements in the universe. For their work, the Burbidges shared the Warner Prize from the American Astronomical Society, in 1959.

During the late 1950s and early 1960s, Burbidge studied the rotation of galaxies. The speed at which a galaxy spins reveals how much matter it contains and how that matter is distributed. Her pioneering work in this field would later lead U.S. astronomer Vera Rubin to develop the concept of dark matter (invisible mass, in contrast to the bright objects astronomers usually study) to explain the way in which galaxies rotate.

In the late 1960s, Burbidge turned her attention

Nucleosynthesis

Nucleosynthesis is the process within stars by which light elements, such as hydrogen and helium, are transformed into heavier elements, such as carbon, oxygen, and iron. Burbidge's analysis of nucleosynthesis explains why the chemical elements present in the universe occur in the amounts in which they do.

Astronomers can determine which chemical elements are present within stars by using spectroscopy. Spectroscopy is a process in which the light emitted by a star is first separated into its various colors. These colors are then compared with the colors produced by known samples of heated elements. In this way, astronomers can determine which elements are present in the star, and the brightness of the colors reveals how much of the element is present compared to the other elements within the star.

Spectroscopy indicated to Burbidge a pattern of stellar evolution in which older stars contain more heavy elements than younger stars. This finding led her and her co-workers to conclude that heavy elements are created from lighter elements within stars as they age.

Most newly formed stars are composed almost entirely of hydrogen. In groups of four, these hydrogen atoms fuse to form helium atoms, releasing energy. Earth's sun undergoes this type of nuclear fusion to produce heat and light. As the star ages, the helium atoms fuse to form heavier elements such as carbon and oxygen. Then, the carbon and oxygen atoms combine to form elements such as magnesium, sodium, silicon, and sulfur As the star grows older, complicated reactions among all these elements result in the production of even heavier elements, such as iron.

Nucleosynthesis within the star ends when the iron stage is reached. Elements that are slightly heavier than iron, such as nickel and cobalt, may be formed during this stage, but elements that are much heavier than iron cannot be obtained by this process because they are broken down by the star's heat as quickly as they are formed.

Elements that are considerably heavier than iron can be formed by a supernova explosion. A supernova occurs when a star several times larger than Earth's sun has reached the end of the iron stage. The star explodes, releasing the elements within it, as well as free neutrons. Elements heavier than iron are produced when lighter elements capture the free neutrons and stabilize.

An important consequence of a supernova explosion is the widespread distribution of elements heavier than iron throughout space. These elements may then come together with the more common lighter elements to form new stars. Earth's sun is considered to be an example of this type of star, and the existence of the solar system, with planets partly composed of elements heavier than iron, is explained by this theory of stellar evolution.

Bibliography

Clayton, Donald D. *Principles of Stellar Evolution and Nucleosynthesis*. New York: McGraw-Hill, 1968.

Harpaz, Amos. *Stellar Evolution*. Wellesley, Mass.: A. K. Peters, 1994.

to the recently discovered objects known as quasars. Quasars, also known as quasi-stellar objects, posed a mystery for astronomers. They seem to be extremely distant and yet very bright. Either the methods used to measure astronomical distances were seriously flawed, or quasars were thought to rely on a source of energy far more powerful than anything previously known. Burbidge's careful measurements of quasars led astronomers to conclude that they are, indeed, very far away. Later, it was believed that they were distant galaxies with vast black holes at their centers releasing enormous amounts of energy.

Honors and Awards

In 1964, Burbidge began her career as a professor in the Department of Astronomy at the University of California, San Diego (UCSD). The same year, she was elected a Fellow of the Royal Society of London. In 1968, the American Academy of Arts and Sciences also elected her a Fellow.

From 1976 to 1978, Burbidge served as the president of the American Astronomical Society. She also became a citizen of the United States at that time. In 1978, she was elected to the National Academy of Sciences.

Burbidge served as the director of the UCSD Center for Astrophysics and Space Science from 1979 to 1988. She was promoted to university professor in 1984 and professor emeritus in 1990.

Major awards presented to Burbidge during this time included the Catherine Wolfe Bruce Medal from the Astronomical Society of the Pacific in 1982, the National Medal of Science from President Ronald Reagan in 1984, and the Albert Einstein Medal from the World Cultural Council in 1988. She was also selected to serve on scientific committees involved in designing the Hubble Space Telescope, an orbiting observatory launched in 1990.

Bibliography

By Burbidge

"Synthesis of the Elements in Stars," *Review of Modern Physics*, 1957 (with Geoffrey Burbidge, William A. Fowler, and Fred Hoyle).

"The Life-Story of a Galaxy" *Stars and Galaxies: Birth, Aging, and Death in the Universe*, 1962.

Quasi-Stellar Objects, 1967 (with Geoffrey Burbidge).

"Watcher of the Skies," *Annual Review of Astronomy and Astrophysics*, Vol 32, 1994.

About Burbidge

Abbott, David. *The Biographical Dictionary of Scientists: Astronomers*. New York: Peter Bedrick Books, 1984.

Uglow, Jennifer S., ed. *The Continuum Dictionary of Women's Biography*. New York: Continuum, 1989.

Moxley, Christina F., ed. *Who's Who of American Women 1995-1996*. New Providence, N.J.: Marquis, 1995.

(Rose Secrest)

Annie Jump Cannon

Discipline: Astronomy

Contribution: Cannon, a pioneer in stellar spectroscopy, developed a method of classifying stellar spectra.

Dec. 11, 1863	Born in Dover, Delaware
1884	Graduates from Wellesley College
1893	Returns to Wellesley to work for Professor Sarah Whiting
1895	Enrolls as a special student at Radcliffe College
1896	Hired by Edward Pickering to work for the Harvard College Observatory
1907	Earns an M.A. degree from Wellesley
1911	Becomes the curator of astronomical photographs at Harvard College Observatory
1918	Appointed an honorary member of the American Association of Variable Star Observers
1918-1924	Publishes "The Henry Draper Catalog"
1922	Discovers a nova while working in South America
1931	Elected an honorary member of the Royal Astronomical Society
1931	Given the Henry Draper Gold Medal by the National Academy of Sciences
1938	Named William Cranch Bond Professor of Astronomy at Harvard
Apr. 13, 1941	Dies in Cambridge, Massachusetts

Early Life

Annie Jump Cannon was born in 1863 as the daughter of William Lee Cannon, a wealthy shipbuilder who served as lieutenant governor of Delaware during the Civil War. As a young student, Annie excelled in school, especially in mathematics. Her mother, Mary Elizabeth Jump Cannon, was an amateur astronomer who taught the young girl to love the stars.

Although few women in her day went to college, Cannon was encouraged to seek higher education because of her excellent scholastic record. She enrolled in Wellesley College, but she was not prepared for the harsh winters in Massachusetts and was sick often during her first year at college. These repeated illnesses left her partially deaf.

After her graduation, Cannon returned home and helped around the house until her mother died in 1893. Most of her friends had married while she was in school and Cannon found that she had little in common with them anymore. She never married and thus was able to put all of her energies into her chosen career: astronomy.

Life in Cambridge

In 1893, Cannon returned to Cambridge, Massachusetts, to work for Sarah Whiting, one of her professors at Wellesley. Cannon then enrolled in Radcliffe College in order to use the telescopes at the nearby Harvard College Observatory. Her work impressed Edward Pickering, the director of the observatory, enough for him to offer her a job analyzing stellar spectra. She moved into a house within a block of the observatory, where she would live for the next four decades.

Cannon's early work involved the study of variable stars, an interest that she kept for the rest of her life. Her analysis of stellar spectra led Cannon to revise dramatically the way in which stellar spectral types were organized and categorized.

Her new system of classification gained general acceptance by 1910 and remains the primary method of designating star types.

In her illustrious career, Cannon classified more than 350,000 stars, surpassing any other individual in history. She discovered more than 300 variable stars. Most of Cannon's stellar spectroscopy work appeared in "The Henry Draper Catalog," which was published in *The Annals of the Harvard College Observatory* from 1918 to 1924.

In 1911 as a reward for her meticulous and accurate work, Cannon was named the curator of the famed photographic plate collection at the Harvard College Observatory, a position that she held for the remainder of her life.

Spectral Classification of Stars

Stars may be categorized by analysis of their spectra. Cannon revised the way in which stellar spectral types are organized and categorized.

A careful analysis of light coming from stars indicates that certain wavelengths, known as spectral lines, are diminished in intensity. The study of these spectral lines is called spectroscopy. Many stars have similar spectra, and thus the idea arose to categorize stars based on this characteristic, a process known as spectral classification.

In an early spectral classification system at Harvard University, a letter of the alphabet was assigned to a star based on the spectral lines of hydrogen observed in that star's light. Cannon revised this system by limiting the letters used to only a few major categories. She then rearranged the letters in order of stellar temperature. Going from hottest to coolest, the spectral types used are O, B, A, F, G, K, and M. Several special types may also be used. Cannon then subdivided each spectral type into ten parts; for example, the sun is spectral type G2.

This method of classifying stellar spectra provides astronomers with a tool for comparing different stars. Cannon's designation, even with comparatively few other parameters, can tell a student of astronomy much about a star and remains one of the most important pieces of information about it.

Bibliography

Robins, Robert R., William H. Jefferys, and Stephen J. Shawl. *Discovering Astronomy*. New York: John Wiley & Sons, 1995.

Bohm-Vitense, Erika. *Introduction to Stellar Astrophysics, Vol. 1*. Cambridge, England: Cambridge University Press, 1989.

Birney, D. Scott. *Observational Astronomy*. Cambridge, England: Cambridge University Press, 1991.

Recognition and Later Years

Women were rare in astronomy in Cannon's day and frequently were not well received. Nevertheless, her work was so spectacular that she received numerous awards and praises from her male colleagues. In 1931 she was awarded the Henry Draper Gold Medal and in 1932 she received the Ellen Richards Research Prize. In 1925 Cannon became the first woman ever to be granted an honorary doctorate from Oxford University. Although she received many awards from around the world, Harvard University did not grant her the same honors until 1938, when she was named the William Cranch Bond Professor of Astronomy.

Cannon never retired. She worked until the age of seventy-six, when heart problems forced her to take a leave of absence from the observatory. She died shortly thereafter.

Bibliography

By Cannon

"The Henry Draper Memorial," *The Journal of the Royal Astronomical Society of Canada*, 1915.

"The Henry Draper Catalog," *The Annals of the Harvard College Observatory*, 1918-1924.

"Astronomical Fellowships for Women," *Circular of Harvard College Observatory*, 1919.

"The Henry Draper Extension," *The Annals of the Harvard College Observatory*, 1925-1936.

"Sarah Frances Whiting," *Popular Astronomy*, 1927.

About Cannon

Campbell, Leon. "Annie Jump Cannon." *Popular Astronomy* 49, 1941.

Veglahn, Nancy J. *Women Scientists*. New York: Facts on File, 1991.

George R. Carruthers

Disciplines: Astronomy and physics

Contribution: Carruthers developed electronic imaging devices and techniques for photographing hydrogen molecules in space, which helped advance understanding of how stars are formed.

Oct. 1, 1939	Born in Cincinnati, Ohio
1964	Earns a Ph.D. from the University of Illinois
1964	Joins the Naval Research Laboratory (NRL)
1969	Patents an electromagnetic radiation image converter
1971	Wins the Arthur S. Fleming Award for scholarly achievement
1972	Develops the ultraviolet camera deployed on Apollo 16
1972	Awarded the Exceptional Scientific Achievement Medal from NASA
1972	Develops an ultraviolet telescope on OAO 3 (Copernicus)
1977	Wins the Samuel Cheevers Award from the National Technical Association
1980	Becomes head of NRL's Ultraviolet Measurements Branch
1982	Becomes a senior astrophysicist at NRL
1982-1991	Develops far-ultraviolet cameras flown on space shuttle missions
2012	Receives National Medal of Technology and Innovation

Early Life

George Robert Carruthers, who would become the most prominent African American in space science was born on October 1, 1939, in Cincinnati. He was the oldest of four children born to George and Sophia Carruthers.

As a young boy growing up in the Cincinnati suburb of Milford, George was inspired by reading Buck Rogers and other space-related comic books. His father, a civil engineer for the United States Air Force, encouraged his son's interest in astronomy. He insisted that George study all forms of science and mathematics and bought him many books. At the age of ten, Carruthers built his own telescope and saved money from his job as a delivery boy to purchase lenses.

When Carruthers was twelve, his father died and the family moved to Chicago, where his mother went to work for the post office. While attending Chicago's Englewood High School, he received encouragement from his science teachers.

He built a telescope that won him first prize at a local science fair.

After graduating from Englewood in 1957, Carruthers went to the University of Illinois at Urbana-Champaign, where he received a B.S. in aeronautical engineering and astronomy in 1961. He continued in graduate school at Illinois, earning an M.S. in nuclear engineering in 1962 and a Ph.D. in aeronautical and astronautical engineering in 1964. The title of his doctoral dissertation was "Experimental Investigations of Atomic Nitrogen Recombination."

The Naval Research Laboratory

After completing his doctorate, Carruthers received a National Science Foundation fellowship in rocket astronomy at the NRL. Two years later he became a research assistant in the E. O. Hurlburt Center for Space Research at NRL. He specifically worked in the fields of far-ultraviolet spectroscopy and photometry. Scientists use ultraviolet light to determine the atoms and molecules present in interstellar space.

In November, 1969, Carruthers was granted a patent for an "Image Converter for Detecting Electromagnetic Radiation Especially in Short Wave Lengths."

Carruthers married in 1973 and became active in a program called Science, Mathematics, Aerospace Research and Technology (SMART), running workshops to train students and teachers, most of whom are members of minorities, in the Washington-Baltimore area. He also served as editor of the journal of the National Technical Association. In 1980, Carruthers became the head of NRL's Ultraviolet Measurements Branch. In 1982 he became a senior astrophysicist at NRL.

Over the years, Carruthers received numerous honors. These include the Arthur S. Fleming Award for Scholarly Achievement from the Washington Jaycees, which he received in 1971, the Exceptional Scientific Achievement Medal from the National Aeronautics and Space Administration (NASA) in 1972, and the Samuel Cheevers Award from the National Technical Association for his work with minority students in 1977.

Bibliography

By Carruthers

"Far-Ultraviolet Photography of Orion: Interstellar Dust," *Science*, 1970 (with R. C. Henry).

"Apollo 16 Far-Ultraviolet Camera/Spectrograph: Earth Observations," *Science*, 1972 (with T. Page).

"Astronomy with the Space Shuttle," *Sky and Telescope*, 1974.

"Far-Ultraviolet Rocket Survey of Orion," *Sky and Telescope*, 1977 (with C. B. Opal).

"The Distribution of Hot Stars and Hydrogen in the Large Magellanic Cloud," *Astrophysical Journal*, 1981 (with T. Page).

Far-Ultraviolet Astronomy from Space

Carruthers worked in developing electronic imaging devices and techniques for photographing hydrogen molecules in space that helped advance an understanding of how stars are made.

In April, 1972, an ultraviolet camera that Carruthers developed was carried to the moon on the Apollo 16 mission. His device was a semiautomatic combination spectrograph and camera with an electron intensifier. It had a Schmidt optical system that focused an image on a potassium bromide cathode that emitted electrons in proportion to the number of ultraviolet photons striking it.

Observing objects in wavelengths shorter than 1,600 angstroms, the camera created the first stellar observatory ever used on the moon and was the first instrument to photograph hydrogen bands around Earth up to 50,000 miles out in space, which helped monitor carbon monoxide and other pollutants in the atmosphere above large cities. It was also used to photograph the Great Magellanic Cloud, the closest galaxy to the Milky Way, among other objects, and it detected hydrogen molecules in deep space.

A modified version of the Apollo camera was carried on the Skylab 4 mission and deployed on the spacewalk of astronauts Eugene Carr and Bill Pogue on Christmas Day, 1973. It was used to photograph the hydrogen halo of Comet Kohoutek in the 1,050-to-1,600-angstrom-wave-length range. Carruthers also developed an ultraviolet telescope that was launched on the third Orbiting Astronomical Observatory (OAO 3, or Copernicus) in August, 1972.

One of his cameras, a cirris cryogenically cooled infrared telescope used to observe Earth's limb and rocket plumes, has flown aboard the space shuttle for the Strategic Defense Initiative (SDI). The first time was in June, 1982, on Columbia on mission STS-4; the project was classified at the time. It flew a second time in Discovery's cargo bay on STS-39 in April, 1991. His far-ultraviolet imaging spectrograph (FUVIS), designed to study the ozone layer in near-earth space was scheduled to fly on a space shuttle mission as part of the Air Force Spartan-281 payload.

Bibliography

"Apollo 16 Far-Ultraviolet Camera/Spectrograph: Earth Observations." George Carruthers and T. Page. *Science* 177, no. 4051 (September 1, 1972).

"Astronomy with the Space Shuttle." George Carruthers. *Sky and Telescope* 48, no. 3 (September, 1974).

"Far-Ultraviolet Stellar Astronomy." George Carruthers. *Astronautics and Aeronautics* 7, no. 3 (March, 1969).

"Far-Ultraviolet Stellar Photometry: A Field in Monoceros," *Astrophysical Journal*, 1993 (with E. G. Schmidt).

About Carruthers

American Men and Women of Science. 12th ed. Vol. 1. New York: Jaques Cattell Press, 1971.

Sammons, Vivian O. *Blacks in Science and Medicine.* Washington, D.C.: Hemisphere, 1990.

Carwell, Hattie. *Blacks in Science: Astrophysicist to Zoologist.* Hicksville, N.Y.: Exposition Press, 1977.

Kessler, James H. et al. *Distinguished African American Scientists of the Twentieth Century.* Phoenix, Ariz.: Oryx Press, 1996.

"Earth's Eye on the Moon." *Ebony* 28, no. 12 (October, 1973).

Emily J. McMurray, ed. *Notable Twentieth-Century Scientists.* New York: Gale Research, 1995.

"NRL's Dr. George Carruthers Honored with the National Medal of Technology and Innovation." *Naval Resource Laboratory*, February 4, 2013. http://www.nrl.navy.mil/media/news-releases/2013/dr-george-carruthers-honored-with-national-medal-of-technology-and-innovation

(Derek W. Elliott)

Gian Domenico Cassini

Disciplines: Astronomy and physics
Contribution: Cassini discovered four satellites of Saturn and the structure of its system of rings and carefully charted the movements of the four brightest satellites of Jupiter. His determination of the astronomical unit established the distance scale for the solar system.

Jun. 8, 1625	Born in Perinaldo, Imperia, Republic of Genoa (now Italy)
1650	Appointed a professor of mathematics at the University of Bologna
1668	Publishes tables of the positions of Jupiter's satellites
1669	Appointed the first director of the Paris Observatory
1671	Discovers Iapetus, the first known satellite of Saturn
1671-1673	Calculates the astronomical unit
1672	Discovers Rhea, a second satellite of Saturn
1673	Takes French nationality
1675	Observes that the ring around Saturn is divided into at least two concentric rings
1679	Completes a chart of the moon that is 11.8 feet in diameter
1684	Discovers Tethys and Dione, two additional satellites of Saturn
1693	Publishes improved ephemerides of Jupiter's satellites
1710	Becomes blind
Sept. 14, 1712	Dies in Paris, France

Early Life

Gian Domenico Cassini (pronounced "ka-SEE-nee"), the first of four generations of astronomers, was born in 1625 in Perinaldo, Republic of Genoa, which is now in Italy. Little is known of his early training, but he seems to have distinguished himself as an industrious observer with telescopes. His mathematical talents and his remarkable breadth of knowledge in the sciences added to his reputation.

At the age of twenty-five, Cassini was asked to join the University of Bologna as a professor of mathematics to succeed Father Bonaventura Cavalieri, the first to have explained in his public lectures the Copernican system and the implications of the discoveries made by Galileo. Since at that time mathematics professors were required to teach Euclidean geometry and the Ptolemaic system of astronomy, the task to which the young Cassini was called assumed great importance.

During the nineteen years in which he remained at Bologna, Cassini considerably advanced astronomical studies with the modest means at his disposal. His duties at the university also included solving problems in hydraulics for the civil authorities and designing fortifications and road systems for the military.

Jupiter and its System of Satellites

While at the University of Bologna, Cassini established a program of observations of the planet Jupiter and its four brightest satellites. The pronounced flattening of the planet indicated a rapid rate of rotation, and Cassini made detailed maps of Jupiter's cloud belts and spots in an effort to measure the rotational period. His value of nine hours and fifty-six minutes is only five minutes longer than the best modern determinations. Cassini extended his methods to other planets—Mars, Venus, and Saturn—in attempts to determine their periods of rotation. He succeeded only with Mars, for which he also noted the changing face of the planet with the seasons.

Cassini was also greatly interested in the movements of the bright satellites of Jupiter. Occasionally, each of the satellites will pass through Jupiter's shadow and thus be eclipsed. Cassini worked steadily on compiling a set of tables that could be used to predict when such eclipses occur. The result was the renowned *Ephemerides bononienses mediceorum syderum ex hypothesibus, et tabules Io*, published in 1668. For the navigator, Jupiter and its system of satellites are a sort of celestial clock, offering a way of determining longitude at sea. Cassini's tables were of commercial and military interest as they permitted accurate maps to be drawn.

Successes at the Paris Observatory

Cassini's work on Jupiter's satellites impressed Jean Picard, a French astronomer who was also an advisor to King Louis XIV of France.

The Scale of the Solar System

Through coordinated observations of the planet Mars from two widely separated stations on Earth, Cassini was able to determine the distance to that planet from Earth. With that distance known, the scale of the entire solar system was established.

The heliocentric models of the solar system developed by Nicolaus Copernicus and later modified by Johannes Kepler provided only the relative scale of the solar system. The distances separating the planets were known only in terms of Earth-sun distance, defined to be one astronomical unit (1 AU). The question addressed by astronomers then became "How long is 1 AU in terms of some standard length?"—for example, a meter or a mile.

The first successful measurement of the size of the astronomical unit was made by a team of astronomers headed by Cassini. Continued improvements in the performance and operation of telescopes made parallax measurements feasible for small angles. Such small parallactic shifts result when a relatively nearby object is viewed against a background of more distant objects. The nearby object's apparent position changes when it is measured from opposite ends of a baseline. The longer the baseline, the larger the apparent shift and the greater the parallax.

Cassini assigned Jean Richer the task of mapping the position of Mars relative to several bright stars at predetermined times. While Richer worked in Cayenne in the French colony of Guiana, Cassini and Jean Picard carried out similar measurements in Paris, 6,213 miles away. Mars was at the time in opposition, so that it was nearer Earth than at other times. The principle of Cassini's method is illustrated above. One observer at Paris (P) observes the direction in which Mars appears, that is, the direction of line PM. The other observer at Cayenne (C) performs a similar measurement and determines the direction of line CM. The length of the line CP joining Cayenne and Paris is known

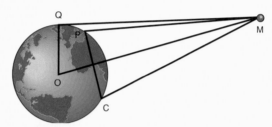

Measuring the Distance to Mars

The distance to Mars (M) is determined from two positions on earth, Paris (P) and Cayenne (C). Knowing the distance between P and C allows all other relevant distances and angles to be determined. The position O corresponds to the observer at M who would measure the maximum angle between the center of Earth (O) and Q. The angle OMQ is called the parallax.

geographically. Thus, two of the angles of triangle PCM and the length of one side are known, and so the lengths of all the other sides can be calculated. Knowing the positions of C and P on Earth's surface, the length of OM can be found. This represents the distance of Mars from the center of Earth (O). Cassini found this to be 75 million kilometers.

The models of Copernicus and Kepler indicated that the distance from Mars to the sun was 1.52 AU; Earth's distance from the sun is defined to be 1 AU. Therefore, the distance that Cassini measured, EM, was equivalent to 0.52 AU. According to Cassini, 1 AU was then equivalent to 140 million kilometers. The scale of the sun's system of planets was now known. Future refinements would alter Cassini's result very little.

Bibliography

Ferris Timothy. *Coming of Age in the Milky Way.*
   New York: Doubleday, 1988.
Morrison, David and Tobias Owen. *The Planetary System.* Reading, Mass.: Addison-Wesley, 1988.
Baugher, Joseph F. *The Space-Age Solar System.*
   New York: John Wiley & Sons, 1988.

The king was building an observatory in 1669, and, at Picard's recommendation the king appointed Cassini as the first director of the Paris Observatory.

Cassini produced an almost uninterrupted stream of astronomical advances. Employing some novel developments in the construction and use of telescopes, he discovered four new satellites of Saturn: Iapetus in 1671, Rhea in the following year, and Dione and Tethys in 1684.

In 1675, Cassini noticed a dark marking in Saturn's ring that separates it into two concentric rings. This division, which still bears Cassini's name, gave him an accurate idea of the constitution of the ring. He correctly surmised that the rings are formed by a swarm of very small satellites that could not be seen separately and that move around the planet with different orbital velocities.

While heading the Paris Observatory, he improved the theory that predicted the position of the sun in the sky, calculated new tables of atmospheric refraction that superseded the one published by Johannes Kepler, and issued, in 1693, a revised ephemeris of Jupiter's satellites, one whose accuracy was markedly better than his own tables of 1668.

Cassini also supervised several projects that brought him, his colleagues, and the observatory worldwide fame. He sent his assistant Jean Richer to Cayenne in the French colony of Guiana. They found that a pendulum of fixed length beat more slowly in Cayenne than in Paris, thus showing that the acceleration of gravity is smaller near the equator than at higher latitudes. This fact suggested that Earth is not a perfect sphere and served as the impetus for future investigations as to the shape of Earth. In another project, Richer's observations of the position of Mars in the sky, combined with observations made at the same time by Cassini and Picard in France, led to a much-improved esti-mate of the distance to Mars and ultimately to the distance scale of the solar system.

Cassini died in Paris, France, in 1712 at the age of eighty-seven.

Bibliography

By Cassini

Ephemerides bononienses mediceorum syderum ex hypothesibus, et tabules Io, 1668.

Connaissance des temps, 1679.

Découverte de la lumiére céleste qui paroit dans le Zodiaque, 1685.

About Cassini

Abetti, Giorgio. *The History of Astronomy.* New York: Henry Schuman, 1952.

Grant, Robert. *History of Physical Astronomy.* New York: Jefferson Reprint, 1966.

Wilson, Colin. *Starseekers.* Garden City, N.Y.: Doubleday, 1980.

Ley, Willy. *Watchers of the Skies.* New York: Viking Press, 1963.

Sheehan, William. *Worlds in the Sky.* Tucson: University of Arizona Press, 1992.

(Anthony J. Nicastro)

Subrahmanyan Chandrasekhar

Disciplines: Mathematics and physics

Contribution: Chandrasekhar showed that not all stars end up as white dwarfs; those retaining a mass above a certain limit undergo further collapse. He also contributed to hydrodynamics, hydromagnetics, and the mathematical theory of black holes.

Oct. 19, 1910	Born in Lahore, India
1930	Receives a B.A. from the University of Madras and formulates the Chandrasekhar limit
1933	Earns a Ph.D. in theoretical physics from Trinity College, University of Cambridge
1944	Elected a Fellow of the Royal Society of London
1952	Appointed a distinguished service professor at the University of Chicago
1952	Serves as managing editor of the Astrophysical Journal
1953	Awarded the Gold Medal of the Royal Astronomical Society
1962	Awarded the Royal Medal of the Royal Society of London
1966	Given the National Medal of Science from the United States
1971	Awarded the Henry Draper Medal from the National Academy of Sciences
1983	Awarded the Nobel Prize in Physics
Aug. 21, 1995	Dies in Chicago, Illinois

Early Life

Subrahmanyan Chandrasekhar (pronounced "chan-drah-SEEK-hahr") was born on October 19, 1910, in Lahore, India, to Chandrasekhara Subrahmanyan Ayyar and Sitalakshmi Ayyar. Sir Chandrasekhara Venkata Raman, a Nobel Prize-winning physicist, was his uncle. Taught at home until he was eleven, Subrahmanyan Chandrasekhar was admitted in 1921 into the Hindu High School in Triplicane, which was considered the best school in Madras. He was regarded as a prodigy, having mastered permutations and combinations, conic sections, coordinate geometry, calculus, and differential equations far ahead of his class.

At fifteen, he became a freshman at the Presidency College of the University of Madras. While studying for his B.A. honors degree, he was inspired by Srinivasa Ramanujan, the mathematical genius who had died only a few years earlier.

Emergence as a Preeminent Astrophysicist

While Chandrasekhar was pursuing mathematical physics in college, his uncle's discovery in 1928 of the Raman effect, which received international acclaim, became a turning point in his life.

Stimulated by a meeting with Arnold Sommerfeld in 1928, Chandrasekhar launched into a study of the new discoveries in atomic physics and statistical mechanics. In 1929 he had his first paper published in the prestigious *Proceedings of the Royal Society of London.* Two other papers were ready

The Chandrasekhar Limit

The Chandrasekhar limit is the mass that a star must have in order to end its life by contracting into an extremely dense white dwarf. A more massive star collapses into an object such as a neutron star or a black hole, which are smaller and denser than a white dwarf.

The evolutionary outcomes for high-mass and low-mass stars can be dramatically different. As a rule, every star eventually tries to generate a white dwarf at its core as it undergoes core contraction. During the 1920s, British physicist Ralph Fowler showed that a white dwarf has the peculiar property that the more massive it is, the smaller its radius. The explanation for this property is that a massive white dwarf has more selfgravity, so that more pressure is required to counter the stronger gravity. To increase the pressure, the degenerate electron gas constituting the white dwarf must be compressed until the pressure is strong enough to balance the gravitational force. This happens only at very high densities.

Chandrasekhar made a crucial modification to this hypothesis to accommodate Albert Einstein's special theory of relativity. Chandrasekhar showed that relativistic effects impose an upper limit on the mass of possible white dwarfs. This limit arises because electrons cannot move faster than the speed of light, and, for sufficiently massive stars, the internal degeneracy pressure cannot prevent the self-gravity of the star from crushing it to zero size. For likely white dwarf compositions, this limit is found to correspond to about 1.4 solar masses.

Suppose that a star attempts to exceed the Chandrasekhar limit, so that even after the initial envelope-

mass loss, it has enough material to try to build a massive white dwarf. As the limit is approached, the core's outer boundary reaches arbitrarily small dimensions, generating enormous gravitational fields above it. To counteract the gravity, the pressure in the shell above the core must rise, yielding densities and temperatures that will drive all thermonuclear reactions to completion. Barring any other intervention, such a star suffers what is known as the iron catastrophe, whereby the envelope is expelled through a supernova explosion while the core turns into a large mass of hot neutrons or, in extreme cases, a black hole.

On the other hand, the final mass of the core in a low-mass star may end up well below the Chandrasekhar limit. The outer shell in such a star may still be dense and hot enough to allow nuclear fusion. The resulting heat will greatly distend its envelope, driving it to the red giant and the red supergiant phases. The surface gravity in these phases is too weak to hold the atmospheric mix of gas and dust, and the mixture is blown out as a stellar wind. Stars in this state are called planetary nebula. The white-hot core left behind is a bare white dwarf, composed mainly of carbon and oxygen.

Bibliography

The Internal Constitution of Stars. A. S. Eddington. Cambridge, England: Cambridge University Press, 1926.

"On Massive Neutron Cores." J. Robert Oppenheimer and G. M. Volkoff. *Physical Review* 55 (1939): 374-381.

to be published in the *Philosophical Magazine*, and several others were in progress.

In 1930 he received his B.A. honors degree and was offered a scholarship to study abroad by the government of India. On his way to England that year, he made the discovery that revolutionized stellar physics. Working on the theory of the evolution of white dwarf stars (such as the sun) from a relativistic standpoint, Chandrasekhar found that there is an upper limit to the mass of a star that will evolve into a white dwarf. A more massive star degenerates into a neutron star or a black hole. This limiting mass came to be known as the Chandrasekhar limit.

Cambridge and the Yerkes Observatory

Chandrasekhar spent the years between 1930 and 1935 at Trinity College, University of Cambridge, where his research flourished in the company of mentors such as Edward Milne, Ralph Fowler, Paul A. M. Dirac, and the great astronomer Arthur Eddington. These years were stimulating and challenging, as well as extremely productive.

Despite their cordial personal relations, Eddington disagreed strongly with Chandrasekhar's conclusions vis-à-vis the fate of white dwarfs. Indeed, so great was Eddington's hold on the astronomical community that for many years Chandrasekhar received awards that carefully avoided citing his work on white dwarfs. Nevertheless, he continued his research on white dwarfs, despite repudiation by Eddington. During this period, Chandrasekhar also carried out research on a variety of subjects, ranging from ionization in stellar atmospheres and the equilibrium of rotating gas spheres to distorted polytropes and relativistic degeneracy.

Between 1935 and 1936, Chandrasekhar spent several months lecturing at the renowned Harvard Observatory. In 1937, he accepted an offer for a position as research associate at the Yerkes Observatory of the University of Chicago in Williams Bay Wisconsin. Over the next ten years, his research encompassed stellar dynamics, dynamical friction, the negative hydrogen ion, and radiative transfer.

The Years at the University of Chicago

In 1952, Chandrasekhar became the Morton Hull Distinguished Service Professor of Astrophysics at the University of Chicago, a position that he held until 1986. During this time, his research shifted among such topics as stellar structure, energy transfer in stellar atmospheres, and black holes. Apart from his outstanding contributions to research, Chandrasekhar was also regarded as an exceptional teacher and an author of outstanding texts, many of which remain classics in their fields.

Chandrasekhar died in Chicago on August 21, 1995, at the age of eighty-four.

Bibliography

By Chandrasekhar
The Mathematical Theory of Black Holes, 1983.
Truth and Beauty: Aesthetics and Motivations in Science, 1987.
Selected Papers, 1989-1996 (7 vols.).

About Chandrasekhar
Wali, C. *Chandra: A Biography of S. Chandrasekhar.* Chicago: University of Chicago Press, 1991.
Magill, Frank N, (ed.). "Subrahmanyan Chandrasekhar." *The Nobel Prize Winners: Physics*, Pasadena, Calif.: Salem Press, 1989.

(Monish R. Chatterjee)

Nicolaus Copernicus

Disciplines: Astronomy and cosmology

Contribution: Copernicus was the founder of modern astronomy. He taught that the sun, not Earth, is the center of the solar system, thus abolishing the ancient Ptolemaic theory of a geocentric universe.

Feb. 19, 1473	Born in Thorn, Prussia (now Toru'n, Poland)
1483	Becomes the charge of his uncle, Lucas Waczenrode, Bishop of Ermeland
1491-1494	Studies classics and mathematics at the University of Cracow
1496	Studies law and astronomy at the University of Bologna
Mar. 9, 1497	Makes his first recorded astronomical observations
1497	Named canon of the Frombork Cathedral
1500	Lectures on mathematics in Rome and studies law and Greek in Bologna and Padua
1503	Receives a Ph.D. in canon law at the University of Ferrara
1506-1512	Serves as personal physician and secretary to his uncle
1506	Returns to Poland and serves as canon at the Frombork Cathedral
1513	Builds an observatory
1514	Privately circulates his revolutionary ideas on astronomy
1543	Publishes *De revolutionibus orbium coelestium*
May 24, 1543	Dies in Frauenburg, Prussia (now Frombork, Poland)

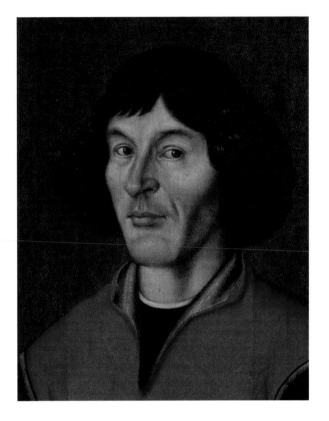

Early Life

The famed astronomer Nicolaus Copernicus (pronounced "koh-PER-nihk-uhs"), also known as Niklas Koppernigk or Mikolaj Kopernik, was born on February 19, 1473 in Thorn, Prussia (now Toru'n, Poland), where he obtained his elementary education. Copernicus was part of a generation that revolutionized Europe's view of the world. What Christopher Columbus did for geography, Copernicus did for astronomy.

Upon the death of his father in 1483 when Copernicus was only ten years of age, he became the ward of his maternal uncle, Lucas Waczenrode, who became the bishop of Ermeland. His uncle's patronage made it possible for Copernicus to attend the Cathedral School in Wloclawek. There, he was thoroughly prepared for his higher education, which began at the University of Cracow, where he was in residence from 1491 until 1494, concentrating on classics and mathematics.

The Italian Years

Copernicus lived at the height of the Renaissance and seemed destined for a career in the Catholic Church, so it was not surprising that his higher education included study for more than a decade in Italy. By 1496, Copernicus was at the world-famous University of Bologna, where he furthered his knowledge of canon and civil law and where he was introduced to the study of astronomy by D. M. de Novara.

On March 9, 1497, Copernicus made his first recorded observation of the heavens. At this time, his uncle named him a canon of Frombork (Frauenburg) Cathedral, a position that he held for the rest of his life and that gave him both an adequate income and the leisure to pursue his studies. Although a canon, Copernicus never took holy orders.

By 1500, Copernicus had lectured in Rome on mathematics and was studying law and Greek at Padua. In 1503, he received a Ph.D. in canon law at the University of Ferrara. At Padua, he studied medicine, indicating that he was a true "universal man" of the Renaissance. Ironically, in his lifetime, Copernicus was more valued as a physician and lawyer than as an astronomer.

Contributions to Astronomy

Copernicus returned to his native land in 1506 and remained there until his death in 1543. For six years, from 1506 to 1512, he was employed as his uncle's personal physician and secretary. Following the death of his uncle, Copernicus continued as a canon at Frombork Cathedral while also maintaining administrative, diplomatic, financial, and medical responsibilities.

On March 31, 1513, Copernicus finished the construction of an observatory, where he pursued his interests in the heavens. Although he was not primarily an observational astronomer—he probably never did more than 100 observations—he did reflect on the findings of others.

In 1514, he circulated privately and largely anonymously his brief text *De hypothesibus motuum coelestium a se constitutis commentariolus* (The Commentariolus," translated 1939), in which he stated some of his revolutionary ideas. Copernicus believed that the cosmology inherited from Aristotle and Ptolemy could not do justice to the new discoveries.

Ptolemaic theory, developed in ancient times, held that Earth was the center of the universe (the geocentric model) and that the sun and the planets rotated around it. Copernicus taught that a heliocentric (or sun-centered) model better explained the evidence. It could account for the rotation of Earth on its axis and the movements of the planets, as well as the fluctuations of Earth's seasons.

A colleague and former pupil, George Joachim Iserin, or Rheticus, encouraged him to expand and publish his ideas in *De revolutionibus orbium coelestium* (1543; On the Revolution of the Celestial Spheres, 1939). Copernicus dedicated his work to Pope Paul III, hoping that this might forestall charges of heresy, because his view of the universe seemed to question the uniqueness of human beings as God's creations placed at the very heart of the cosmos.

Copernicus rightly predicted the impact of his teaching, for it would require major rethinking of the role of humans in the universe.

By postponing the publication of his research, he personally avoided controversy and a heresy trial. He saw his work in print only on his deathbed.

As anticipated, *De revolutionibus* was condemned for running contrary to scientific and religious orthodoxy. In 1616, it was placed on the *Index*, a list of books forbidden for Catholics to read, and it remained there until 1835.

Copernicus, one of the world's great scholars, died in Frauenburg (Frombork) on May 24, 1543. Building on his work, Galileo, Tycho, and Johannes Kepler proved Copernicus right and joined him in laying the foundations of modern astronomy.

The Heliocentric System

Copernicus taught that the sun, not Earth, is the center of the solar system. All planets, including Earth, rotate around the sun in regular orbits and according to predictable schedules. This view, the heliocentric system, became the basis of modern astronomy.

Until the time of Copernicus, the accepted cosmology (theory of the structure and evolution of the universe) was one based on the teachings of two celebrated Greek philosopher-scientists of antiquity: Aristotle and Ptolemy, or Claudius Ptolemaeus. Named the geocentric or Ptolemaic system, it had been in vogue for more than a millennium.

The work of Ptolemy, a brilliant geographer, mathematician, and astronomer working in Alexandria, had given the model great credibility among Muslim and Jewish scientists as well as Christians. Ptolemy had done many amazing things, such as estimating the size of Earth, describing its surface, and locating places by longitude and latitude. His central hypothesis, however, was that Earth, as the center of the universe, was stationary and that the sun, the planets, and the stars, like the moon, orbited it. It was this central doctrine that Copernicus came to question.

Although Copernicus was not primarily an observational astronomer, he was a splendid mathematician and an inexhaustible scholar who was thoroughly familiar with the research done by others. On this basis, Copernicus came to have trouble with the Ptolemaic system. Too many facts could not be accommodated, and efforts to incorporate them simply made the Ptolemaic model more complex and unwieldy.

For example, the Ptolemaic system did not do justice to the simple phenomenon of the seasons, nor did it furnish good explanations for the movement of the then-known planets. The behavior of Mercury and Venus could only be understood if their orbits were inside that of Earth, which itself was rotating around the sun. The orbits of such outer planets as Mars, Jupiter, and Saturn became more understandable if they were seen as circumnavigating the sun outside Earth's own orbit. If, as Copernicus came to believe, Earth rotates on its axis and orbits the sun, then these other phenomena could be better explained, as well as the shifting star patterns in the night sky.

The Copernican cosmology was strongly opposed on two grounds. First, it went contrary to the accepted scientific views of the time. It was believed that the "ancients" were superior to the "moderns" in wisdom and that their authority was to be accepted passively. Second, it seemed contradictory to the religious teachings of Scripture and tradition. Making Earth only one of several planets circling the sun (and hence not at the center of the universe) was seen as diminishing the dignity and importance of humans as divine creations.

Although Copernicus' view faced opposition from both scholars and the public, it eventually prevailed for three reasons. First, it explained the behavior of the solar system better than any previous model. Second, it predicted where further findings in astronomy could be made, so it was instrumental in paving the way for Galileo, Tycho Brahe, and Johannes Kepler. Third, it had the value of simplicity, in keeping with the law of parsimony that the least complicated explanation that does justice to the data is to be preferred.

Without the work of Copernicus, the modern revolution in astronomy would have been impossible.

Bibliography

The Astronomical Revolution: *Copernicus, Kepler, Borelli*. Alexander Koyre. Translated by R. E. W. Maddison. Paris: Hermann, 1973.

The Grand Tour: A Traveler's Guide to the Solar System. Ron Miller. New York: Workman, 1993.

The Planets: Exploring the Solar System. Roy A. Gallant. New York: Four Winds Press, 1989.

Solar System Evolution: A New Perspective. Stuart Ross Taylor. Cambridge, England: Cambridge University Press, 1992.

Bibliography

By Copernicus

De hypothesibus motuum coelestium a se constitutis commentariolus, 1514 ("The Commentariolus" in Three Copernican Treatises, 1939).

De revolutionibus orbium coelestium, 1543 (On the Revolution of the Celestial Spheres, 1939).

About Copernicus

Armitage, Angus. *Copernicus: The Founder of Modern Astronomy*. New York: T. Yoselaff, 1957.

Gingerich, Owen. *The Eye of Heaven: Ptolemy, Copernicus, Kepler*. New York: American Institute of Physics, 1993.

Hoyle, Fred. *Nicholas Copernicus: An Essay on His Life and Work*. New York: Harper & Row, 1973.

Adamczewski, Jan. Translated by Edward J. Piszner. *Nicolaus Copernicus and His Epoch*. Philadelphia: Copernicus Society of America, 1970.

(C. George Fry)

Sir Arthur Stanley Eddington

Disciplines: Astronomy and physics

Contribution: Eddington made important advances in the understanding of the motions, distribution, and structures of stars. His measurements during the 1919 solar eclipse were crucial in establishing Albert Einstein's general theory of relativity.

Dec. 28, 1882	Born in Kendal, England
1902-1905	Studies at Trinity College, University of Cambridge
1906	Appointed chief assistant at the Royal Observatory
1906	Elected a Fellow of the Royal Astronomical Society
1912-1917	Serves as secretary of the Royal Astronomical Society
1913	Appointed Plumian Professor of Astronomy at Cambridge
1914	Named director of the Cambridge Observatory
1914	Elected a Fellow of the Royal Society of London
1919	Heads an expedition to the island of Príncipe to study an eclipse
1921-1923	Serves as president of the Royal Astronomical Society
1923	Publishes *The Mathematical Theory of Relativity*
1930	Knighted
1936-1944	Serves as foreign secretary of the Royal Astronomical Society
1938	Awarded the Order of Merit
Nov. 22, 1944	Dies in Cambridge, England

Early Life

In 1884, when Arthur Stanley Eddington was not yet two years old, his father died during a typhoid epidemic. This left his mother, Sarah Ann Eddington, to rear Arthur and his older sister with very limited means.

As a child, Arthur was drawn to mathematics and science. He learned the multiplication table up to twenty-four times twenty-four before he learned to read. When loaned a small telescope at the age of ten, he used it every night to explore the sky.

Fortunate enough to have good teachers and combining his impressive mental ability with huge amounts of hard work, Eddington earned various awards and scholarships and was able to enter Owens College at the University of Manchester before he turned sixteen. He earned a bachelor's degree in physics in 1902 and went on to Trinity College at the University of Cambridge, where he earned a second bachelor's degree in 1905, as well as a master's degree in 1909.

A Working Astronomer

After receiving his degree in 1905, Eddington began research in physics at the Cavendish Laboratory, but he made little progress. The following year, he accepted the position of chief assistant at the Royal Observatory. There, he began a study of stellar motion.

In 1913, Eddington was elected to Cambridge's Plumian Professorship, and the following year he was appointed director of the Cambridge Observatory. In 1914, he published his first book, *Stellar Movements and the Structure of the Universe.* His work helped to establish the modern picture of the Milky Way as a rotating disk of several hundred billion stars and the "spiral nebulas" as distant galaxies similar to that of Earth.

General Relativity

As a Quaker, Eddington was exempt from combat in World War I, and the Astronomer Royal, Sir Frank Dyson, arranged for Eddington to be exempt from military service altogether.

Thus Eddington, as secretary of the Royal Astronomical Society, was available to receive Albert Einstein's landmark paper on general relativity in 1915; this was the only copy to reach England during the war. Mastering the formidable mathematics required, Eddington was soon giving lectures on the meaning of general relativity.

General relativity predicts that the path of starlight passing near the sun should be bent, and it was expected that this effect could be seen during a total eclipse of the sun. Eddington was selected to head an expedition to the island of Príncipe to photograph the solar eclipse of May, 1919. His results, along with those of a second expedition to Brazil, supported Einstein's prediction.

Later, Eddington showed that the static universe that Einstein artificially built into his theory is unstable and that the theory more properly predicts that the universe expands. This brought theory and experiment into agreement, for the American astronomer Edwin Hubble had shown that observational data supported the utterly unexpected result that the universe is expanding. In 1923, Eddington published his famous book, *The Mathematical Theory of Relativity.* It is said that more people learned general relativity from that book, than by any other way.

Other Work

Eddington also studied Cepheid variable stars. This led him to his pioneering study of stellar structure and to the mass-luminosity relation.

His models implied that the density of a white dwarf star was more than 50,000 times that of water, a result that most scientists considered absurd. Eddington showed that according to general relativity, light leaving the surface of such a dense white dwarf should be gravitationally redshifted (shifted toward the red end of the spectrum). Measurements were made that confirmed this prediction, thus vindicating both Einstein and Eddington.

Eddington's final years were spent in a somewhat controversial and largely unfruitful effort

Verifying the General Theory of Relativity

Albert Einstein's general theory of relativity predicts that the path of a light ray will bend noticeably if it travels near a large mass. This effect is observable as the deflection of starlight during a total solar eclipse.

According to Einstein's theory, mass causes the fabric of space to curve so that it is no longer flat. The path of a light ray in flat space is a straight line. If it encounters a patch of curved space, however, this path must bend with the space.

By analogy, one can picture a golf ball rolling due south toward a cup. If the ball just catches the rim of the cup and then rolls back out, it begins to head southwest. Traveling through a patch of curved space (the rim of the cup) has changed its direction.

Eddington studied the total solar eclipse of May 29, 1919. During this event, the sun appeared in front of bright stars of the Hyades cluster. Photographs taken during the eclipse were compared with photographs taken earlier, when the Hyades were in the night sky. This comparison showed that the apparent positions of the stars had shifted by about the amounts that Einstein had predicted. Einstein's theory of gravitation was thereby shown to be a more correct description of nature than that of Sir Isaac Newton.

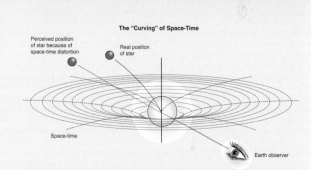

Eddington helped prove Einstein's general relativity theory, which predicts that space curves. For example, the gravity of the sun can bend the light coming from a star to be in a location other than its actual one.

Bibliography

Black Holes and Warped Spacetime. William J. Kaufman III. San Francisco: W. H. Freeman, 1979.

Relativity for the Million. Martin Gardner. New York: Macmillan, 1962.

Was Einstein Right? Clifford M. Will. New York: Basic Books, 1986.

to unify all physical theories into a single fundamental theory.

Eddington published more than a hundred scientific papers, as well as a dozen books. He was knighted and received more than a dozen honorary doctorates. Eddington's works have had lasting value, and he is still viewed as one of the great scientists of his time. Eddington died in 1944.

Bibliography

By Eddington

Stellar Movements and the Structure of the Universe, 1914.

Report on the Relativity Theory of Gravitation, 1918.

The Mathematical Theory of Relativity, 1923.

The Expanding Universe, 1933.

Relativity Theory of Protons and Electrons, 1936.

About Eddington

Chandrasekhar, Subrahmanyan. *Eddington: The Most Distinguished Astrophysicist of His Time.* Cambridge, England: Cambridge University Press, 1983.

Kilmister, C. W. *Men of Physics: Sir Arthur Stanley Eddington.* London: Pergamon Press, 1966.

Chandrasekhar, Subrahmanyan. *Truth and Beauty: Aesthetics and Motivations in Science.* Chicago: University of Chicago Press, 1987.

(Charles W. Rogers)

The Mass-Luminosity Relation

Eddington found that the luminosities of normal stars are proportional to approximately the fourth power of their masses.

Prior to Eddington's work, it was generally believed that a clear understanding of how stars produce energy would be necessary before anything useful could be surmised about their internal structures.

Eddington simply assumed that, somehow, enough energy was produced in the star's core to produce the star's luminosity. He then supposed that at any given point inside a star, the pressure of the weight of the overlying layers pushing down must be balanced by the sum of the gas pressure added to the pressure of the radiation streaming up from the center of the star. Solving the resulting equations led directly to the mass-luminosity relation.

By comparing his mass-luminosity relation with the actual masses and luminosities of stars, Eddington was able to deduce that the temperature at the sun's center is millions of Kelvins and that the pressure is tens of millions of atmospheres.

According to his model, stars more than fifty times as massive as the sun should be unstable and are therefore very rare. Eddington also guessed that a star's energy comes from the nuclear process of converting hydrogen to helium. This prediction was verified in the late 1930s, when some of the laws of nuclear fusion were first worked out.

Bibliography

McCrea, Sir William. "Arthur Stanley Eddington." *Scientific American* (June, 1991).

Kaler, James B. *Stars.* New York: W. H. Freeman, 1992.

Kaufmann III, William J. *Stars and Nebulas.* San Francisco, W. H. Freeman, 1978.

Sandra Faber

Disciplines: Astronomy and cosmology
Contribution: Faber studied the formation, structure, and evolution of galaxies. She is best known for her discovery of a new method for determining the distances to galaxies, as well as for her investigations into the large-scale motion of galaxies.

Dec. 28,1944	Born in Boston, Massachusetts
1966	Receives a B.A. in physics from Swarthmore College
1967	Marries Andrew Leigh Faber
1972	Receives a Ph.D. in astronomy from Harvard University
1972	Begins work at the Lick Observatory at the University of California, Santa Cruz
1975	Helps develop the Faber-Jackson relation
1977	Promoted to associate professor and astronomer at the Lick Observatory
1979	Promoted to full professor
1979	Concludes that galaxies are surrounded by pockets of invisible matter
1985	Wins the American Astronomical Society's Dannie Heineman Prize
1986	Elected to the National Academy of Sciences
1990	Helps establish the Keck Observatory
2012	Receives the Bruce Gold Medal from the Astronomical Society of the Pacific
2012	Receives the National Medal of Science

Early Life

Sandra Moore was born in Boston on December 28, 1944. Her mother, Elizabeth, was a homemaker who was very interested in medicine. Her father, Donald, was an amateur astronomer who often took Sandra stargazing. Sandra was the only child of older parents. They and their friends encouraged her to read widely and supported her interest in the sciences, which included rock collections, fossils, botany, and biology.

Student Days

Moore entered Swarthmore College with no particular goal in mind. She did not see how a woman could pursue such questions as the origin of the universe and still have a normal family life.

Sarah Lippincott, an astronomer at the observatory there, offered Moore a role model of an independent, professional woman who was able to create a life for herself. Lippincott's lack of a faculty position made Moore resolve that she must go on to obtain a Ph.D. so that she would not be limited. While at Swarthmore, she also met Andrew Leigh Faber. They were married on June 9, 1967.

After receiving her B.A. in physics from Swarthmore, Faber went on to graduate school at Harvard University. The next year, her husband also attended Harvard, to study applied physics. Since he had only a one-year deferment from service in the military, he had to find a job. Andrew Faber got a position at the Naval Research Laboratory in Washington, D.C. By this time, Sandra had completed her coursework for her degree

and, unwilling to live a long-distance marriage, managed to get an office at the Naval Research Laboratory. Unfortunately, her interests lay in a different direction from those of the other astronomers, and she found herself quite isolated. She was invited to work at the Department of Terrestrial Magnetism with Vera C. Rubin and Kent Ford, where she finished her dissertation and received her Ph.D. in 1972.

Research on Galaxies

Sandra Faber accepted a position as assistant professor and astronomer at the Lick Observatory

Dark Matter

Faber concluded that galaxies are surrounded by invisible mass known as dark matter.

The big bang theory proposes that the universe began with a gigantic explosion about 13 billion years ago. This has important implications for the future of the universe. Like a spaceship trying to escape from Earth, the universe has three possibilities: it can expand forever, it can stop expanding and begin deflating, or it can expand forever but at a decreasing rate. To determine which of these futures lies ahead, it is necessary to determine the density of the universe, which determines the gravitational attraction.

The critical density is the density necessary for the universe to continue expanding at a decreasing rate. Cosmologists denote the ratio of the actual to critical densities by the symbol Ω. If Ω is less than one, the universe is open and will expand forever; if Ω is greater than one, the universe is closed and will eventually collapse. Measurements of the mass of galaxies occupying a region of space have obtained a value for Ω much less than one.

Observations, however, indicate that galaxies are surrounded by an extensive, invisible outer halo, or galactic corona. Most of the mass of the galaxy seems to be contained in this so-called dark matter.

This material can only be detected by its gravitational effects; it emits no radiation of any type. Galaxies may contain as much as ten times more dark matter than luminous matter, and the fraction for large-scale systems may be even greater. Dark matter makes a major contribution to the average density. The nature of dark matter is still unknown, but understanding it holds the key to understanding the future of the universe.

Bibliography

Chaisson, Eric and Steve McMillan. *Astronomy Today*. Englewood Cliffs, N.J.: Prentice Hall, 1993.
Gribbin, John and Martin Rees. *Cosmic Coincidences: Dark Matter, Mankind, and Anthropic Cosmology*. New York: Bantam Books, 1989.
Trefil, James. *The Dark Side of the Universe: A Scientist Explores the Mysteries of the Cosmos*. New York: Charles Scribner's Sons, 1988.
Barrow, John D. and Joseph Silk. *The Left Hand of Creation: The Origin and Evolution of the Expanding Universe*. New York: Basic Books, 1983.
Jastrow, Robert. *Red Giants and White Dwarfs*. New York: W. W. Norton, 1990.

at the University of California, Santa Cruz. Using high-resolution spectra of galaxies, she studied the velocities of their internal stars. In 1975, with graduate student Robert Jackson, she developed the Faber-Jackson relation, which later developed into a fundametal way of calculating distances between galaxies. In 1979, with John Gallagher, she published a review concluding that galaxies are surrounded by enormous pockets of invisible matter.

In the 1980s, Faber collaborated with six other astronomers in the Seven Samurai project, collecting data on elliptical galaxies. In 1990, they discovered the Great Attractor, a concentration of clumped galaxies and matter that exerts a steady gravitational pull on an area of space.

In the 1990s, she helped establish the Keck Observatory on Mauna Kea in Hawaii. She received the Dannie Heineman Prize for astrophysics, became one of the few female members of the National Academy of Sciences, and was elected a member of the wide-field camera design team for the Hubble Space Telescope. She now is a full professor and interim director of Lick Observatory at the University of California, Santa Cruz. She studies the evolution of galaxies by augmenting the power of large telescopes. Working with David Koo and Raja Guhathakurta, she used the DEIMOS (Deep Imaging Multi-Object Spectograph) to survey 50,000 galaxies. Currently she is working on the CANDELS project, creating a rich database for further research of galaxies using the Hubble Telescope.

Bibliography

By Faber

"Variations in Spectral-Energy Distributions and Absorption-Line Strengths Among Elliptical Galaxies," *Astrophysical Journal*, 1973.

"Ten-Color Intermediate-Band Photometry of Stars," *Astronomy and Astrophysics Supplement*, 1973.

"Velocity Dispersions and Mass-to-Light Ratios for Elliptical Galaxies," *Astrophysical Journal*, 1976 (with R. E. Jackson).

"Spectroscopy and the photometry of elliptical galaxies. V—Galaxy streaming toward the new supergalactic center," *Astrophysical Journal*, 1988 (with D. Lynden-Bell et al.).

"Galaxy Luminosity Functions to z~1 from DEEP2 and COMBO-17: Implications for Red Galaxy Formation," *Astrophysical Journal*, 2007 (with S. M. Faber, et al.).

About Faber

Faber, Sandra M. sv "Sandra M. Faber" http://www.astro.ucsc.edu/faculty/profiles/singleton.php?&singleton=true&cruz_id=smfaber

Bagne, Paul. "Interview with Sandra Faber." *Omni* (July, 1990).

Pasachoff, J. "Interview with Sandra Faber." *Journey Through the Universe*. New York: W. B. Saunders, 1992.

Lightman, Alan and Roberta Brawer. *Origins: The Lives and Worlds of Modern Cosmologists*. Cambridge, Mass.: Harvard University Press, 1990.

"President Obama Honors Nation's Top Scientists and Innovators" December 21, 2012, http://www.whitehouse.gov/the-press-office/2012/12/21/president-obama-honors-nation-s-top-scientists-and-innovators

(Linda L. McDonald)

Hippolyte Fizeau

Disciplines: Astronomy and physics

Contribution: Fizeau developed ingenious and important techniques for the study of light, many of which are still in use today. He made the first accurate measurement of the speed of light in air.

Sept. 23, 1819 Born in Paris, France

1837-1842   Studies physics at the Collège de France and astronomy at the Paris Observatory

1840   Begins his investigations into heliography, an early type of photography

1845   With Léon Foucault, takes the first clear photographs of the surface of the sun

1848   Describes the effect of motion on light emitted from stars

1849   Measures the speed of light

1851   Measures the shift in the speed of light through a moving substance such as water

1856   Awarded the Triennial Prize by the Institut de France

1860   Made a member of the Académie des Sciences

1866   Awarded the Rumford Medal by the Royal Society of London

1878   Elected president of the physics section of the Académie des Sciences

Sept. 18, 1896 Dies in Venteuil, France

Early Life

Armand-Hippolyte-Louis Fizeau (pronounced "fee-ZOH") was the eldest son of a prosperous physician. Hippolyte desired to follow in his father's footsteps and began medical training, but his studies were interrupted by health problems. When Fizeau was sufficiently recovered, his interest had shifted to the physical sciences.

One of his courses of study was in astronomy, taken at the Paris Observatory, where the famous astronomer Dominique-François Arago taught. Arago recognized Fizeau's abilities brought Fizeau's work to the attention of the scientific community.

Much of Fizeau's early research was done in collaboration with others, such as Léon Foucault. Fizeau improved Louis-Jacques-Mandé Daguerre's heliography ("light drawing") process, an early type of photography. In 1845, Fizeau and Foucault made what were probably the first clear photographs of the surface of the sun.

Further Research

Fizeau and Foucault were able to confirm some predictions of the wave theory of light. In one experiment, they worked with infrared rays, invisible rays produced by warm objects. They showed that these "heat" rays obey the same laws as visible light and that they have a longer wavelength than visible light waves.

In another investigation, the two scientists tried to establish whether light travels more slowly when passing through a transparent substance such as glass or water. Before finishing these experiments, however, Fizeau and Foucault broke up their partnership over a personal dispute. Each continued to work on the problem, and in 1850 each submitted a paper to the Académie des Sciences. They both found that light does travel more slowly in water than in air

Measuring the Speed of Light

In 1849, Fizeau invented a mechanism that would enable him to determine the speed of light. A large toothed wheel spun rapidly, and a beam of light sent through the spaces was reflected by a mirror. If the wheel spun rapidly enough, the reflected light hit a tooth, which had moved in the time that it took the light to make the round trip. Knowing the distance to the fixed mirror and the speed of the wheel, Fizeau was able to calculate the speed of light.

Measuring the Speed of Light

Fizeau performed the first measurement of the speed of light on Earth.

Ole Rømer had estimated the speed of light by observations of the moons of Jupiter. Essentially, he used the moons as clocks to measure delays across the space from Jupiter to Earth. A controlled experiment on Earth, however, was not done until Fizeau's effort in 1849.

Fizeau's method was clever but difficult to perform. The accompanying diagram shows his experimental scheme. A toothed wheel interrupts a beam of light at regular intervals as it spins. The light is then reflected from a distant mirror (in Fizeau's case, a mirror 5.3 miles from his father's house at Suresnes). By the time that the pulse of light returns, the toothed wheel may have advanced far enough to block the light by a tooth, and the observer sees nothing. If one speeds up the rotation of the wheel, however, the time for the round trip of light is enough for the next gap in the wheel to rotate into place, and the observer sees the reflection in the mirror.

Knowing the rate of rotation, one can determine the time required for a round trip and thereby calculate the

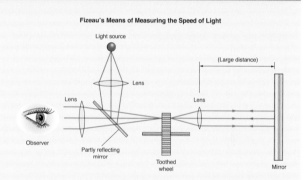

Fizeau's Means of Measuring the Speed of Light

speed of light. Great experimental skill and perseverance were necessary to make this apparatus work.

Fizeau's value for the speed of light was 195.73 miles per second, about 5 percent greater than today's accepted value. His idea became the basis for more accurate measurements by Alfred Cornu and Albert Abraham Michelson.

Bibliography

Dibdin, Frederick. *Essentials of Light*. London: Cleaver-Hume, 1961.

Sobel, Michael I. *Light*. Chicago: University of Chicago Press, 1987.

Tipier, Paul. *Physics*. New York: Worth, 1976.

Important Work in Optics

In 1848, Fizeau published a paper showing that the movement of an object affects the observed frequency of waves given off by that object. Fizeau did not know that Christian Doppler had published a paper on the same subject six years before. Since 1868, this Doppler-Fizeau effect has been used in astrophysics to measure the speed of stars relative to Earth.

In 1851, Fizeau found a way to measure the shift in the speed of light through a moving substance such as water. This was important in the historic controversy over the existence of the "ether," the substance that was thought to carry light waves, just as air carries sound waves.

Fizeau is mainly remembered for the ingenious experimental techniques that he invented. The Fizeau interferometer is still widely used.

Honors and Awards

Fizeau was awarded the Triennial Prize by the Institut de France and the Rumford Medal of the Royal Society of London. He was elected to the Académie des Sciences and became president of its physics section in 1878.

He died on September 18, 1896, in Venteuil, France, from cancer of the jaw.

Bibliography

By Fizeau

"Sur les effets résultant de certains procédés employés pour abréger le temps nécessaire à la formation des images photographiques," *Comptes rendus*, 1843.

"Sur le phénomène des interférences entre deux rayons de lumière dans le cas de grandes differences de marche," *Comptes rendus*, 1845 (with Léon Foucault).

"Sur une expérience relative à la vitesse de propagation de la lumière," *Comptes rendus*, 1849.

"Notes sur l'expérience relative à la vitesse comparative de la lumière dans l'air et dans l'eau," *Comptes rendus*, 1850 (with L. Breguet).

"Recherches sur la vitesse de propagation de l'électricité," *Comptes rendus*, 1850 (with E. Gounelle).

About Fizeau

Coulston Gillispie, Charles (ed.). *Dictionary of Scientific Biography.* Vol. 5. New York: Charles Scribner's Sons, 1970.

Asimov, Isaac. "Fizeau, Armand Hippolyte Louis." *In Isaac Asimov's Biographical Encyclopedia of Science and Technology.* New rev. ed. New York: Avon Books, 1976.

(Tom R. Herrmann)

Léon Foucault

Disciplines: Astronomy, invention, physics, and technology

Contribution: Foucault was the first to make an accurate determination of the velocity of light. He also took the first detailed pictures of the sun's surface and measured Earth's rotation using a swinging pendulum.

Sept. 18, 1819	Born in Paris, France
1843	Develops a regulator for arc lamps
1845	Makes the first daguerreotype of the sun's surface
1848	Shows how the brain combines two separate colors presented to individual eyes into one image
1850	Conducts pendulum experiments demonstrating the rotation of Earth
1850	Compares the velocity of light in air and water
1851	Receives the Cross of the Legion of Honor
1852	Invents the gyroscope
1853	Receives the Docteur des Sciences Physiques
1855	Becomes a physicist at the Paris Observatory
1855	Receives the Copley Medal of the Royal Society of London
1857	Develops a method for silvering glass to improve telescope mirrors
1862	Makes the first precise measurement of the velocity of light
1865	Elected to the Académie des Sciences
Feb. 11, 1868	Dies in Paris, France

Early Life

Jean-Bernard-Léon Foucault (pronounced "few-KOH") was born the son of a bookseller in Paris, France, on September 18, 1819. He had generally poor health and was therefore educated at home. He studied medicine with the desire to become a surgeon. Studies in physics followed, leading him to the field that dominated his later life.

Foucault published texts on geometry, arithmetic, and chemistry, and he coauthored a course textbook on clinical microscopy at the École de Médecine, where he served as an assistant. He wrote to a general audience about the latest from the world of science as a reporter for the *Journal des Débats* in 1845.

One of Foucault's earliest achievements was the development of a regulator for arc lamps. The regulator made it possible to use electricity, rather than gas, to supply artificial light to microscopes. Later improvements in the regulator allowed the introduction of arc lamps in theaters.

Foucault went on to invent other devices throughout his career, and he contributed greatly to the fields of astronomy and navigation. His interest in astronomy led him, with the help of French physicist Hippolyte Fizeau, to make the first detailed daguerreotype (an early form of photograph produced on a silver plate or a silver-covered copper plate) of the sun's surface.

The Earth's Rotation

Foucault had employed a pendulum clock to rotate his camera, and thus follow his subject, to photograph the entire sun in 1845. He noted that the pendulum behaved strangely over a period of time, maintaining the same movement relative to Earth's

Foucault's Pendulum

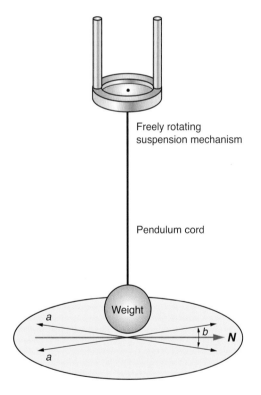

Freely rotating
suspension mechanism

Pendulum cord

Weight

a

a

b

N

The pendulum shows the rotation of Earth relative to the path of a swing pendulum over time. Arrows a show the path of a swinging pendulum, and arrow b shows the apparent direction of rotation of the plane in which the pendulum swings.

axis while the plane of swing appeared to rotate slowly. These observations led to his first pendulum experiments relative to the rotation of Earth.

The pendulum experiment was repeated at the Paris Observatory in 1851. This experiment also related the circle described by the swinging pendulum to the latitude of the experimental station. Additional repetitions were completed at numerous sites around the world between 1851 and 1853. The experiment was conducted at the Pantheon in Paris in 1852 using a 219.8-foot long pendulum with a 61-kilogram ball.

Foucault's pendulum experiment was the first direct demonstration of the Earth's rotation. Data collected from the experiment allowed Foucault to develop an equation relating the apparent angular rotation of the plane of a pendulum with the angular velocity of Earth and the latitude of the experimental station.

Foucault invented the gyroscope in 1852, having realized that a rotating body would behave in the same way as a pendulum. He was rewarded with the Copley Medal from the Royal Society of London in 1855 for his achievements with the pendulum and the gyroscope.

The Velocity of Light

In 1850, Foucault, working with Fizeau, succeeded in using a rotating mirror apparatus developed by Francois Arago, another French physicist, to make a comparative evaluation of the velocity of light (C) in air and water. Foucault and Fizeau demonstrated that the velocity of light in air is faster than that in water, thus supporting the wave theory of light first proposed by Christiaan Huygens in 1678. This finding was in contradiction to Sir Isaac Newton's predictions based on the particle theory of light.

Later modifications to Arago's rotating mirror apparatus enabled Foucault to make the first accurate determination of C in 1862. His apparatus used five mirrors, with a total light-path length of 66 feet.

The Rotation of the Earth

Foucault was the first to demonstrate, by direct means, that Earth rotates.

Foucault's pendulum experiments made it possible to define the rate of rotation as a function of latitude. Scientists can now explain most of the apparent motion of the sun, moon, and earth system by the rotation of Earth.

Foucault's pendulum apparatus functioned similarly to that of the apparatus shown in the figure on the previous page. The pendulum swing path rotates clockwise when viewed from above, while Earth rotates in a counterclockwise direction ("eastward").

The Earth's rotation affects the duration of exposure to the sun, the length of day and night, the temperature of the planet surface, the strength of the gravitational field, and the degree of bulge along the equator. The earth's rotation does not, however, contribute to the forces that raise the tides.

The Earth's rate of rotation accounts for moderate surface temperatures that are, for the most part, conducive to life as humans know it. A slower rate of rotation, such as that of Mercury, would have a strong impact on life on Earth. Surface temperatures on Mercury range from a low of absolute zero to a high of 420 degrees Celsius (790 degrees Fahrenheit). The temperature extremes result from longer exposure of the planetary surface to the sun and longer periods over which the opposite side of the planet is not exposed to the sun.

One complete rotation of Earth defines the length of a day. A lower rate of rotation would result in longer days and longer nights, while a faster rate would have the opposite effect.

The rotation of Earth produces a gravitational field. This phenomenon can be explained by physical laws studied and developed by Johannes Kepler, Galileo, and Sir Isaac Newton. Slower rates of rotation result in weaker gravitational fields, while increases in the rate of rotation yield stronger fields.

In 1687, Newton hypothesized that the rotation of Earth around a north-south axis would result in centrifugal forces and that these forces could be expected to produce a bulge in Earth's surface along the equator. Newton's hypothesis was proven to be correct; the difference between Earth's polar and equatorial radii is about 13.4 miles, and Earth's shape is more accurately defined as spheroidal rather than spherical.

Foucault's direct demonstrations of Earth's rotation led to the quantification of the rate of rotation. They also led to the development of the gyroscope and of modern astronomy.

An understanding of Earth's rotation, and that of other celestial bodies, has contributed to the development of space travel and the use of artificial satellites. A thorough understanding of planetary motion and natural forces will result in further developments in astronomy and space travel.

Bibliography

Feynman, Richard P., R. Leighton, and M. Sands. *The Feynman Lectures on Physics*. 5th ed. Vol. 1. Reading, Mass.: Addison-Wesley, 1975.

Gordon, R. *Physics of the Earth*. New York: Holt, Rinehart and Winston, 1972.

Munk, W. *The Rotation of the Earth: A Geophysical Discussion*. Cambridge, England: Cambridge University Press, 1975.

His measurement of 185,168.615 miles per second was within 1 percent of the actual value of 186,282.4 miles per second.

Astronomy

Foucault went to work at the Paris Observatory in 1855, and, by 1857, he had developed methods for silvering glass, thus improving the quality of telescope mirrors and enabling astronomers to make more detailed observations of the heavens.

He designed a photometer in 1855 and developed a birefringent prism in 1857, making it possible to obtain plane polarized light into the ultraviolet range. Modern telescopic astronomy was developed largely on the basis of optical techniques pioneered by Foucault.

Continuing developments in astronomy and industry required a mechanism that would drive machinery at a constant speed. Foucault responded with the invention of high-quality regulators in 1860. His heliostat enabled astronomers to keep telescopes pointed at the sun, while they used his siderostat to follow the stars.

Foucault's work in astronomy, as well as his accomplishments with light and Earth's rotation led to his election to the Royal Society of London in 1864 and the Academie des Sciences in 1865. He died in 1868.

Bibliography

By Foucault

Cours de microscopie complementaire des études médicates, 1844–1845 (with Alfred Donné; textbook on clinical microscopy).

Sur les vitesses relatives de la lumière dans l'air et dans l'eau, 1853 (on the relative velocity of light in air and water).

Recuil des travaux scientifiques de Léon Foucault, 1878.

About Foucault

Porter, Roy. ed. *The Biographical Dictionary of Scientists*. Oxford, England: Oxford University Press, 1994.

Millar, David et al. *Chambers Concise Dictionary of Scientists*. Cambridge, England: W&R Chambers/Cambridge University Press, 1989.

Williams, Trevor ed. *Collins Biographical Dictionary of Scientists*. New York: Harper Collins, 1994.

Coulston Gillispie, Charles. ed. *Dictionary of Scientific Biography*. New York: Charles Scribner's Sons, 1972.

(Kyle L. Kayler)

Herbert Friedman

Disciplines: Astronomy and physics

Contribution: Friedman pioneered rocket astronomy by including sensors on rockets fired high into the atmosphere or into space. He studied the emission of X-rays by the sun and from outside the solar system.

Jun. 21,1916	Born in New York City
1940	Receives a Ph.D. in physics from The Johns Hopkins University
1940	Works as a physicist at the United States Naval Research Laboratory
1949	Provides the first scientific proof that X-rays come from the sun
1956	Discovers evidence for the existence of extrasolar X-rays
1957	Launches the first telescope into space
1958	Discovers solar sources of X-rays and ultraviolet radiation
1960	Elected to the National Academy of Sciences
1960	Leads a team that takes the first X-ray photographs of the sun
1963	Becomes chief scientist at the E. O. Hulburt Center for Space Research
1964	Receives the National Medal of Science
1964	Finds that one extrasolar source of X-rays coincides with the Crab Nebula
1987	Given the Wolf Prize in Physics
1992	Receives the Massey Medal from the Royal Society of London
Sep. 9, 2000	Dies in Arlington, Virginia

Early Life

Herbert Friedman was born in New York City, New York, where his father was an art dealer. As a boy, Friedman attended public schools in Brooklyn. He loved art and decided early to be an artist. As an undergraduate at Brooklyn College, he majored in art until his junior year, when a professor convinced him to switch to physics.

Friedman graduated from Brooklyn College in 1936, but he could not find employment in physics and so sought a job as a commercial artist. The next year, he was accepted into graduate school in physics at The Johns Hopkins University, where he earned his Ph.D. in 1940.

Also in 1940, he married Gertrude Miller and was employed at the United States Naval Research Laboratory in Washington, D.C. At first, Friedman worked in the metallurgy division at the laboratory.

Rocket Astronomy

Study of the moon, planets, sun, and stars has, until only recently, been affected by distortion and other limitations caused by Earth's atmosphere. Sending instruments into the atmosphere or into space aboard a rocket overcomes these problems, giving scientists a clearer, more detailed understanding of the universe.

During the 1930s Robert H. Goddard experimented with rockets with the intent of using them to study Earth's upper atmosphere. E. O. Hulburt of the United States Naval Research Laboratory contemplated using Goddard's rockets to study the physics of the influence of the sun on Earth's ionosphere, but this first potential effort at "rocket astronomy" was never realized because of the beginning of World War II.

The German V-2 rockets that were captured at the end of the war, and more efficient rockets developed later, provided Friedman and his colleagues with the opportunity to send instruments high into the atmosphere. Different gases in the atmosphere at different levels block some wavelengths of energy, while allowing others to pass through to Earth-bound telescopes. For example, the ozone layer above Earth filters out ultraviolet light that can be harmful to life on the surface. At the same time, however, knowing about the wavelengths of energy coming from the sun and other objects in space can tell scientists much about the nature of those objects.

Design of experiments in early rocket astronomy was limited by the lack of precise control of rocket movements, but Friedman and his colleagues developed approaches that worked. During an eclipse of the sun, for example, they could send rockets aloft while only the outer portions of the sun were visible and then again when the whole sun was visible. Similarly, they could measure energy coming from the region of the Crab Nebula and then measure it again as the moon was passing in front of the Nebula. By using the moon to block out portions of the sun or the Crab Nebula, Friedman could ultimately identify the regions from which the radiation was coming.

Rocket astronomy remains important, but with the Hubble telescope and other instruments orbiting Earth, rocket astronomy progressed to satellite astronomy. With rockets, measurements could be taken only for a few seconds to a few minutes at a time. With instruments orbiting Earth, measurements could be taken continuously. The Japanese satellite YOHKOH can provide quality X-ray images of the sun continuously at two-second intervals.

The knowledge of the universe is growing rapidly. In 1958, Friedman proposed establishing astronomical observations on satellites orbiting Earth. In part as a result of his pioneering efforts, his dreams and predictions have come true. Perhaps the future will see another of Friedman's dreams come true—a permanent telescope facility on the moon.

Bibliography

A New Sun: The Solar Results from Skylab. Washington, D.C.: National Aeronautics and Space Administration NASA SP-402.

Giovanelli, R. G. *Secrets of the Sun.* New York: Cambridge University Press, 1984.

Lang, Kenneth R. *Sun, Earth, and Sky.* New York: Springer-Verlag, 1995.

Radiation Studies

During World War II, Friedman's efforts were focused on electron optics, X-ray analysis, and the development of radiation-detection devices. One of his inventions, an electronic X-ray diffractometer, was crucial to the rapid manufacture of quartz plates for radio circuits, which were needed for both military and civilian use.

His efforts during the war were also significant in helping to make available radiation-detection devices needed in the aftermath of the atomic bombs used against Japan. In 1945, Friedman received the Navy Distinguished Service Award for his contributions toward speeding up the production of materials needed during the war.

Early Efforts in Rocket Astronomy

Friedman began his tenure at the Naval Research Laboratory as what he called a "bench" scientist, who "rarely looked up at the sky." Soon, however, he came under the influence of Edward O. Hulburt, who introduced Friedman to natural science and inspired him with his studies of the ionosphere.

With the capture of several German V-2 rockets at the end of World War II, Friedman gained an opportunity to change astronomy as it was then known. The military wanted to test these rockets but did not want to launch them with an explosive warhead. Since they were designed to carry the weight of the explosives, something of similar weight had to be added to the rockets.

Friedman suggested adding instruments that would assist in high-altitude studies of the ultraviolet and X-ray spectrum of energy from the sun that is blocked by Earth's atmosphere. The V-2 rocket flights were brief, the most successful lasting only 450 seconds and climbing to 105.6 miles. One of these, however, provided the first proof that X-rays come from the sun.

With the firing of the last V-2, Friedman turned to smaller, more efficient rockets to carry his instruments aloft. Experiments in 1956 provided evidence for the production of X-rays elsewhere in the universe. Under Friedman's direction, the hard X-rays of solar flares were observed and proved to create radio blackout. Friedman demonstrated that X-rays come from the sun's corona and that ultraviolet radiation comes from the sun's surface (photosphere) and atmosphere (chromosphere).

During project Sunflare II, a team led by Friedman measured temperatures in the sun's corona as high as 190,000,000 degrees Fahrenheit during periods of intense coronal activity. In 1960 he and his colleagues obtained the first X-ray pictures of the sun during a five-minute rocket flight. In 1964, he found that one source of X-rays elsewhere in the universe coincides with the Crab Nebula, a remnant of a supernova. In 1968, he obtained evidence of X-ray pulsations from the neutron star in the Crab Nebula.

Teamwork, Persistence, and Luck

Friedman worked as part of a team at the Naval Research Laboratory, first as a team member and later as a team leader. An incredibly modest man, he never failed to credit the team effort. His work in astrophysics reveals the vision of the artist as well as the precision of the scientist. There were many failures—including one V-2 rocket that traveled horizontally instead of upward, landing in Mexico. However, persistence and carefully planned experiments resulted in many discoveries.

These findings earned for Friedman many honors, including the National Medal of Science, the coveted Wolf Prize in Physics, and honorary doctorates from the Universities of Tübingen and Michigan.

Serendipity also played a role in Friedman's successes. For example, the launching of the Soviet Union's Sputnik satellite meant that funding would be available for his experiments, and a rocket that failed to go off as planned was launched late and coincided with a solar flare.

Bibliography

By Friedman

The Amazing Universe, 1975.

Sun and Earth, 1985.

The Astronomer's Universe: Stars, Galaxies, and Cosmos, 1990.

"From Ionosonde to Rocket Sonde," *Journal of Geophysical Research,* 1994.

About Friedman

Tucker, Wallace and Karen. *The Cosmic Inquirers: Modern Telescopes and Their Makers.* Cambridge, Mass.: Harvard University Press, 1986.

Moritz, C. ed. *Current Biography.* New York: H. W. Wilson, 1963.

Jauhar, Sandeep. "Herbert Friedman, 84, Leader in Astronomy, Dies." *New York Times,* September 13, 2000.

Land, Barbara. *The Telescope Makers: From Galileo to the Space Age.* New York: Thomas Y. Crowell, 1968.

Tucker, Wallace and Riccardo Giaconni. *The X-Ray Universe.* Cambridge, Mass.: Harvard University Press, 1985.

(Jerome A. Jackson)

Galileo

Disciplines: Astronomy, cosmology, invention, mathematics, and physics

Contribution: Galileo is best remembered for his use of the telescope to make astronomical observations to support the sun-centered concept for planetary motion.

Feb. 15, 1564	Born in Pisa, Republic of Florence (now Italy)
1581	Enters the University of Pisa as a medical student
1583	Uses a pendulum to invent a pulse-measuring device
1588	Invents a hydrostatic balance
1589	Appointed to the chair of mathematics at the University of Pisa
1589	Demonstrates his principle of falling objects
1592	Named chair of mathematics at the University of Padua
1593	Invents the basic thermometer
1596	Invents a military and geometric drafting compass
1609	Constructs a telescope and observes the moon
1610	Observes the moons of Jupiter
1610	Appointed chief mathematician and philosopher of Tuscany
1616	Called to Rome and warned not to teach the theory of Nicolaus Copernicus
1632	Publishes a book on Ptolemaic and Copernican systems
1633	Tried for heresy in Rome and recants
Jan. 8, 1642	Dies in Arcetri, Republic of Florence

Early Life

Galileo (pronounced "ga-lih-LAY-oh") was the first child born to Vincenzo and Giulia Galilei. The date of his birth is recorded as February 15, 1564, in Pisa. His father was an accomplished musician who both taught and composed music. Galileo's mother came from a noble family. She was often critical of her husband's inability to provide for their family, which grew to include seven children. It was not a happy household.

By the time that Galileo was ten, his father recognized that he was an extraordinary child. Galileo was able to play both the lute and the organ. His father tutored him in the classical languages of Greek and Latin, but the boy needed further instruction. It was decided that Galileo would be educated at the monastery at Vallombrosa. After four years of training, his father removed him from the monastery just before he took his final vows.

In 1581 Galileo began his studies at the University of Pisa. It was in his first year of study that he was introduced to the scientific philosophy of Plato and Aristotle. At once, he rebelled at these outdated philosophers and questioned the logic of his teachers. As his education progressed, his interest gradually changed from medicine to mathematics and science. He soon became convinced that mathematical principles would replace the logic of Aristotle. This was a relatively dangerous position to hold at this particular time in history.

Galileo was not a model student. He was boastful and arrogant toward his professors and his fellow students. He had a brilliant mind, but he did not fit in well with the accepted academic behavior.

Lack of money to pay for his education forced Galileo to leave the University of Pisa without a degree. He found work tutoring other students in mathematics. It was also during this period that he developed his lifelong interest in the physical sciences. As a result of studying Archimedes' principle of water displacement, Galileo invented a hydrostatic balance. Along with it, he published his first scientific work, which described how his balance could measure the density of metals and fluids.

First Academic Appointment

The year 1589 saw Galileo achieve his first success: He was appointed to the chair of mathematics at Pisa. It was during this appointment that he successfully defended his principle of falling objects in a public demonstration that took place from the famous Leaning Tower of Pisa. He proved that objects fall at a constant rate regardless of how light or heavy they were.

Galileo's career was on the rise, and inventions such as the thermometer and the military compass earned him the prestigious chair of mathematics at the University of Padua. Over the next several years, he would solidify his position as a great scientist and mathematician.

Principles on the Mechanics of Motion

Had Galileo never used a telescope, science would have remembered him for his brilliant discoveries that dealt with motion.

Early in his career, Galileo became fascinated with motion and the way in which it was explained by Aristotle. He was convinced that Aristotle was wrong. Galileo's demonstration that objects of different weights dropped from the Leaning Tower of Pisa fall at the same rate helped make his reputation as one of the leading scientists of his day. Throughout his career, he would never lose sight of the beauty of motion and the laws that govern it.

In his final work, *Discorsi e dimostrazioni mathematiche intorno a due nuove scienze attenenti alla meccanica* (*Discourses Concerning Two New Sciences* 1914), published in 1634, Galileo summarized his thoughts on motion. He also covered several other topics, including the strength and resistance of various materials used in construction. The majority of the book is devoted to motion. He incorporated many of his earlier concepts that were unpublished. He also refined several of his ideas about the acceleration of falling objects, such as that resistance to air plays an important role in an object's velocity. Galileo also introduced incline planes and pendulums to prove his point of uniform motion.

Galileo viewed motion as three parts: uniform motion, naturally accelerated motion, and violent motion as seen in projectiles. His clue to understanding motion was found by observing nature itself and experimentally duplicating that motion.

Perhaps the most important aspect of motion to come out of the discourses was the "times-squared law." Galileo states that if a body falls from rest with uniformly accelerated motion, the spaces that it covers in given increments of time are the squares of those times. He was able to prove this law by rolling a metal ball down an inclined plane and timing its travel rate over a constant distance. By varying the angle of the plane, he proved that the spaces traversed were always the squares of the times.

The concept of inertia, that objects in motion tend to remain in motion, is clearly indicated by Galileo. This concept would become a critical part of Sir Isaac Newton's first law of motion. Another aspect of motion that is found in the discourses deals with the combination of uniform motion and accelerated motion. An object traveling with such motion would trace a semi-parabolic path. This fact had tremendous implications when dealing with projectiles such as bullets and cannonballs. The military had a particular interest in this information to improve the efficiency of its artillery weapons.

Galileo's achievements in the understanding of motion can be seen when his astronomical discoveries are combined with his basic physics experiments. His contemporary Johannes Kepler developed three laws of motion that govern the movement of the planets around the sun. Galileo, in his basic physics experiments, showed how motion is both regular and predictable. When this is added to Kepler's laws, one can clearly see that a force does govern the motion of the planets. A fine example of this was seen in Galileo's observations of Jupiter's four moons. Although Galileo hinted at, and described, the effects of such a force, he could not pinpoint its exact source. It was left to Newton to describe the force of gravity mathematically.

Bibliography

Drake, Stillman. *Galileo: Pioneer Scientist*. Toronto: University of Toronto Press, 1990.

Hazen, Robert M. and James Trefil. *The Physical Sciences: An Integrated Approach*. New York: John Wiley & sons, 1996.

Hall, A. R. *The Revolution in Science: 1500-1750*. London: Longman, 1983.

Lindberg, D.C. ed. *Science in the Middle Ages*. Chicago: University of Chicago Press, 1978.

Galileo's Use of the Telescope

The telescope gave seventeenth century scientists the ability to see far beyond the limits of human sight.

Galileo did not invent the telescope, but he made improvements to its design and used it for scientific purposes. History records that Galileo was not the first person to gaze at the moon with a telescope; that distinction probably goes to the Englishman Thomas Harriot. It was Galileo, however, who made the first scientific observations of the moon with a telescope and then published his findings.

For almost four months, Galileo made nightly observations of the moon. He noted the presence of mountain peaks and craters. Large, dark, and somewhat circular features were taken to be "seas." In almost every respect, he was looking at a world similar to Earth—which should not have been possible according to the science of Plato and Aristotle. Galileo was providing physical evidence that would rock the foundation of the Catholic Church's teachings. It was dangerous ground on which Galileo was walking, and he needed to exercise great caution when making his discoveries known.

In Galileo's effort to construct the finest telescopes, he continuously worked to improve them. Increasingly powerful instruments were desired, and each new telescope brought additional discoveries. As Galileo looked into the Milky Way, he saw thousands of stars never before observed by anyone. The universe that he was viewing in his telescope appeared to be infinite, with countless numbers of stars. Nothing in the writings of Plato or Aristotle could explain this fact.

Galileo's most important astronomical discovery came on January 7, 1610. As he observed Jupiter, he noticed the presence of three bright stars forming a straight line with the planet. The following night, this configuration had changed, and every night thereafter a new association would appear. It was only after a fourth moon was discovered that he came to the correct conclusion. Jupiter and its four moons were a model in miniature of the solar system as described by Nicolaus Copernicus and Johannes Kepler. No longer could the heavens circle a stationary Earth at the center of the universe. Human thinking would have to change in order to conform with Galileo's discovery.

Within two weeks of the confirmation of Jupiter's moons, Galileo published his work *Sidereus Nuncius* (1610; The Sidereal Messenger, 1880). In it, he discussed his observations of the moon and Jupiter's moons. There would be more to come: Saturn was later observed as being three objects rather than one, which confused Galileo. Venus proved to be no problem; he observed it in its crescent phase and correctly determined its position to be between the sun and Earth.

As with any discovery, sometimes the unexpected happens and it is not recognized for what it is. This was the case with Neptune. Galileo definitely observed Neptune on December 28, 1612, and on January 28, 1613, but he failed to recognize it as a planet. It would be another 234 years before its official discovery.

The significance of Galileo's use of the telescope lies not in the timing of the actual discoveries but in the publishing of his observations. His reports were accurate, and his interpretations provided strong support for the Copernican model of a sun-centered universe.

Bibliography

Finochiaro, Maurice A. *The Galileo Affair*. Berkeley: University of California Press, 1989.

Fermi, R and G. Bernardini. *Galileo and the Scientific Revolution*. Greenwich, Conn.: Fawcett, 1965.

Shea, W. R. *Galileo's Intellectual Revolution*. New York: Macmillan, 1972.

Wallace, William A., ed. *Reinterpreting Galileo*. Washington, D.C.: Catholic University Press, 1986.

Koestler, A. *The Sleepwalkers: A History of Man's Changing Vision of the Universe*. London: Hutchinson, 1959.

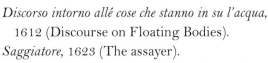

The Starry Messenger

The year 1609 would be the turning point in Galileo's career. In this year an important invention was gradually becoming known all across Europe. A Dutch lens-maker had made the first telescope. When Galileo heard of the optical principles involved, he quickly understood how it worked and made one for himself. It was an instrument with a tremendous potential. The obvious application was for the military; it could give advanced warning of an enemy's approach. Galileo saw its scientific potential and used it to gain both fame and wealth.

A more important achievement came when Galileo turned the telescope toward the moon. Instead of seeing a smooth, perfect world as described by Aristotle, he saw a world much like that of Earth: the moon had craters, "seas," and mountains. Clearly Aristotle was wrong and a new view of the universe was born. The astronomical discoveries of Galileo led him into conflict with the teachings of the Catholic Church, which supported a universe as described by Plato and Aristotle. In the Church's model, Earth was the center of the universe, and everything moved around it in perfect circles. What Galileo saw in his telescope shattered that view and supported the sun-centered universe of Nicolaus Copernicus.

Galileo's boastful and arrogant character brought him into direct conflict with the Catholic Church. He was tried as a heretic in 1633, and all of his writings were banned. As a sick old man, he apologized for his scientific beliefs and affirmed the correctness of Earth-centered universe of Aristotle. Although Galileo was disgraced and lost respect from some fellow scientists, he continued his work in physics until his death in 1642.

Bibliography

By Galileo

Sidereus Nuncius, 1610 (The Sidereal Messenger, 1880; also known as The Starry Messenger).

Discorso intorno allé cose che stanno in su l'acqua, 1612 (Discourse on Floating Bodies).

Saggiatore, 1623 (The assayer).

Dialogo sopra i due massimi sistemi del mondo, tolemaico e copernicano, 1632 (*Dialogue Concerning the Two Chief World Systems, Ptolemaic and Copernican*, 1661).

Discorsi e dimostrazioni mathematiche intorno a due nuove scienze atteneti alla meccanica, 1634 (*Discourses Concerning Two New Sciences …*, 1914).

About Galileo

Reston, James Jr. *Galileo: A Life*. New York: HarperCollins, 1994.

Shapere, Dudley. *Galileo: A Philosophical Study*. Chicago: University of Chicago Press, 1974.

Sharratt, Michael. *Galileo: Decisive Innovator*. Oxford, England: Blackwell Scientific Publishers, 1994.

Drake, S. *Galileo: Pioneer Scientist*. Toronto: University of Toronto Press, 1990.

(Paul P Sipiera)

Margaret Geller

Disciplines: Astronomy and physics
Contribution: Geller studied the distribution of galaxies in space and discovered the Great Wall, a group of galaxies that is the largest known structure in the universe.

Dec. 8, 1947	Born in Ithaca, New York
1970	Earns a bachelor's degree from the University of California, Berkeley
1970-1973	Receives a National Science Foundation Fellowship
1972	Earns a master's degree from Princeton University
1974-1976	Receives a fellowship to the Harvard-Smithsonian Center for Astrophysics
1975	Earns a Ph.D. from Princeton
1976-1980	Employed as a research associate at the Harvard-Smithsonian Center for Astrophysics
1983	Begins working at the Smithsonian Astrophysical Observatory
1985	Begins large-scale galaxy survey with John P. Huchra
1988	Promoted to professor at Harvard
1989	With Huchra, discovers the Great Wall, a long sheet of galaxies
1990-1995	Receives a MacArthur Fellowship
1991-present	Senior Scientist at Smithsonian Astrophysical Observatory
1995	Fellow of American Physical Society
1996-1998	Chair of Astrophysics Screening Panel for the National Academy of Sciences

Early Life

Margaret Joan Geller was born in Ithaca, New York, on December 8, 1947. Her parents were Seymour Geller and Sarah Levine Geller. She received a bachelor's degree from the University of California, Berkeley, in 1970.

As a graduate student, Geller received a fellowship from the National Science Foundation from 1970 to 1973. Her graduate studies were done at Princeton University in Princeton, New Jersey, where she received a master's degree in 1972 and a Ph.D. in 1975. Her doctoral thesis concerned the distribution of galaxies within clusters.

Fellowships and Professorships

Geller received a fellowship in theoretical physics to the Harvard-Smithsonian Center for Astrophysics from 1974 to 1976. She was a research associate at the same institution from 1976 to 1980. She was a senior visiting fellow at the Institute for Astronomy in Cambridge, England, from 1978 to 1982.

The Large-Scale Distribution of Galaxies

Instead of being evenly distributed throughout space, galaxies are grouped into very large structures that astronomers find difficult to explain.

Astronomers believe that the universe began billions of years ago in an enormous explosion known as the big bang. Evidence for the big bang is found in the cosmic background radiation of the universe. This background exists in the form of microwaves radiating from the most distant regions of the universe. Because the source of these microwaves is so far away and have thus taken so long to reach Earth, they are believed to be the remnant of the energy of the big bang.

The fact that the cosmic background radiation is constant in all directions indicates that the universe began with matter evenly distributed everywhere. As the universe expanded, gravity caused matter to form into various structures. These structures include galaxies, clusters of galaxies, and superclusters of clusters. The age of the universe does not allow enough time for gravity to have formed structures much larger than superclusters. Because of this, astronomers predicted that, on a large scale, galaxies would be evenly distributed throughout the universe.

In 1985, Geller began collecting evidence that this prediction was wrong. Her large-scale maps of galaxies showed that they were grouped into long, curved sheets surrounding "bubbles" of empty space. The largest of these sheets, known as the Great Wall, is 15 million light-years thick, 200 million light-years wide, and at least 500 million light-years long. Because the ends of the Great Wall went beyond the borders of Geller's maps, it may actually be much longer. It is the largest structure known to exist.

The Great Wall is probably not the only structure of its size. Other astronomers have studied regions of space that are much narrower than the area mapped by Geller but which include galaxies that are much more distant. These studies suggest that a series of Great Walls exist throughout the universe in what has been described as a "honeycomb" structure.

Given the apparent uniformity of the universe at the time of the big bang, these enormous structures are difficult to explain. Most astronomers believe that dark matter is involved. Dark matter consists of unknown, unseen particles that are believed to make up more than 90 percent of the mass of the universe. Dark matter could have been unevenly distributed at the time of the big bang without disturbing the smoothness of the cosmic background radiation. The gravitational force of this uneven dark matter could have been responsible for the formation of large structures such as the Great Wall.

The dark matter explanation for these structures causes its own problems for astronomers. If dark matter is cold, containing slow-moving particles, theoretical models of the expansion of the universe have difficulty accounting for the creation of large structures. If dark matter is hot, containing fast-moving particles, these models do not accurately predict the way in which smaller structures are formed. Geller suggested that some fundamental gap may exist in the knowledge of astronomers that could explain these difficulties.

Bibliography

Colliding Galaxies: The Universe in Turmoil. Barry Parker. New York: Plenum Press, 1990.

The Large-Scale Structure of the Universe. P. J. E. Peebles. Princeton, N.J.: Princeton University Press, 1980.

The Vindication of the Big Bang: Breakthroughs and Barriers. Barry Parker. New York: Plenum Press, 1993.

Geller served as an assistant professor at Harvard University in Cambridge, Massachusetts, from 1980 to 1983. In 1983, she started working at the Smithsonian Astrophysical Observatory, also in Cambridge. She returned to Harvard as a professor of astronomy in 1988.

Mapping Galaxies

In 1985, Geller began an ambitious project with astronomer John P. Huchra to map the three-dimensional positions of 15,000 galaxies. Although the two-dimensional positions of these galaxies were already known, each galaxy's distance from Earth had to be determined individually. This was done by measuring the redshift of each galaxy.

The redshift of an object in space is the degree to which the light from the object is shifted toward the red end of the spectrum. The amount of redshift is determined by the speed at which the object is moving away from Earth. Because the universe is expanding, more distant objects are moving away more quickly. By measuring the redshift of a galaxy, Geller and Huchra were able to tell how quickly it was moving away and therefore how distant it was.

Geller and Huchra expected to find that galaxies were uniformly distributed in space. Instead, they were surprised to discover relatively thin sheets of galaxies surrounding large empty spaces. The first results of their study were published in 1986.

The Great Wall

In 1989, Geller and Huchra found the longest sheet of galaxies that they had ever encountered. Known as the Great Wall, it was the largest structure ever discovered by astronomers. Other astronomers soon found evidence for a series of Great Walls separated by vast empty spaces.

Geller was awarded the Newcomb-Cleveland Prize from the American Academy of Arts and Sciences in 1989. She won a MacArthur

Fellowship in 1990. Her current work is leading the HectoMAP project mapping clusters of the galaxy and she still works with dark matter leading a project called SHELS. Geller has also dedicated herself to the public education of science and has made several short films including *Where the Galaxies Are* and *So Many Galaxies…So Little Time.*

Bibliography

By Geller

Large Scale Structures in the Universe, 1987 (with A. C. Fabian and A. Szalay).

"The Great Wall and Beyond," *Reviews in Modern Astronomy*, 1997.

"μ-PhotoZ: Photometric Redshifts by Inverting the Tolman Surface Brightness Test," *Astrophysical Journal* (with Michael J. Kurtz, Daniel G. Fabricant, William F. Wyatt, and Ian P. Dell'Antonio) 2007.

"Dust Obscured Galaxies in the Local Universe," *Astrophysical Journal* (with Ho Seong Hwang) 2013.

About Geller

Bartusiak, Marcia. "Mapping the Universe." *Discover* 11 (August, 1990).

McMurray, Emily J. ed. *Notable Twentieth-Century Scientists*. Detroit: Gale Research, 1995.

"Margaret Geller," Array of Contemporary American Physicists, http://www.aip.org/history/acap/biographies/bio.jsp?gellerm

"Margaret J. Geller," https://www.cfa.harvard.edu/~mjg/

Who's Who of American Women. New Providence, N.J.: Marquis, 1993.

(Rose Secrest)

Alan H. Guth

Disciplines: Cosmology and physics

Contribution: Guth proposed that early in its life, the universe underwent a sudden inflation, an idea that helped resolve serious dilemmas in cosmology.

Feb. 27, 1947	Born in New Jersey
1969	Receives bachelor's and master's degrees in physics from the Massachusetts Institute of Technology (MIT)
1971	Becomes an instructor at Princeton University
1972	Earns a Ph.D. in physics from MIT
1974-1977	Obtains a fellowship at Columbia University
1977-1979	Becomes research associate at Cornell University
1979-1980	Becomes research associate at the Stanford University
1980	Appointed a professor of physics at MIT
1981	Named a Alfred P. Sloan Foundation Fellow
1984-1990	Staff physicist at the Harvard Smithsonian Center for Astrophysics
1989	Named chair of astrophysics for the American Physical Society
1992	Wins the Julius Edgar Lilienfeld Prize of the American Physical Society
1992	Becomes Victor Weisskopf Professor of Physics at MIT
2012	Awarded the Fundamental Physics Prize

Early Life

Alan Harvey Guth was born in New Brunswick, New Jersey, in 1947. His father, Hyman Guth, ran a small business, and neither his father nor his mother, Elaine Cheiten Guth, had an interest in science. Nevertheless, young Alan enjoyed intellectual matters, especially mathematics, and his recreational reading in high school included books about cosmology.

Guth entered the Massachusetts Institute of Technology (MIT) as a physics major. Particle physics and the fundamental forces of nature fascinated him. He pursued both theoretical and experimental physics, working on lasers at Bell Laboratories in Murray Hill one summer. He finished both his bachelor's and his master's degrees in 1969. In 1972, he completed his Ph.D. also at MIT. In 1971, he married Susan Tisch and they had two children.

Academic Career

While completing his doctoral requirements, Guth held a temporary instructorship in Princeton University's physics department. In 1974, he began a fellowship at Columbia University, which was the normal career step for a young physicist. When the fellowship expired in 1977, he became a research associate at Cornell University.

The Inflationary Universe

Guth proposed that inflation took place in the very early history of the universe, when it briefly grew at an enormously faster pace than it does today.

The original big bang cosmological model, proposed in the 1930s, explained the universe as the debris sprayed uniformly in all directions when a huge "primal atom" exploded about 10 to 20 billion years ago. Three serious concerns plagued this model: the horizon, smoothness, and flatness problems.

The horizon problem arises because if the uniform expansion described by this model were correct, it is not clear why every region of the universe should look the same. The fast uniform expansion rate would quickly separate regions too far for communications, being restricted by the speed of light, and so different initial conditions could have produced regions with different physical laws. Why, then, do physical laws appear to be the same everywhere in the universe?

The smoothness problem comes from the existence of galaxies, which evolved from unevenness in the distribution of matter in the early universe. Although there are myriad galaxies, the universe is still extremely uniform. Therefore, the early universe must have been even more uniform, but the original big bang theory gave no hint as to why.

The flatness problem pertains to the density of matter in the universe. The critical point of density, omega, is defined as the ratio of observed density and the density required to bring the universe's expansion to a halt and reverse it. Below an omega of 1, the universe is closed and will eventually collapse back to a single point. Above an omega of 1, the universe will expand forever. If omega equals 1, the universe will expand at an ever-decreasing rate, like a ball rolling down a gently, uniformly decreasing slope. Omega seems close to 1, mysteriously.

Inflation solves parts of these problems. According to Guth, the universe did not expand at a steady rate in the beginning. Instead, it puffed out 10 times, ballooning from the size of a proton to the size of a grapefruit in 10-35 seconds. Since then, it has expanded uniformly. He proposed that the observable universe, the result of this inflation, is only part of a larger, unobservable universe.

Guth's model argues that the universe grew from a much smaller area than that proposed by the original big bang model. Thus, during the crucial early expansion, the matter remained in close contact, sharing the same initial conditions. This idea answers the horizon problem. Quantum fluctuation in the small inflationary stage could also have produced sufficient density variations to produce galaxies within a universe that is still smoothly textured on today's large scale. Finally, the universe may be flat, having an omega of 1, in the 10 to 20 billion light-years that are visible, but not in the larger universe beyond. Likewise, children in the United States growing up in the Great Plains region may think the world a very flat place until they see the mountain ranges of the west or east.

Bibliography

Silk, Joseph. *The Big Bang.* New York: W. H. Freeman, 1989.

Hawking, Stephen W. *A Brief History of Time: From the Big Bang to Black Holes.* New York: Bantam Books, 1988.

Barrow, John D. *The Origin of the Universe.* New York: Basic Books, 1994.

Most physicists make the transition to industry or a junior professorship at this point, but Guth was unable to land a permanent position. Instead, he spent a year conducting research in elementary particles at the Stanford Linear Accelerator Center (SLAC) south of San Francisco.

Becoming a Cosmologist

As a researcher, Guth had dedicated himself to well-defined physical problems that could be treated mathematically, and had avoided speculative cosmological questions. Yet cosmology slowly gained a hold on him. A lecture by Princeton University cosmologist Robert Dicke in 1978 piqued his interest. Dicke pointed out serious problems with the standard cosmological theory, the big bang model, which assumed that the universe has expanded from a primal explosion.

A Cornell colleague, Henry Tye, intrigued Guth with a problem in grand unification theories (GUTs), which attempt to explain the fundamental forces of nature. These theories often required the existence of a bizarre heavy particle, called a magnetic monopole, but the two men calculated that early in the history of the universe, an impossibly high number of these magnetic monopoles had to have been created in order to fit the requirements of GUTs.

The Inflationary Universe and Fame

On December 6, 1979, Guth had an inspiration: a sudden acceleration, or inflation, of the universe's expansion would remove the magnetic monopole problem. In the following months, he also realized that an inflationary universe would also help solve the cosmological problems described by Dicke.

The idea attracted enthusiastic support. Although others had thought of it independently, inflation became associated with Guth. Soon he was a celebrity in the scientific community. In 1980 he was hired by MIT, and he stayed there, eventually being promoted to a prestigious chair as Victor Weisskopf Professor of Physics in 1992.

He now works with Edward Farhi exploring the possibilities of creating a new universe by igniting inflation in a hypothetical laboratory. This research has opened up many opportunities for exploring the theory of spacetime and a possible quantum theory of creation.

Bibliography

By Guth

"Inflationary Universe: A Possible Solution to the Horizon and Flatness Problems," *Physical Review D*, 1981.

"The Birth of the Cosmos" *Origins and Extinctions: Based on a Symposium on Life and the Universe, Held at the National Academy of Sciences*, Washington, D.C., April 30, 1986, 1988.

The Inflationary Universe: The Quest for a New Theory of Cosmic Origins. Perseus Publishing, 1997. (Donald E. Osterbrock and Peter H. Raven, eds.).

"Starting the Universe: The Big Bang and Cosmic Inflation" in *Bubbles, Voids, and Bumps in Time: The New Cosmology*, 1989 (James Cornell, ed.).

About Guth

"Alan Guth," MIT Department of Physics, http://web.mit.edu/physics/people/faculty/guth_alan.html

Lemonick, Michael. *Light at the Edge of the Universe: Leading Cosmologists on the Brink of a Scientific Revolution*. New York: Villard Books, 1993.

Overbye, Dennis. *Lonely Hearts of the Cosmos: The Scientific Quest for the Secret of the Universe*. New York: HarperCollins, 1991.

Lightman, Alan and Roberta Brawer. *Origins: The Lives and Worlds of Modern Cosmologists*. Cambridge, Mass.: Harvard University Press, 1990.

The Inflationary Universe: The Quest for a New Theory of Cosmic Origins. Perseus Publishing, 1998.

(Roger Smith)

George Ellery Hale

Disciplines: Astronomy, invention, and physics

Contribution: Hale, one of the key figures of modern astronomy, helped found astronomical observatories, journals, and scientific organizations. He discovered the sun's magnetic field and the sunspot polarity cycle.

Jun. 29, 1868	Born in Chicago, Illinois
1889	Invents the spectroheliograph
1890	Graduated from the Massachusetts Institute of Technology (MIT)
1892	Appointed an associate professor at the University of Chicago
1895	Founds the *Astrophysical Journal*
1895	Appointed the director of the Yerkes Observatory
1899	Helps found the American Astronomical Society
1902	Elected to the National Academy of Sciences
1904	Awarded the gold medal of the Royal Astronomical Society
1904	Appointed the director of Mount Wilson Observatory
1908	Discovers magnetic fields in sunspots
1916	Appointed chair of the National Research Council
1916	Awarded the Bruce Medal of the Astronomical Society of the Pacific
1919	Discovers the twenty-two-year sunspot cycle
1932	Awarded the Copley Medal of the Royal Society of London
Feb. 21, 1938	Dies in Pasadena, California

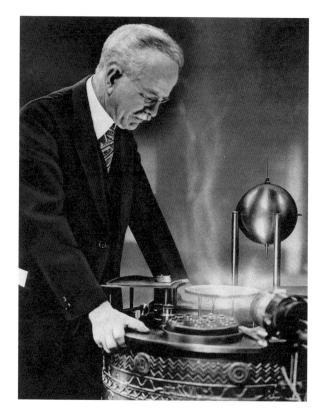

Early Life

George Ellery Hale was born in Chicago in 1868. He was the son of William Ellery Hale and Mary Scranton Browne. Through his father, a wealthy designer and builder of elevators for Chicago skyscrapers, young Hale developed an early interest in mechanical apparatus and various types of machinery. After a neighbor interested him in astronomy, Hale obtained a Clark telescope, and, by the age of sixteen, he had succeeded in photographing the solar spectrum.

Resolving to make astronomy his life's work, he entered the Massachusetts Institute of Technology (MIT) in 1886, where he studied physics, chemistry, and mathematics. At the same time, he volunteered as an assistant at the Havard College Observatory under Professor Edward Pickering. Hale also began constrution of his own solar observatory at Kenwood, near the family home in Chicago.

Hale's first important contribution to astronomy was the conception and construction of the spectroheliograph, a device for observing sunlight at one particular spectral line, or wavelength. This was his senior thesis at MIT.

On June 5, 1890, Hale married Evelina S. Conklin, and he began a year or two of intermittent travel, to California and Europe.

The Yerkes Observatory

In 1892, Hale founded the journal *Astronomy and Astro-Physics* and was appointed an associate professor of astrophysics at the newly established University of Chicago. Later that year, learning of the availability of a 40-inch refracting disk, Hale persuaded Chicago trolley-car magnate Charles T. Yerkes to provide funds to build an observatory for the university. The Yerkes Observatory, located in Williams Bay Wisconsin, opened in 1897, with Hale as its first director.

Meanwhile, in 1895 Hale and James Edward Keeler had founded the *Astrophysical Journal*, which quickly became the preeminent journal in its field.

In 1899, he helped establish the American Astronomical and Astrophysical Society; the name was subsequently shortened to the American Astronomical Society. Elected to the National Academy of Sciences in 1902, Hale soon became involved in efforts to organize international cooperation among astronomers; these efforts eventually led to the formation of the International Astronomical Union.

Mount Wilson Observatory

With the Yerkes Observatory well established, Hale next turned his organizational talents toward

Magnetic Fields in the Sun

Because the sun is a rotating ball of ionized gas with convection currents, it possesses a magnetic field. The presence of a magnetic field can be detected by the Zeeman effect, which causes spectral lines to be split.

In 1896, the Dutch physicist Pieter Zeeman had discovered, in the laboratory, that spectral lines emitted in the presence of a magnetic field are split into several components. Moreover, the spacing of these components is proportional to the strength of the magnetic field. Thus, Hale's 1908 observation of split lines in the spectra of sunspots enabled him to deduce the presence of strong magnetic fields there (roughly 1,000 gauss, as compared to about 0.5 gauss at the surface of Earth).

The solar magnetic field is complicated by the fact that the sun rotates somewhat faster at the equator than at higher latitudes; therefore the magnetic field lines become twisted and knotted. Sunspots are magnetic disturbances wherein the magnetic field causes the surface temperature to be somewhat lower than in the surrounding photosphere. This makes sunspots appear dark by comparison.

Although the eleven-year cycle of sunspot activity (from maximum to maximum) had previously been noted by others, Hale and his co-workers also discovered that the polarity of the magnetic field reverses over this cycle. Thus, the complete cycle of solar magnetic activity is now referred to as a twenty-two-year cycle.

Bibliography

Zeilik, Michael, Stephen A. Gregory, and Elske V. P. Smith. *Introductory Astronomy and Astrophysics.* 3d ed. Philadelphia: W. B. Saunders, 1992.

Menzel, Donald H. *Our Sun.* Cambridge, Mass.: Harvard University Press, 1959.

Wentzel, Donat G. *The Restless Sun.* Washington, D.C.: Smithsonian Institution Press, 1989.

Foukal, Peter V. "The Variable Sun." *Scientific American* (February, 1990).

founding a second observatory, this time to house a 60-inch reflector. For sponsorship, he approached the Carnegie Institute of Washington. The new observatory would be located atop Mount Wilson, above Pasadena, California, with Hale its first director. Hale's initial observing program at Mount Wilson involved photographing the spectrum of sunspots and other features of the sun's atmosphere. These were his most scientifically productive years.

During this period, Hale also became involved in Pasadena civic and cultural affairs. In 1906, he became a trustee of the relatively unknown Throop Polytechnic Institute in Pasadena. He used his influence to transform the school into an excellent technical college, which eventually became known as the California Institute of Technology (Caltech). He also persuaded railroad baron Henry Huntington to use his huge collection of books and paintings to found the Huntington Library and Art Gallery.

Always desirous of an ever-larger telescope, Hale obtained the support of the Carnegie Institute and Los Angeles businessman John D. Hooker as benefactors for the development of a 100-inch mirror for Mount Wilson. This telescope became operational in 1917 and was the instrument used by Edwin Hubble, Harlow Shapley, and others in their discovery of the extragalactic universe. In 1919 Hale, in collaboration with Walter S. Adams, discovered the twenty-two-year sunspot cycle.

Later Life

Hale was always of a rather highly strung, nervous temperament and he had occasionally suffered breakdowns. Finally in 1923, he found it necessary to resign as director at Mount Wilson and go into semiretirement to a less strenuous life. Nevertheless, he kept quite active, especially with writing and with plans for a 200-inch telescope. This time, the funding was to be provided jointly by the Rockefeller Foundation and by Carnegie. The telescope would be owned by Caltech and installed at Mount Palomar, near San Diego. Hale was chair of the Joint Observatory Council until his death on February 21, 1938. Upon its commission in 1948, it was named the Hale Telescope in his honor.

Bibliography

By Hale

"The Astrophysical Journal," *Astronomy and Astro-Physics*, 1892.

"The Yerkes Observatory of the University of Chicago," *Astronomy and Astro-Physics*, 1892.

"The Spectroheliograph," *Astronomy and Astro-Physics*, 189.

"Preliminary Results of an Attempt to Detect the Magnetic Field of the Sun," *Astrophysical Journal*, 1913.

About Hale

Adams, Walter. S. "Biographical Memoir of George Ellery Hale." *Biographical Memoirs, National Academy of Sciences* 21 (1940).

Wright, Helen. *Exploring the Universe: A Biography of George Ellery Hale.* New York: E. P. Dutton, 1966.

Term, Joseph S. "George Ellery Hale: The Thirteenth Bruce Medalist." *Mercury*, (May/June, 1992).

Lankford, John and Ricky L. Slavings. "The Industrialization of American Astronomy 1880-1940." *Physics Today* 49, no. 1 (January, 1996).

(George W. Rainey)

Edmond Halley

Disciplines: Astronomy, mathematics, and physics

Contribution: Halley was the first person to predict successfully and explain the motion of comets. This was the first application of Sir Isaac Newton's laws of motion.

Oct. 29, 1656	Born in Haggerston, near London, England
1676	Observes and catalogs stars from the island of St. Helena
1678	Publishes a catalog of 341 southern sky stars
1678	Elected a Fellow of the Royal Society of London
1678	Granted an M.A. degree from Oxford University
1682	Observes the comet that would eventually bear his name
1687	Pays for the publication of Newton's *Philosophiae Naturalis Principia Mathematica*
1698-1701	Makes a series of voyages to study Earth's magnetism
1703	Appointed Savilian Professor of Geometry at Oxford University
1716	Predicts the 1761 and 1769 transits of Venus
1718	Notes the direct motion of the stars Sirius, Aldebaran, and Arcturus
1720	Appointed Astronomer Royal of England
Jan. 14, 1742	Dies in London, England
1758	The comet returns, as Halley had predicted, in 1705

Dr. Halley

Early Life

Edmond Halley, whose name is sometimes spelled Edmund, was born near London, England, on October 29, 1656. He was educated at St. Paul's School in London and later at Queen's College at Oxford University.

From an early age, it appeared that Halley was very interested in mathematics and science. By the age of twenty, he had published a scientific paper that discussed planetary orbits, which appeared in the *Philosophical Transactions* of the Royal Society of London. It was the beginning of Halley's great career.

Halley the Astronomer

Halley's interest in astronomy was greatly influenced by his association with the Astronomer Royal, John Flamsteed. It was Halley, along with Robert Hooke, who helped Flamsteed with the design and construction of the Royal Astronomical Observatory at Greenwich, London.

Later, Halley assisted Flamsteed in his astronomical observations that led to the completion of a catalog of northern hemisphere stars. Excited by this work, Halley decided to compile a similar catalog for the stars of the southern hemisphere. To do so, he traveled to the island of St. Helena in the South Atlantic Ocean.

The idea of observing and cataloging the southern stars so fascinated Halley that he left his studies at Oxford and sailed to St. Helena as quickly as possible. There, he cataloged more than 300 stars and observed a transit of the planet Mercury. Upon his return to England, Oxford University granted him a degree in recognition of his work. In 1678 Halley's southern stars catalog was published and he was elected to the Royal Society of London.

During his time at Oxford, Halley began his friendship with Sir Isaac Newton. Together, they would solve the problem of the nature and motion of comets. Halley's interest in comets came from his observation of the bright comet of 1682 that appeared over London. Most people at this time feared comets as bad omens or "bringers of doom."

Halley looked on comets from a scientific point of view. He saw them for what they actually are—members of the solar system that are governed by the same laws as the planets. In cooperation with Newton, he was able to correctly predict their motion.

Halley's Other Scientific Achievements

Halley's scientific career was not limited to comets. His interests covered Earth's magnetic field and its relationship to aurora displays, the design and construction of diving bells, and the development of statistical tables on mortality rates. Among his other accomplishments were the development of meteorological charts in 1688.

Solving the Mystery of Comets

Comets generally follow elliptical paths around the sun and are governed by the law of gravity. Their motion is predictable.

Almost a hundred years before the time of Halley, the Danish astronomer Tycho Brahe recognized the true motion of comets. Beyond that, however, Brahe did little to help understand their true relationship to the sun and the planets. Halley thought that he could do better.

The first thing that Halley did was to list the brightest comets with sufficient observations to plot their motion. From these data, he was able to determine that three such comets might actually be a single object. They appeared at roughly seventy-five-year intervals: 1531, 1607, and 1682). If this were true, then comets were not supernatural objects of evil but ordinary objects that moved about the sun.

Although Halley had a good idea of how comets moved, he needed a force to move them, and Sir Isaac Newton's law of gravity provided it. When Halley applied Newton's formula to his observations, he was able to predict the motion of the 1682 comet. If Halley were correct, then the comets of 1531, 1607, and 1682 would be the same one. His data suggested that the comet would return in 1758. It did so, putting to rest once and for all the idea of an Earth-centered universe and superstitions about the nature of comets. Today, it is known as Halley's comet.

Bibliography

Comet. Carl Sagan and Ann Druyan. New York: Random House, 1985.

Comets. Russell Ash and Ian Grant. London: Ash and Grant Limited, 1973.

In 1701 Halley also developed the first magnetic charts. These were especially good and remained in use long after his death in 1742.

Halley also attempted to develop a means for determining longitude at sea by using measurements of the moon's motion. He devoted the last years of his life to making accurate measurements of the moon's orbital motion. His observations confirmed that the moon deviates from its predicted motion, which later astronomers would tie into the gravitational interactions between Earth and the moon.

Although Halley achieved widespread recognition from his discovery of the motion of comets, many of his basic astronomical observations went unpublished. Halley was best at making observations and compiling data. The fact that he correctly predicted the return of the 1682 comet earned him the honor of having it named Halley's comet. Today, that honor goes to the first person to observe a new comet.

Bibliography

By Halley

Catalogus stellarum Australium, 1679.

"Breslau Table of Mortality," *Philosophical Transactions,* 1693.

"Astronomiae cometicae synopsis," *Philosophical Transactions,* 1705 (A Synopsis of the Astronomy of Comets, 1705).

Tabula astronomica, 1749 (Astronomical Tables, 1752).

About Halley

Ronan, Colin A. *Edmond Halley: Genius in Eclipse.* Garden City, N.Y.: Doubleday, 1969.

Louis Baldwin. *Edmond Halley and His Comet.* Bend, Oreg.: Maverick, 1985.

(Paul P. Sipiera)

Stephen Hawking

Disciplines: Astronomy, cosmology, and physics

Contribution: Hawking did ground-breaking research into black holes and the birth of the universe. He brought the evolution of the cosmos to the public through his books, which are intended to explain complicated scientific ideas to nonscientists.

Jan. 8, 1942	Born in Oxford, England
1959	Enters University College at Oxford University
1963	Diagnosed with amyotrophic lateral sclerosis (ALS)
1965	Receives a Ph.D. from the University of Cambridge
1968	Joins the staff of the Institute of Theoretical Astronomy
1970	Begins research on black holes
1974-present	Invested as a Fellow in the Royal Society of London
1977- present	Chair of gravitational physics at Cambridge
1978	Receives the Albert Einstein Award
1979-2009	Lucasian Professor of Mathematics at Cambridge
1979	Nominated as "Man of the Year" by the Royal Association for Disability and Rehabilitation
1988	Publishes *A Brief History of Time*
2006	Awarded the Copley Medal by the Royal Society
2009-present	Director of Research of Department of Applied Mathematics and Theoretical Physics at the University of Cambridge

Early Life

Stephen William Hawking was born on January 8, 1942. He was reared and educated in England. His father, a physician, wanted him to study chemistry and physics but Hawking's great love was mathematics. He entered University College at Oxford University in 1959 to study physics but he put little effort into his studies.

During his studies at Cambridge, Hawking was diagnosed with amyotrophic lateral sclerosis (ALS, which is popularly known as Lou Gehrig's disease) and was given two years to live. ALS is an incurable disease characterized by loss of motor neuron function. Hawking also became engaged to Jane Wilde.

He applied to and was accepted at Caius College, at the University of Cambridge, under a research fellowship. Hawking became a theoretical physicist, a thinking job for which having ALS would not be a disability. ALS did, however, direct his interests, for the area of physics that he chose did not require lecturing. In 1962, he started research on general relativity and cosmology.

Cosmology and Black Holes

From 1970 to 1974 he concentrated on black holes. At that point in time, his work was theoretical, since he was not sure that black holes really existed. A black hole is an area in space where the gravitational pull on matter is so strong that nothing can escape, not even light.

Scientists have since collected observational evidence that black holes do exist. Cygnus X-l is a system in which a normal star orbits an unseen companion. X-ray radiation has been observed falling off the normal star toward the companion. The X-rays resemble water running down a drain because they spiral as they near the unseen companion. The unseen companion is a black hole. Its gravity is pulling the X-rays from the normal star into itself.

In 1974, Hawking realized that black holes are not really completely black. He discovered radiation leaking from a black hole. As the radiation leaks, the black hole becomes smaller. The smaller it gets, the faster it leaks radiation. Finally, it will explode. This phenomenon is comparable to the big bang theory, widely accepted as an explanation of the beginning of the universe.

Hawking, however, changed his mind about the beginning of the universe. In 1983, he and Jim Hartle proposed a new theory, the no-boundary proposal. The no-boundary proposal is akin to a human's understanding of Earth. The surface of Earth is finite, but it has no boundary. In other words, one cannot fall off it. The beginning of the universe would be similar to the North Pole. It is a point on Earth, and, although one could call it the beginning, it actually has no beginning or end.

Hawking, the Man

Until 1985, Hawking could still speak, although it was very difficult to understand him.

A bout of pneumonia in 1985, however, required that a hole be cut in his trachea so that he could breathe. This procedure, known as a tracheostomy, destroyed his ability to speak. Walt Waltosz, a software expert in California, sent Hawking a program by which he could select words from a screen and send them to a voice synthesizer. He soon used this form of communicating exclusively.

Despite losing his voice, more and more people began listening to what Hawking had to say. In the 1980s he became regarded as the most brilliant theoretical physicist since Einstein.

Evolution of the Universe

Cosmologists are especially interested in the beginning of the universe and its possible end.

Hawking based his cosmology research on the works of famous scientists such as Aristotle, Galileo, Johannes Kepler, Sir Isaac Newton, and particularly Albert Einstein. Einstein taught that matter and energy are interchangeable; that is, matter can be converted into energy (as in burning wood) and energy can be converted to matter.

Hawking's early research was based on Einstein's general theory of relativity. In the very early stages of the universe, everything was energy; there was no matter. The gravity of the universe had compressed everything to infinite density, creating what is called a singularity. This singularity was the beginning of space-time.

The general theory of relativity, however, was based on classical physics, and, at a singularity, the laws of physics break down. The general theory would have to be modified to take into account the uncertainty principle of quantum mechanics, which states that one cannot measure both the position and speed of a particle. The more one knows about the position of an object, the less one knows about its speed. The more one knows about the speed of an object, the less one knows about its position. This modification ruled out a singularity.

Hawking revised his description of the beginning of the universe. He described a finite universe with no singularities. Space-time is like Earth's surface: Earth has a definite amount of surface area but no singularity (edge or boundary). This proposal is known as the No-Boundary theory. Hawking described the universe as having a beginning and an end, much like lines of latitude begin and end at the poles. Hawking proposed that the big bang was a normal point in space-time, much like the North Pole is a regular point on Earth's surface. If this is the case, the laws of physics hold and predictions can be made about the state of the universe.

Theoretical physics seeks to find a unified theory to explain every aspect of physics, chemistry, and biology. This theory would be a mathematical representation of the underlying principles of all science. Hawking believed that such a unified theory would be found.

While cosmologists are interested in the evolution of the universe, particularly the beginning and possible end of space-time as it is currently known, they are also interested in learning as much about the present universe as possible, including studies of the life cycle of stars. When a star's fuel runs out and thermonuclear reactions are no longer strong enough to overcome the gravity between its particles, it sometimes collapses. The star's own gravity causes it to fall in on itself. When this happens, a black hole is formed.

Bibliography

Hawking, Stephen W. *Black Holes and Baby Universes and Other Essays*. New York: Bantam Books, 1993.

Hawking, Stephen W. *A Brief History of Time: From the Big Bang to Black Holes*. New York: Bantam Books, 1988.

White, Michael. *Stephen Hawking: A Life in Science*. New York: E. P. Dutton, 1992.

As time went on, his fame increased. Hawking began writing for popular presses about understanding science, and his books became bestsellers. He has been honored in science fiction and his contributions widely celebrated in popular culture. He has guest starred in several episodes of the television show *The Big Bang Theory* and in an opening scene of an episode of the television series *Star Trek: The Next Generation*, he is shown with Einstein and Newton as a holographic image.

Black Holes

A black hole is an area where the gravitational field is so strong that it pulls everything into it and not even light can escape. Inside a black hole is a point called a singularity where matter is infinitely dense.

Black holes do not simply appear; they must be made from matter or energy. A black hole may be the result of the death of a star. If the star's thermonuclear reactions are not strong enough to overcome the gravitational attraction between its particles of matter, gravity wins the "tug of war" and the star collapses in on itself. The matter compresses infinitely during the process of collapse. A point of infinitely dense matter called a singularity is formed; it is a place where space-time ends. This point is rather like the singularity described by the big bang theory of the birth of the universe.

A black hole has a border called the event horizon. Astronauts could fly into a black hole, but once they passed the event horizon, they could never come out. If they sent a radio message describing what they saw, the radio waves could not exit the black hole once the event horizon had been passed. Scientists will never know what the inside of a black hole looks like because once something crosses the event horizon, it too is compressed by gravity.

The star system Cygnus X-1 consists of a black hole and a companion star. The companion star is a normal star that can be seen with a telescope. When it is viewed with an X-ray telescope, however, one finds that the X-rays are being pulled off the star and toward a region in space that is apparently empty. Observing the X-rays over a longer period shows that they begin to spiral toward an unknown area, much like water spirals down a drain. The region into which the X-rays are being pulled is a black hole. In 1974, Hawking discovered that black holes are not completely black. Radiation can leak out of the black hole at the same time that it is pulling other radiation and matter into it. He suggested searching for black holes by looking for regions in space that are apparently empty but that have radiation coming from them.

As energy leaks from the black hole, it becomes smaller. The smaller that it gets, the weaker its gravity becomes and the more radiation will leak out and at a faster rate. The black hole becomes increasingly smaller and the radiation leaks increasingly faster until finally a tremendous explosion results.

This type of phenomenon offers one explanation for the birth of the universe known as the big bang theory. In the beginning, all matter was energy. The energy that began the universe was borrowed from the intense gravitational pull on everything in the universe until it had infinite density. This infinite density is the singularity that may have been the origin of the universe. Energy was converted into matter during the explosion called the big bang.

Bibliography

Hawking, Stephen, W. *Black Holes and Baby Universes and Other Essays.* New York: Bantam Books, 1993.

Hawking, Stephen, W. *A Brief History of Time: From the Big Bang to Black Holes.* New York: Bantam Books, 1988.

White, Michael. *Stephen Hawking: A Life in Science.* New York: E. P. Dutton, 1992.

With his pop icon status Hawking has also become a spokesperson for those with disabilities, and in 2012 opened the Paralympic Games in London.

Bibliography

By Hawking

The Large Scale Structure of Space-Time, 1973 (with G. F. R. Ellis).

A Brief History of Time: From the Big Bang to Black Holes, 1988.

The Nature of Space and Time, 1996 (with Roger Penrose).

A Briefer History of Time, 2008 (with Leonard Mlodinow).

The Grand Design, 2012.

About Hawking

Kraus, Gerhard. *Has Hawking Erred?* London: Janus, 1993.

"Professor Stephen Hawking" University of Cambridge Department of Applied Mathematics and Theoretical Physics, http://www.damtp.cam.ac.uk/people/s.w.hawking/

"Stephen Hawking," http://www.hawking.org.uk.

Stephen Hawking: A Life in Science. Michael White. New York: E. P. Dutton, 1992.

Simon, Sheridan. *Stephen Hawking: Unlocking the Universe*. Minneapolis: Dillon Press, 1991.

(Linda E. Roach)

Sir John Herschel

Disciplines: Astronomy, chemistry, mathematics, and technology

Contribution: Herschel, a noted astronomer, conducted extensive observations of stars and nebulas, making many discoveries and cataloging his findings.

Mar. 7, 1792	Born in Buckinghamshire, England
1813	Becomes a member of the Royal Society of London
1816	Graduated from the University of Cambridge with an M.A.
1819	Discovers hypo (sodium thiosulfate), a fixing agent for use in photography
1820	Completes the large reflector telescope needed for his observations
1821	Awarded the Copley Medal of the Royal Society of London
1826	Receives the gold medal of the Royal Astronomical Society
1827	Elected president of the Royal Astronomical Society
1831	Receives knighthood
1834	Moves to the Cape of Good Hope for southern sky research
1838	Returns to England
1845	Elected president of the British Association for the Advancement of Science
1850	Receives a government position as master of the mint
1864	Publishes a catalog of 5,079 nebulas and stellar clusters
May 11, 1871	Dies in Kent, England

Early Life

With prominent astronomers Sir William and Caroline Herschel as his father and aunt, John Frederick William Herschel was introduced to astronomy in childhood. At first a poor musician, William devoted his spare time and genius to becoming a self-educated astronomer of international fame. In sharp contrast, John's education at Eton and individual tutoring led to the University of Cambridge.

At Cambridge, John Herschel studied and excelled in mathematics. His fellow classmates George Peacock and Charles Babbage would become famous mathematicians. This trio initiated the Analytical Society, an association devoted to importing the analysis of continental mathematicians (such as Joseph-Louis Lagrange and Pierre-Simon Laplace) to English schools. Toward this end, Herschel and Peacock translated a calculus treatise. Next, Herschel published a book on finite difference calculus examples.

Concurrently, he passed his examinations at the top of his class.

Herschel submitted several mathematical papers to the Royal Society of London and became a fellow in 1813. He advanced in chemistry as well and even studied law. While there, Herschel's association with scientist William Wollaston and astronomer James South further motivated his decision to pursue astronomy.

Cataloging the Sky

Upon his graduation, Herschel directed his efforts toward his father's work, sidereal astronomy. This involved the design and construction of an improved reflective telescope, especially of the key component: a carefully ground and polished 18-inch mirror. His mathematical expertise proved significant in solving several optical problems. Along the way, he discovered the Herschel effect and created numerous measuring devices. With his new tool, Herschel launched his career as an observational astronomer. In collaboration with South, he began an award-winning reassessment and study of the binary stars from 1821 to 1823.

Herschel, who was knighted in 1831, refined and corrected his father's work, cataloging all nebulas and stellar systems of the northern sky by 1833. In an inspired move, he then ventured south. Packing his telescope, equipment, and texts, Herschel, his family, and mechanic John Stone journeyed to the Cape of Good Hope in South Africa, a British colony with an observatory that offered the best location for southern sky research. Herschel and Stone worked rapidly to set up his imported reflector. On March 4, 1834, the painstaking process of observation, charting, and drawing began.

At Cape Town, South Africa, Herschel also conducted several botanical expeditions, introduced educational reforms, and contributed to the Cape Philosophical Society. Species of flora have received his name.

Later Life

After his triumphant return in 1838, he was made a baronet and published a large number of papers. He independently developed the medium of photography but was not given proportional credit. In 1839, Herschel produced the first glass photograph, twenty years after discovering sodium thiosulfate, a photographic fixing agent known as hypo.

Herschel was awarded a government position as master of the mint and recommended that Great Britain adopt a decimal currency system. His areas of interest, publications, and honors became innumerable. Sir John Herschel died on May 11, 1871, in Hawkhurst, Kent, and was buried at Westminster Abbey near Sir Isaac Newton.

Bibliography

By Herschel

A Collection of Examples of the Application of the Calculus of Finite Differences, 1820.

A Treatise on Astronomy, 1830.

Results of Astronomical Observations, Made During the Years 1834-38 at the Cape of Good Hope, 1847.

A General Catalog of Nebula and Clusters of Stars, 1864.

Sir John Herschel: Scientific Papers, 1912 (2 vols.).

About Herschel

Clerke, Agnes M. *The Herschels and Modern Astronomy.* London: Cassell, 1901.

Buttman, Gunther. *The Shadow of the Telescope: A Biography of John Herschel.* New York: Charles Scribner's Sons, 1970.

(John Panos Najarian)

Mapping the Stars

Herschel recorded and charted the stellar and nebular objects in both hemispheres.

The term "monumental" best characterizes the extensive number of observations that Herschel conducted. The result was a succession of catalogs. In the final count, he had listed 5,079 nebulas and 10,300 double stars, a large portion being his own discoveries.

For the Southern Hemisphere, Herschel meticulously recorded the position and brightness of more than 2,100 binary stars, 1,707 nebulas, and 68,948 stellar objects. Most notable are his drawings of the Magellanic Clouds and the Eta Carinae Nebula. In this nebula, he recorded a brief eruption, an increase in brightness, followed by a decline.

His observation of the Great Magellanic Cloud yielded the record "collection of detached or loosely connected Clusters and Nebulae." As with these "nebulae," Herschel did not realize the extragalactic nature of many of the objects that he saw. For example, the apparent "star cluster" that he observed south-east of the star alpha-Erdani is actually a major galaxy, NGC 782. He also named several of Saturn's and Uranus' moons.

In the process of observation, Herschel created tools for measuring characteristics of stars exactly. To measure brightness, he created the astrometer, which determined the relative intensity of light from a star in contrast to the full moon. These measurements set a standard for future astronomers to refine and interpret.

Bibliography

Pasachoff, Jay M. A*stronomy: From the Earth to the Universe.* 4th ed. Philadelphia: W. B. Saunders, 1995.

Burnham, Robert Jr. *Burnham's Celestial Handbook.* 3 vols. Mineola, N.Y.: Dover, 1978.

The John Herschel Bicentennial Symposium Proceedings. South Africa: Royal Society of South Africa, 1992.

Sir William Herschel

Disciplines: Astronomy and cosmology

Contribution: Herschel perfected reflecting telescopes, discovered Uranus, cataloged 800 double stars and 2,500 star clusters and nebulas, calculated the rotation time of Mars, and proved the universality of the law of gravity.

Nov. 15, 1738	Born in Hanover, Hanover (now Germany)
1757	Moves to England and works as a musician
1772	His sister Caroline joins him in England and becomes his partner in astronomical work
1773	Begins to construct telescopes
1779-1784	Conducts "sweeps" of the heavens and catalogs stars
Mar. 13, 1781	Discovers Uranus
1781	Correctly calculates the rotation time of Mars
May, 1782	Named Royal Astronomer
1785-1789	Builds the world's largest telescope
1786	Moves to Observatory House, in Berkshire, England
1787	Discovers Mimas and Enceladus, moons of Saturn
1787	Discovers Titania and Oberon, moons of Uranus
1801	Proposes the term "asteroid" for bodies between Mars and Jupiter
1816	Knighted
1821	Publishes the last of his catalogs
Aug. 25, 1822	Dies in Berkshire, England

Early Life

Frederick William (originally Friedrich Wilhelm) Herschel was born on November 15, 1738, in Hanover as the third of six surviving children of Isaac Herschel. With little opportunity for formal education, William became an oboist with the Hanoverian Guards at the age of fourteen, touring England with the regiment in 1756. He learned English and made important contacts.

The French occupation of Hanover encouraged Herschel to seek refuge in Britain in 1757. For years, he supported himself by teaching, performing, conducting, and composing music in Leeds, Durham, Doncaster, and Halifax. Herschel secured employment as an organist at the Octagon Chapel and settled in Bath. His professional interest in music caused him to read Robert Smith's *Harmonics* (1749), and he next became acquainted with Smith's *A Compleat System of Opticks in Four Books* (1738), which changed his life.

Sidereal Astronomy

Herschel's major contribution to his profession was in founding the science of sidereal astronomy, the study of the universe beyond the solar system.

To this discipline, Herschel brought three main components: a passion for technical competence (seen in the construction of ever better and larger telescopes); a method for the rigorous, detailed, and documented observations of the heavens (seen in his catalogs of the stars); and a model for understanding the data discovered through imaginative and bold theorizing (seen in his paradigm of how the universe originated and operates). These contributions made Herschel the founder of observational cosmology.

This scientific method enabled Herschel to solve the mystery of nebulas. Named from a Latin root meaning "mists," these cloudy patches in the night sky had long defied explanation. Some thought that they were "self-luminous fluids." Others suggested that they were star clusters. Using superior refractory telescopes, Herschel located more than 2,500 nebulas, and, with the improved clarity of his observations, he determined them to be star clusters.

Having decided on their nature, Herschel turned to their behavior. By focusing on double stars Herschel noted the power of attraction, which provided the first proof that the law of gravity propounded by Sir Isaac Newton applied outside the solar system. This was a major accomplishment, both for theoretical science and for astronomy.

Next, Herschel attempted to measure the distance of these star clusters from Earth and each other. The Italian astronomer Galileo had assumed that all stars were equal in luminosity, the sun being the norm for all. For him, this meant that the dimmer a star, the farther it was from Earth, and the brighter it was, the nearer it was.

Initially, Herschel shared this notion. By 1793, however, he abandoned all thought of any correlation between the dimness and the distance of a star. The universe was more complex than Galileo had imagined, with stars differing vastly in size, brightness, distance, and distribution. This insight enhanced a sense of the diversity inherent in galaxies.

Not content to merely find, map, and measure stars, nor simply to describe their appearance and behavior, Herschel turned fearlessly to trying to formulate the principles of cosmological evolution. As a cosmologist, one who studies the general structure and evolution of the universe, Herschel devised a paradigm to explain the origin and growth of the universe. When the world began, Herschel thought, stars tended to be solitary and widely distributed. As the law of gravity took effect, over a period of great time, these isolated stars were drawn closer together, creating those clusters called nebulas.

By his combination of dogged perseverance and brilliant analysis, Herschel laid the basis of not only the systematic observation of the world beyond the solar system but also its rational explanation. Although his achievements have been surpassed, his role as the founder of sidereal astronomy will never be eclipsed.

Bibliography

Taylor, Roger John. *Galaxies: Structure and Evolution.* Cambridge, England: Cambridge University Press, 1993.

Henbest, Nigel. *The Guide to the Galaxy.* Cambridge, England: Cambridge University Press, 1994.

Hoskin, Michael A. *William Herschel and the Construction of the Heavens.* New York: W. W. Norton, 1963.

Building Better Telescopes

By reading Smith's work, Herschel learned how to build telescopes. Joined by his sister and collaborator, Caroline Lucretia Herschel, he began constructing reflecting telescopes in 1773. These instruments had considerable light-gathering power, and, by 1782, the Royal Observatory took note of the superiority of Herschel's telescopes. Between 1785 and 1789, with government support, Herschel built what was then the world's largest telescope. These powerful tools brought the heavens down to Earth.

Finding Uranus and Fame

With his great reflective telescopes, Herschel swept the heavens, producing detailed star catalogs, with a particular interest in double stars. From their power of mutual attraction, he inferred that Sir Isaac Newton's law of universal gravity applied outside this solar system.

On March 13, 1781, Herschel discovered a planet that he named "Georgium Sidus" in honor of King George III but it was renamed "Uranus" by Johann Bode of the Berlin Observatory. Herschel became instantly world-famous as the first recorded discoverer of a planet. He was given the Copley Medal, elected a Fellow of the Royal Society of London, received by King George III, named Royal Astronomer, and awarded an annual pension of £200.

Now able to devote himself to science, Herschel settled at Observatory House in Slough, Berkshire, in 1786. Assisted in his research by his sister, Herschel achieved a brilliant career in astronomy. Although self-taught and entering this occupation only in midlife, he made enormous contributions to both solar and astral astronomy.

Exploration of the Solar System

In solar astronomy, Herschel confirmed the existence of infrared rays, calculated correctly the rotation time of Mars, proposed the name "asteroid" for the bodies bound between Mars and Jupiter, and predicted the discovery of the minor planets Juno (1804) and Vesta (1807). Herschel formulated the "trade winds theory" to explain Jupiter's mysterious belts and discovered two satellites of Saturn (Mimas and Enceladus) and two moons of Uranus (Titania and Oberon).

Contributions to Sidereal Astronomy

While Herschel won popular acclaim for the discovery of Uranus, his enduring professional reputation rested on his contributions to sidereal astronomy ("sidereal" means "pertaining to the stars"). He is regarded as the founder of the science of galactic structure, pertaining to the origin, evolution, and behavior of star systems.

By December, 1781, Herschel had become fascinated by the milky patches in the night sky called nebulas, and he studied the work on that topic by Charles Messier, who had located one hundred of them. Through his three vast "sweeps" of the heavens, Herschel increased that number to more than 2,500.

Not only an observational astronomer, Herschel was a also natural historian, and, in his later life, he gave much thought to cosmology.

Family Life

In May, 1788, at the age of fifty, Herschel married Mary Pitt, the wealthy widow of one of his neighbors. Their son, John Frederick William Herschel, was as noted for mapping the skies of the Southern Hemisphere as his father had been for charting the heavens of the Northern Hemisphere. William Herschel's sister, Caroline, was the first notable female astronomer, discovering more than eight comets.

Knighted in 1816 and honored throughout the world, Sir William Herschel died peacefully at home in Slough, Berkshire on August 25, 1822.

Bibliography

By Herschel

"Account of a Comet," *Philosophical Transactions of the Royal Society of London*, 1782 (also as The Discovery of Uranus, 1782).

"Account of Some Observations Tending to Investigate the Construction of the Heavens" and "On the Construction of the Heavens," *Philosophical Transactions of the Royal Society of London*, 1784 and 1785 (published together as *The Structure of the Universe*, 1784–1785).

"Catalogue of a Second Thousand of New Nebulae and Clusters of Stars: With a Few Introductory Remarks on the Construction of the Heavens," *Philosophical Transactions of the Royal Society of London*, 1789.

Dreyer, J. L. E ed. *The Scientific Papers of Sir William Herschel*, 1912 (2 vols.).

Lubbock, Constance A. ed. *The Herschel Chronicle*, 1933.

About Herschel

Armitage, Angus. *William Herschel.* Garden City, N.Y.: Doubleday, 1963.

Sidgwick, J. B. *William Herschel: Explorer of the Heavens.* London: Faber & Faber, 1953.

Hoskin, Michael A. *William Herschel: Pioneer of Sidereal Astronomy.* New York: Sheed & Ward, 1959.

(C. George Fry)

Ejnar Hertzsprung

Disciplines: Astronomy and physics

Contribution: A pioneer in the detailed study of light from stars, Hertzsprung is most remembered for discovering the relationship between the brightness and temperature of stars. He also made the first measurement of the distance to another galaxy.

Oct. 8, 1873	Born in Frederiksberg, Denmark
1898	Graduated from the Polytechnical Institute in Copenhagen
1898	Moves to St. Petersburg, Russia, to begin work as a chemist
1901	Studies photochemistry in Leipzig, Germany
1902	Returns to Denmark as an astronomer at the University of Copenhagen
1909	Accepts a position in astrophysics at Göttingen University
1909	Moves to the Potsdam Astrophysical Observatory
1913	With Henry Norris Russell, recognized for inventing the diagram that bears their names
1919	Appointed associate director of Leiden Observatory, later becoming its director
1929	Awarded the Gold Medal of the Royal Astronomical Society
1937	Awarded the Bruce Gold Medal of the Astronomical Society of the Pacific
1944	Retires from Leiden Observatory
Oct. 21, 1967	Dies in Roskilde, Denmark

Early Life

Ejnar Hertzsprung was born in Frederiksberg, Denmark, in 1873. His father, Severin Hertzsprung, had studied astronomy at the University of Copenhagen but decided that he could not support his family well by pursuing science. Therefore, he took a position with the Danish government, rising rapidly to director of the state life insurance company. Severin retained his love for astronomy and mathematics, however, and Ejnar became interested in these sciences, too.

Although he studied chemical engineering and worked as a chemist after his graduation from college, Ejnar Hertzsprung decided to make astronomy his life's work. In 1902, he began work at the observatory of the University of Copenhagen and at the Urania Observatory in Frederiksberg.

Early Research

In 1905 and 1907 Hertzsprung published two papers that are now considered classics. The title

Hertzsprung was the first astronomer to measure the distance to the Small Magellanic Cloud.

for both was "Zur Strahlung der Sterne," which translates as "On the Radiation of the Stars." These papers dealt with spectroscopy, the study of which colors (or wavelengths) make up the light from glowing objects. Hertzsprung showed that stars that have a particular kind of light spectrum are more luminous than the rest. His research laid the foundation for methods of finding the distances to far-off stars and galaxies.

The Famous Diagram

Hertzsprung's extensive studies showed him that stars can be classified into two overall categories. He knew the absolute brightness of thousands of stars and from their spectra could determine the temperature of each.

In 1911, Hertzsprung made a plot to show the relation of the brightness (or magnitude) to the temperature. On such a plot, stars fall into two overall categories. Most stars fall on what is called the main sequence area of the graph, but some, such as blue giant stars and red dwarf stars, fall on a much different part of the plot.

Both Hertzsprung and Henry Norris Russell are given credit for this important discovery, and the diagram has long been known as the Hertzsprung-Russell (or H-R) diagram.

Measuring Intergalactic Distance

After conducting research at several institutions and in many countries, Hertzsprung eventually settled at the Leiden Observatory in the Netherlands, where he remained for twenty-five years. It was during this time that he made a groundbreaking measurement of the distance to an object outside the Milky Way. Hertzsprung used a discovery by fellow astronomer Henrietta Swan Leavitt to estimate the distance to the Small Magellanic Cloud and Hertzsprung's method became widely used for these long-distance measurements.

A Long and Fruitful Career

Hertzsprung was still doing astronomical measurements after his ninetieth birthday. In his long and productive career, he held both himself and his students to very high standards of accuracy in observation. He cared deeply about the education of young astronomers and affected the direction of astronomy for decades. His contributions place him among the great astronomers of history. Hertzsprung died in 1967 at the age of ninety-four.

The Measurement of Cosmic Distances

Hertzsprung made the first true measurement of a distance to an object beyond the Milky Way.

The only way to measure the distance to a star directly is the method of parallax. As Earth orbits the sun, stars that are far away do not appear to move, but the apparent position of an object nearby seems to move against the background of faraway stars. One observes the position of the star in relation to the very distant background, when Earth is at opposite sides of the sun (six months apart in time). By measuring the angle 0 and knowing Earth-sun distance (A), one can use trigonometry to find the distance to the star (L). This method works only for stars closer than 100 light-years away. (A light-year is the distance light travels in one year, or about $5.87849981 \times 10^{12}$ miles.) Other methods must be used for objects at greater distances.

Henrietta Swan Leavitt studied a class of stars that grow brighter and dimmer with time. She found a relationship between the period of variation of these Cepheid variable stars and their average brightness.

Hertzsprung applied Leavitt's observation to some of the Cepheid stars in Earth's galaxy, the Milky Way, whose distance from Earth was known. When he compared these stars to similar stars in the Small Magellanic Cloud, outside the Galaxy, he was able to calculate that it was 32,600 light-years from Earth.

Hertzsprung's measurement was groundbreaking, but it did contain an error: he did not know that there are actually two classes of Cepheid variables, which act in different ways. With this correction, and accounting for intergalactic dust, the currently accepted distance is about 160,000 light-years away. By comparison, the Milky Way is 50,000 light-years in diameter.

Bibliography

Snow, Theodore P. *The Dynamic Universe.* 3d ed. New York: West, 1988.

Stott, Carole ed. *Images of the Universe.* Cambridge, England: Cambridge University Press, 1991.

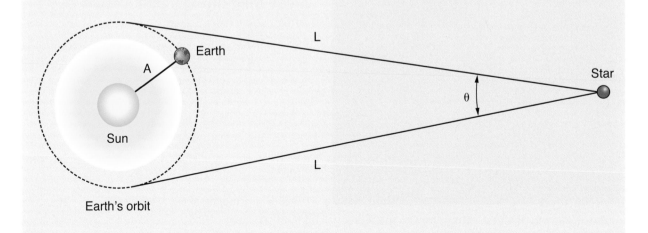

Bibliography

By Hertzsprung

"Zur Strahlung der Sterne," *Zeitschrift für wissenschaftliche Photographie*, 1905.

"Zur Strahlung der Sterne," *Zeitschrift für wissenschaftliche Photographie*, 1907.

"Effective Wave-Lengths of 184 Stars in the Cluster N.G.C. 1647," *Astrophysical journal*, 1915.

"On the Relation Between Mass and Absolute Brightness of Components of Double Stars," *Bulletin of the Astronomical Institutes of the Netherlands*, 1923.

"The Pleiades," *Monthly Notices of the Royal Astronomical Society*, 1929.

About Hertzsprung

Gillispie, Charles Coulston, ed. *Dictionary of Scientific Biography*. Vol. 6. New York: Charles Scribner's Sons, 1972.

Neilse, Axel V. "Ejnar Hertzsprung—Measurer of Stars." *Sky and Telescope* 35 (1968).

McMurray, Emily J. ed. *Notable Twentieth-Century Scientists*. New York: Gale Research, 1995.

(Tom R. Herrmann)

Antony Hewish

Discipline: Astronomy

Contribution: Along with Sir Martin Ryle, Hewish won the Nobel Prize in Physics, for the development of new techniques in radio astronomy. His observations of pulsars provided evidence for the existence of neutron stars.

May 11, 1924	Born in Cornwall, England
1935	Attends King's College, London
1942	Enters the University of Cambridge
1943-1946	Serves Britain's effort during World War II in radar development
1948	Joins Ryle's team at the Cavendish Laboratory at the University of Cambridge
1952	Completes his Ph.D. ionospheric fluctuations
1961	Becomes a lecturer at the University of Cambridge
1964	Discovers interplanetary scintillation of small radio sources
1965	Detects a radio source in the Crab Nebula
1967	Discovers the first pulsar
1968	Elected Fellow of the Royal Society of London
1971	Becomes a professor of radio astronomy at Cambridge
1974	Wins the Nobel Prize in Physics
1989	Retires from the University of Cambridge

Early Life

Antony Hewish was born in Fowey, Cornwall, England, in 1924. He was the youngest of three sons, and his father was a banker. Hewish attended the University of Cambridge in 1942 but World War II interrupted his studies in 1943. He spent the next three years engaged in the development of airborne radar counter-measure devices with Martin Ryle.

Interplanetary Scintillation

After the war, Hewish returned to the University of Cambridge and graduated in 1948. Two distant stars had just been discovered through radio waves, and Hewish realized that they would scintillate, or twinkle, as a result of effects of the Earth's upper atmosphere, as did visible stars as a result of effects of the lower atmosphere. This twinkling could be used to understand the size and electron density of clouds in the ionosphere, a significant achievement at a time before the development of spacecraft.

The planets do not twinkle because they appear larger than the stars from the Earth. Hewish realized that by using an interferometer, consisting of two radio telescopes separated by 56 miles, the apparent size of radio sources could be known. This technique, which can also determine the velocity of solar wind, is called interplanetary scintillation (IPS).

In 1965, using IPS, Hewish and S. E. Okoye discovered a compact source of radio brightness inside the Crab Nebula. They hypothesized that this brightness is the remains of a star that was observed exploding by Chinese astronomers in 1054.

"Little Green Men" and Pulsars

One of Hewish's research students, Jocelyn Bell (later Bell Burnell), noted in 1967 during a routine sky survey that fluctuating signals were being received at regular intervals. Often, such signals would be detected by the observatory, but they would keep time with the rotation of Earth, and not with the sidereal time of the heavens, which differs from the solar day as a result of the motion of Earth in its orbit. Ruling out interference from satellites and other observatories, Hewish and Bell concluded that the signals probably had a heavenly origin.

Initially, it was suspected that the source might be a lighthouse belonging to an interstellar civilization, warning spaceships of the location of some hazard to navigation. Hewish and Bell therefore named their first few sources LGM-1 through LGM-4, the "LGM" prefix standing for "Little Green Men." However, Hewish could not detect any Doppler shift in the signals, which would be expected if the signaling object were orbiting something else. Instead, Hewish adopted Thomas Gold's hypothesis that a neutron star was causing the pulses.

The resulting term "pulsar" for the source of such signals is not credited to any individual; it

What Causes a Pulsar?

A rotating neutron star is the best explanation for clocklike-pulsed radio sources in space.

After a star has run out of nuclear fuel, it collapses as a result of gravitational attraction. For some stars, this collapse can be halted by the Pauli exclusion force, which prevents some kinds of particle from being in identical states of motion. What remains after the collapse is a small object that consists largely of protons and electrons smashed together to make neutrons.

The rotational energy and the magnetic energy of the collapsed star are conserved. The neutron star therefore has a tremendous rate of rotation and a powerful magnetic field. Because of its immense density, the rapid rotation does not tear the star apart.

In order to explain the repetition of pulses detected in space, Hewish adopted Thomas Gold's lighthouse model. The region close to the pulsar is called its magnetosphere. As the star spins, the magnetic field spins along with the pulsar, and it induces a electrical field on the surface of the star, like a huge electrical generator. The electrical field pulls electrons from the crust, which are accelerated by the rotating field lines.

These electrons emit radio signals in a tight beam along the field lines. As the pulsar generates electromagnetic radiation, the torque of the accelerating particles acts as a brake on the rotation, decreasing the period between pulses. The discovery of pulsars confirmed the scientific account of the evolution of stars.

Bibliography

Lorimer, Duncan. "Clocks in the Cosmos." *Physics World* (February, 1996).

Lyne, A.G. and F. G. Smith. *Pulsar Astronomy.* Cambridge, England: Cambridge University Press, 1990.

A rapidly rotating neutron star generates a strong magnetic field that sends out radiation. The resulting radio waves can be detected on Earth.

Anatomy of a Pulsar

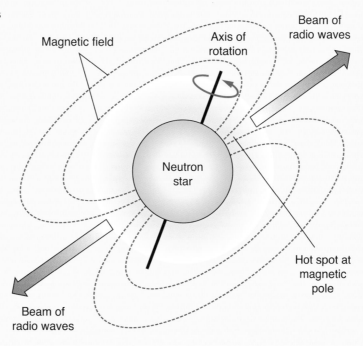

was first used in a publication a month after the first paper published by Hewish, Bell, and their colleagues on their discovery, in a 1968 volume of *Nature*. Over the next thirty years, more than 700 pulsars were discovered.

Later Life

Hewish was awarded the Nobel Prize in Physics in 1974, along with Sir Martin Ryle, who had pioneered the work in radio telescope interferometry. Hewish continued to be active in radio astronomy until he retired from the University of Cambridge in 1989.

Bibliography

By Hewish
"Observation of a Rapidly Pulsating Source," *Nature*, 1968 (with S. J. Bell, J. D. H. Pilkington, P. F. Scott, and R. A. Collins).
"Pulsars," *Scientific American*, 1968.
"Pulsars: Twenty Years After," *Mercury*, 1989.

About Hewish
"Antony Hewish." *The Nobel Prize Winners; Physics*, edited by Frank N. Magill. Pasadena, Calif.: Salem Press, 1989.
Greenstern, George. *Frozen Star*. New York: Charles Scribner's Sons, 1989.
Woolgar. S. W. "Writing an Intellectual History of Scientific Development: The Use of Discovery Accounts." *Social Studies of Science* (1976).

(*Drew L. Arrowood*)

Sir Fred Hoyle

Disciplines: Astronomy, cosmology, and physics
Contribution: A controversial figure, Hoyle is best known as the co-author of the steady state cosmological theory. He also made key contributions to astrophysics, especially in helping to explain how elements are made in stars and supernovas.

June 24, 1915	Born in Bingley, England
1936	Receives a B.A. in mathematics from the University of Cambridge
1939	Earns an M.A. in physics from the University of Cambridge
1940-1945	Helps develop radar for the British navy
1945-1956	Lectures in mathematics at the University of Cambridge
1950	Publishes *The Nature of the Universe*, a book on cosmology
1957	Elected a member of the Royal Society of London
1958-1972	Serves as Plumian Professor of Astronomy and as professor of experimental philosophy
1967	Founds the Institute of Theoretical Astronomy at Cambridge
1969	Named a foreign associate of the National Academy of Sciences
1969-1972	Acts as a professor of astronomy at the Royal Institution of Great Britain
1972	Knighted
1974	Receives the Gold Medal from the Royal Society of London
1975-1985	Investigates the possibility that life exists in interstellar space
Aug. 20, 2001	Dies in Bournemouth, England

Early Life

Sir Fred Hoyle was born in Bingley, England, in 1915. His mother, a former schoolteacher, and his father, a cloth merchant, were determined that he receive a good education, an ambition that young Hoyle did not share. He later claimed that frequent truancy from ages ten to twelve allowed him to explore science on his own.

Nevertheless, Hoyle finished high school and won a scholarship to the University of Cambridge in 1933, where he studied mathematics. He graduated in 1936 and stayed at Cambridge to study physics with Rudolf Peierls and Paul A. M. Dirac, both leading theorists. He received a master's degree in 1939 and married Barbara Clark, with whom he had a son, Geoffrey, and a daughter, Elizabeth. Hoyle was about to begin a fellowship at St. John's College, Cambridge, when World War II started; instead, he helped modify radar to detect aircraft and submarines for the Royal Navy.

The Creation of Elements

Hoyle resumed his Cambridge fellowship as a lecturer in the mathematics faculty in 1945, where he quickly gained a reputation as an energetic, unconventional thinker. Despite a heavy teaching load, he developed a theory with Maurice Pryce during the war to explain the production of light elements in stars. He also predicted an energy state of carbon that had never been detected (experiments soon proved him correct) and pointed out that more helium existed in the universe than could be accounted for by theory.

During the late 1940s and 1950s, Hoyle spent several terms at the California Institute of Technology (Caltech) and at the Mount Wilson and Mount Palomar Observatories. He worked closely with Margaret Burbidge, Geoffrey Burbidge, and William A. Fowler to explain how supernovas form heavy elements. Their collaboration culminated in a landmark paper in astrophysics published in 1957, "The Synthesis of Elements in Stars."

Cosmology

The prevailing cosmological theory in the 1940s held that the universe grew from an exploding primeval atom. During a radio lecture in 1949, Hoyle referred to the theory as the "big bang." The name stuck, even though Hoyle only intended it to be a picturesque description.

In fact, Hoyle thought the big bang theory to be seriously flawed. Beginning in 1946, he worked with Thomas Gold and Hermann Bondi on what became the chief rival theory of the big bang. Called the steady state cosmological theory, it proposes that the universe had no sudden beginning. Instead, matter is continuously created over trackless time. Hoyle's original version of the theory differed somewhat from that of Gold and Bondi, and he modified it significantly between 1960 and 1980.

The steady state theory has sparked continuous and harsh criticism, much to Hoyle's astonishment.

Steady State Cosmology

The steady state cosmological theory proposes that matter in the universe is continuously created over time, rather than having arisen suddenly as suggested in the big bang model.

Serious problems troubled the early version of the big bang cosmological model: It proposed a universe three billion years old, younger than many stars in it, a clear contradiction; it could not account for the formation of galaxies; and it did not explain the distribution of elements well. Such difficulties led Hoyle, Thomas Gold, and Hermann Bondi to consider a universe without a finite age. Gold realized that such a theory requires that matter constantly be created in order to fill the empty space opened by the observed recession of galaxies as the universe expands.

Bondi and Gold rested their version of the theory on an axiom that they called the perfect cosmological principle, which assumes that the universe is uniform everywhere in space and time. As the universe expands and old matter drifts away, new particles materialize spontaneously to maintain the uniformity. They rejected Albert Einstein's treatment of mass in the general theory of relativity in favor of a version of Ernst Mach's principle that attributes the properties of mass to the influence of matter elsewhere in the universe.

In his version of the steady state model, Hoyle treated the cosmological principle not as an axiom but as a result of his calculations, which he based on the general theory of relativity. He did so by incorporating a new term into Einstein's field equations, which Hoyle called the C-field. This field produces new matter and fuels the expansion of the universe. He calculated that new matter, in the form of hydrogen, emerges slowly—about three atoms per cubic yard every million years. In an infinitely old universe, he argued, enough matter accumulates to produce new galaxies at a rate to replace old galaxies that have receded beyond observation. Using steady state principles, Hoyle and his colleagues were able to account for the abundance of helium in the universe and the existence of heavy elements, and explain why the laws of physics depend on a single direction of time.

Hoyle and Jayant Narlikar modified the steady state model in response to criticism from cosmologists and to new observational evidence. Their "quasi steady state" theory proposes an oscillating universe in which fields of negative pressure produce new particles in spurts rather than at a continuous rate. The oscillations last about 40 billion years. Hoyle calculated that the Milky Way is about 300 billion years old and that current observational instruments afford astronomers a look backward in time of about 600 billion years.

The quasi steady state, according to Hoyle, accounts for the physical properties of the universe at least as well as the big bang model, but he did not claim that his theory settles all problems. He argued that future cosmological theories will make use of ideas from both the big bang and the steady state model.

Bibliography

North, John. *Astronomy and Cosmology*. New York: W. W. Norton, 1995.

Narlikar, Jayant. *The Structure of the Universe*. London: Oxford University Press, 1977.

Bondi, Hermann. *The Universe at Large*. New York: Doubleday, 1960.

Although early on Hoyle attracted important supporters, the discovery in 1965 that microwave radiation pervades the universe, as predicted by big bang theory cosmologist George Gamow, has been widely thought to invalidate the steady state theory.

Hoyle remained undeterred, however, and developed his modified "Quasi Steady State" theory with Jayant Narlikar. Hoyle insisted that this theory, in comparison to the big bang model, is simpler in form, has fewer untestable properties also accounts for the cosmic background radiation. In fact, he denounced big bang cosmology as metaphysics or a kind of religious fundamentalism.

The Origin of Life

In 1967, Hoyle was elected Plumian Professor of Astronomy at Cambridge, a prestigious position. He also brought a decade of effort to fruition by opening and heading the Institute of Theoretical Astronomy. Five years later, however, the academic politics connected with the institute and the building of new telescopes soured him on British academic science. He resigned his professorship in 1972.

The resignation freed time for writing and lecturing. Hoyle had already acquired renown at both. He had published more than two dozen science fiction novels (some co-authored with his son) and popular astronomy books. He lectured and wrote about overpopulation, Stonehenge, and nuclear energy.

In 1975, he began studying the possibility that life originated in interstellar space. With Chandra Wickramasinghe, he wrote a series of books theorizing not only that life came from outer space but also that disease-causing organisms continue to reach Earth ferried on comets and meteors. This "panspermia" theory began to receive serious, if hesitant, attention from the scientific establishment in the mid-1990s.

Nucleosynthesis of Elements

Hoyle and his colleagues tailored the modern theory of element building to explain the known abundance of elements in the universe. They concluded that element creation is part of the evolution of stars and that it varies with stellar age, type, and size.

Typically, a star converts hydrogen to helium during fusion as protons, which normally repel one another, are forced together. When the hydrogen is used up, the star's core contracts, and, in the increased heat and density, helium nuclei fuse into carbon, oxygen, and nitrogen nuclei. When the helium is exhausted, the core shrinks, escalating temperatures and densities. In several processes of proton accumulation, carbon burns to form sodium, magnesium, neon, and oxygen and silicon burns to produce heavier elements such as sulfur, calcium, nickel, and iron. In some stars, iron accumulating in the core damps the fusion reaction and a supernova follows. The star collapses inward under the pull of gravity, forming a neutron star, and a shock wave with a dense flux of neutrons spreads outward, forging the nuclei of metals such as gold, copper, mercury, lead, and uranium. Elements heavier than uranium also form but are unstable and decay into lighter elements.

Bibliography

Rolfs, Claus E. and William S. Rodney. *Cauldrons of the Cosmos*. Chicago: University of Chicago Press, 1988.

Ferris, Timothy. *Coming of Age in the Milky Way*. New York: William Morrow, 1988.

Murdin, Paul. *End in Fire: The Supernova in the Large Magellanic Cloud*. New York: Cambridge University Press, 1990.

Bibliography

By Hoyle

A Contradiction in the Argument of Malthus, 1963.
Galaxies, Nuclei, and Quasars, 1965.
Man in the Universe, 1966.
Rockets in Ursa Major, 1969 (with Geoffrey Hoyle).
Steady-State Cosmology Re-visited, 1980.

About Hoyle

Rees, Martin, "Fred Hoyle," *Physics Today*,
    November 2001, http://ptonline.aip.org/
    journals/doc/PHTOAD-ft/vol_54/
    iss_11/75_2.shtml?bypassSSO=1.
Overbye, Dennis. *Lonely Hearts of the Cosmos.*
    New York: HarperCollins, 1991.
Lightman, Alan and Roberta Brawer. *Origins: The
    Lives and Worlds of Modern Cosmologists.* Cam-
    bridge, Mass.: Harvard University
    Press, 1990.
Horgan, John. "The Return of the Maverick."
    Scientific American 272: 46-47 (1995).

(Roger Smith)

Edwin Powell Hubble

Discipline: Astronomy

Contribution: Hubble provided evidence that galaxies consist of ordinary stars and he measured the distances of galaxies, showing that more-distant ones have larger recession velocities.

Nov. 20, 1889	Born in Marshfield, Missouri
1910	Earns a B.S. in astronomy and mathematics at the University of Chicago
1913	Earns a B.A. in jurisprudence and Spanish at Oxford University on a Rhodes scholarship
1913-1914	Teaches high school Spanish and physics in New Albany, Indiana
1914-1917	Works at Yerkes Observatory and earns a Ph.D. from the University of Chicago
1917-1919	Serves in the U.S. Army, rising to the rank of major
1919	Begins his career as an astronomer at Mount Wilson Observatory, California
1942-1946	Works at the U.S. Army Ballistics Research Laboratory at Aberdeen, Maryland
1946-1953	Chairs the Research Committee for Mount Wilson and Palomar Observatories
1949	Becomes the first to use the 200-inch telescope at Mount Palomar Observatory, California
Sept. 28, 1953	Dies in San Marino, California

Early Life

Edwin Powell Hubble, the third of seven surviving children, was the son of an insurance agent. The Hubble family moved from Marshfield, Missouri, to Evanston, Illinois, in 1898 and two years later to Wheaton, west of Chicago.

Edwin's seventh-grade teacher was Harriet Grote, later to become the mother of Grote Reber, the radio astronomy pioneer who built the first true radio telescope. Edwin excelled in both academics and athletics at Wheaton High School. There he was a track star and graduated at the age of sixteen.

Entering the University of Chicago, Hubble won letters in track and basketball and majored in astronomy and mathematics. After his graduation in 1910, he received a Rhodes scholarship and studied jurisprudence and Spanish at Oxford University, England. In 1913 he rejoined his family in Louisville and passed the Kentucky bar examination. Instead of practicing law, however,

he spent a year teaching physics and Spanish, and coaching basketball at New Albany High School in Indiana.

Yerkes Observatory

After a year of teaching, Hubble enrolled in graduate astronomy studies at the University of Chicago and became an assistant at the Yerkes Observatory in Williams Bay, Wisconsin, which was operated by the university.

Before arriving at Yerkes, Hubble attended an American Astronomical Society meeting and heard Vesto Slipher present his discovery of the apparent shift of spectrum lines from faint patches of light called nebulas. All these lines were shifted toward the red end of the spectrum, and Slipher interpreted this redshift as the result of a recession velocity of the nebulas.

Although Yerkes had the largest refracting telescope in the world, with a 40-inch lens, Hubble began a program of nebular photography on a 24-inch reflecting telescope. Soon, he made his first discovery. By comparing his photographs with earlier ones, he found a nebula that had changed over a few years. He expanded this observation into his Ph.D. thesis, "Photographic Investigations of Faint Nebulae," in which he classified nebular types and suggested that spiral nebulas are probably outside the Milky Way. After completing his thesis in 1917, Hubble volunteered for service in the U.S. Army, rising to the rank of major.

His last assignment in the military was at the University of Cambridge, where he studied the statistical methods of the renowned astronomer Arthur Eddington.

Mount Wilson Observatory

After his discharge in 1919, Hubble accepted an invitation to work at the Mount Wilson Observatory in California, where a new giant reflecting telescope was just being readied for service.

Hubble's Law of the Expanding Universe

Hubble established the proportional relationship between the recession velocities of galaxies and their distances, showing that the universe is expanding and has a finite age.

Even before Hubble identified stars in nebulae in 1924 and showed that some are galaxies containing several hundred billions of stars, the recession velocities of these nebulas had been measured by Vesto Slipher in 1912. Slipher observed that the absorption lines in their spectra were shifted toward the longer wavelengths, a phenomenon called redshift. A similar effect with sound waves was observed by Christian Doppler in 1842, in which the pitch of a sound source is lowered as it moves away from an observer as a result of the stretching of waves in relation to the observer.

A Doppler interpretation of the redshift makes it possible to calculate the speed of recession of galaxies. All galaxies were found to have red-shifts except for a few of the nearer ones, whose local motion within a cluster of galaxies gives them a small blueshift (a shift toward the blue end of the spectrum). Willem de Sitter used Albert Einstein's equations of general relativity to develop an idealized model of the universe in 1917 that predicts redshifts for distant light sources, suggesting an expanding universe.

When Hubble found Cepheid variables among the stars in galaxies, he was able to estimate their distances. Henrietta Swan Leavitt had shown that the luminosity of a Cepheid variable increased with the period of its pulsation. This period-luminosity law made it possible to estimate distances by comparing the apparent brightness of a star with its intrinsic luminosity, since brightness decreases with distance for a given luminosity. For distances out to about six million light-years, Hubble showed that recession velocity (V) is proportional to distance (D), giving Hubble's law (V = HD), with a constant ratio of V to D known as Hubble's Constant (H).

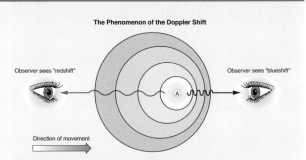

The Phenomenon of the Doppler Shift

Observer sees "redshift"   Observer sees "blueshift"

Direction of movement

Light waves appear more blue when moving toward an observer and more red when moving away from an observer. Here, A represents the Andrmeda Nebula, the light source.

Further confirmation of Hubble's Law depended on greater distances and fainter galaxies whose stars could not be distinguished. Hubble developed other methods of estimating distances, such as the brightness of an entire galaxy compared to the brightness of a closer galaxy whose distance is known from its Cepheids. His colleague Milton Humason was able to measure redshifts for these more distant galaxies, and the velocity-distance relation was confirmed out to about one hundred million light-years.

Hubble's law implies that galaxies began expanding at the same time and place, but with different speeds, so that the faster ones are proportionally further away. The rates measured by Hubble imply that this expansion began about two billion years ago, contradicting estimates of more than four billion years for the age of Earth. Later corrections to the period-luminosity law suggest that the universe has been expanding for about ten to fifteen billion years. The expanding universe is the basis for modern big bang theories.

Bibliography

Whitney, C. *The Discovery of Our Galaxy.* New York: Alfred A. Knopf, 1971.

Smith, Robert. *The Expanding Universe: Astronomy's "Great Debate," 1900-1931.* Cambridge, England: Cambridge University Press, 1982.

His first great discovery with this 100-inch telescope was the detection of a Cepheid variable star in the great spiral nebula in Andromeda on October 5, 1923. Ten years earlier, Henrietta Swan Leavitt had shown how such variables can be used to estimate distances. By the end of 1924, Hubble had found twelve Cepheids in the Andromeda Nebula and derived a distance of about a million light-years, confirming that it was outside the Milky Way and thus a separate galaxy of stars.

In 1925, Hubble introduced the first significant classification system for galaxies in three main categories: irregulars, spirals, and ellipticals. He measured the distances of several other nearby galaxies from their Cepheids and then began to develop other methods of estimating the locations of more distant galaxies.

In 1929, he made his most important discovery by showing that the distances of these galaxies are proportional to their radial velocities as measured by his colleague, Milton Humason. This relationship was confirmed by Hubble and Humason between 1931 and 1936 to about 100 million light-years. Hubble's Law implies that the universe is uniformly expanding.

After 1936, Hubble attempted to measure the distribution of galaxies in order to determine the overall geometry of space. This work led him to some doubts about inferring radial velocities from redshifts, and he preferred to refer to "apparent velocities." In 1941, he used redshift data to determine the direction of the rotation of galaxies relative to their spiral arms.

During World War II, Hubble was chief of ballistics at the U.S. Army's Ballistics Research Laboratory at Aberdeen, Maryland. After the war, he helped to plan for the new 200-inch reflecting telescope at Mount Palomar Observatory and in 1949 became the first person to use it.

Hubble died following a cerebral thrombosis on September 28, 1953, in San Marino, California, at the age of sixty-three.

Bibliography

By Hubble

"Extra-Galactic Nebulae," *Astrophysical Journal*, 1926.

"Distance and Radial Velocity Among Extra-Galactic Nebulae," *Proceedings of the National Academy of Sciences*, 1929.

Red Shifts in the Spectra of Nebulae, 1934.

The Observational Approach to Cosmology, 1937.

"The Law of Red-Shifts," *Monthly Notices of the Royal Astronomical Society*, 1953.

About Hubble

Humason. M. L. "Edwin Hubble." *Monthly Notices of the Royal Astronomical Society* 114 (1954).

Osterbrock, Donald E., Joel A. Gwinn, and Ronald S. Brashear. "Edwin Hubble and the Expanding Universe." *Scientific American* 269 (July, 1993).

Kron, Richard G. ed. *Evolution of the Universe of Galaxies: Edwin Hubble Centennial Symposium*. San Francisco: Astronomical Society of the Pacific, 1990.

(Joseph L. Spradley)

Sir William Huggins

Disciplines: Astronomy and physics

Contribution: By applying the principles of spectrum analysis to stellar light, Huggins determined the chemical constitutions of various stars and nebulas.

Feb. 7, 1824	Born in London, England
1854	Joins the Royal Astronomical Society
1856	Builds an observatory attached to his house at Tulse Hill
1862	Begins a collaboration with William Allen Miller and devises a star spectroscope
1863-1864	Publishes work on the spectra of terrestrial elements and stars
1864	Observes the gaseous nature of the nebula Draco
1865	Elected a Fellow of the Royal Society of London
1867	Receives a gold medal, jointly with Miller, from the Royal Astronomical Society
1876	Begins seriously to photograph his observations
1891	Becomes president of the British Association for the Advancement of Science
1897	Knighted at Queen Victoria's diamond jubilee
1900	Becomes president of the Royal Society of London
1902	Receives the Order of Merit
May 12, 1910	Dies at London, England

Early Life

William Huggins was born in 1824 in Stoke Newington, London. He entered the City of London School in 1837 but left there two years later to continue his education under private tutors. He studied classics, mathematics, and modern languages, but his primary interests lay in science. He had intended to go to the University of Cambridge but instead he took over the business of his father, a silk mercer and linen draper. This occupied his time for about twelve years until 1854, when Huggins decided to devote most of his time to the microscope and telescope. In 1856, he built an observatory attached to his house at Tulse Hill, where he conducted all of his astronomical studies.

A New Method

Aside from conventional observations of the sun and planets, Huggins also wanted to examine the peculiar behavior of starlight when refracted by a prism. To accomplish this, he and his neighbor, William Allen Miller, built a device called a spectroscope. They found that a star's spectrum carries a large amount of information about what gaseous chemicals exist in its atmosphere.

Huggins also applied this method of spectrum analysis to other celestial bodies. He observed several nebulas, including the large nebula in the constellation Orion. He also studied comets and novas, using his spectroscope to discover what elements existed in them.

A New Field

Huggins' work helped to unite the two scientific areas of astronomy and physics into a new field of study: astrophysics. Huggins and Miller had published ten papers on their findings by 1866. Their efforts brought them recognition from the Royal Astronomical Society, and in 1865 Huggins was elected a Fellow of the Royal Society of London.

The scientific community understood the importance of Huggins' work in this field. He received honorary degrees from both Cambridge and Oxford, as well as from prestigious universities in Scotland and Ireland. The Royal Society of London lent him several instruments to use at his Tulse Hill observatory, and in 1890 he was granted a civil pension.

Later Career

Huggins' contributions to science continued after his initial research with Miller. He entered into another productive collaboration in 1875, when he married Margaret Lindsay Murray, who was twenty-six years his junior. His wife worked with him over the next thirty-five years, taking part in many astronomical observations.

During this period, Huggins developed methods of photographing stellar spectra. He

Spectrum Analysis of Stars

The arrangement of dark lines visible in stellar spectra indicates which gases are present around the star.

By analyzing the spectrum of a star's light, Huggins sought to determine some of the elements existing in its atmosphere. He understood that some elements, when burned, produce bright bands of light in their spectra and that the dark bands of the sun's spectrum are caused by the absorption of light by various elements present in its atmosphere. Huggins perceived that the same is true for stars.

Huggins found that comparing the spectra of stars to those of terrestrial elements indicated what elements existed in those stars. He found that the light of the brightest stars originates from some internal hot source and passes through an atmosphere composed of absorbent gases. He concluded that many of these are elements often found on Earth, such as hydrogen, sodium, magnesium, and iron.

Huggins applied spectrum analysis to nebulas,

which were widely held to be merely groups of stars. He found that some do not emit normal spectra, only the bright bands of light. This indicates that some of these mysterious bodies are indeed giant masses of luminous gas.

Spectrum analysis gave science an effective method for discovering the constitutions of stars and other celestial bodies.

Bibliography

Stars and Their Spectra: An Introduction to the Spectral Sequence. James B. Kaler. Cambridge, England: Cambridge University Press, 1987.

Stellar Spectroscopy, Normal Stars. Margherita Hack. Trieste, Italy: Observatorio Astronomico, 1969.

The Theory of Stellar Spectra. New York: Gordon and Breach, 1970.

also published work on the nature of novas. He held a number of scientific posts and received numerous awards, including a knighthood. He continued his observations in his advanced years, but he gave them up in 1908 and returned some of his instruments to the Royal Society of London.

He and his wife published a collection of his scientific papers in 1909, and he died the following year after an operation.

Bibliography

By Huggins

On the Results of Spectrum Analysis Applied to the Heavenly Bodies, 1866.
The Scientific Papers of Sir William Huggins, 1909.

About Huggins

Hearnshaw, J. B. *The Analysis of Starlight.* Cambridge, England: Cambridge University Press, 1986.
Lee, Sidney ed. "Huggins, Sir William." *Dictionary of National Biography: Supplement*, 1901-1911, London: Oxford University Press, 1912.
Gillispie, Charles Coulston, ed. "Huggins, William." *Dictionary of Scientific Biography*, New York: Charles Scribner's Sons, 1970.

(Jacob D. Hamblin)

Christiaan Huygens

Disciplines: Astronomy, invention, mathematics, physics, and technology

Contribution: During Huygens' exceptionally productive career, he discovered the rings of Saturn, invented the pendulum clock, and was instrumental in the development of the wave theory of light.

Apr. 14, 1629	Born in The Hague, the Netherlands
1645	Studies at the University of Leiden
1647	Studies at the University of Breda
1654	Publishes his first mathematics paper, on circles
1655	Builds his first telescope with his brother
1655	Discovers Saturn's rings and its moon, Titan
1655	Receives an honorary Doctor of Laws degree from the University of Angers
1656	Builds a pendulum clock
1657	Publishes a treatise on probability
1663	Elected a Fellow of the Royal Society of London
1666-1681	Lives in Paris and pursues scientific investigations
1678	Writes *Traité de la lumière* (Treatise on Light, 1912), which is published in 1690
1682	Returns to The Hague as a result of ill health
Jul. 8, 1695	Dies in The Hague, the Netherlands

Early Life

Christiaan Huygens (pronounced "HOY-gehnz") was born in The Hague in 1629. His father was a very influential man who was friends with the philosopher René Descartes. Huygens did not have formal schooling in his early years, but instead studied at home. From the age of fifteen, he read the works of Descartes, which were to have a profound impact on his later views of science.

At the age of sixteen, Huygens was sent to the University of Leiden to study law. In 1647, he transferred to the new University of Breda, which his father directed. In 1654, he published a paper on a new way to determine the area of circles accurately.

Astronomy and the Pendulum Clock

In 1655, Huygens worked with his brother to develop a better way of grinding lenses. Together, they built a telescope, with which he studied Saturn. That same year, Huygens discovered Saturn's largest moon, Titan. He also was able to see that Saturn's strange appearance was attributable to a disk around the planet in the same plane as Titan's orbit.

Huygens published his discovery of Saturn's moon in 1656. For fear of ridicule, however, he did not wish to publish his finding of its rings without further study. In order to prove that he saw the rings first, in case someone else reported them in the meantime, he encoded the discovery in an anagram in his paper about Saturn's moon. He realized that the rings were likely composed of individual particles.

Huygens was also one of the first people to measure the rotational period of the planet Mars by timing the passage of surface markings across the face of the planet. He used a micrometer of his own invention to measure the angular sizes of the planets.

Extending the work of Galileo, Huygens developed a weight-driven pendulum clock in 1656, the first truly reliable timepiece. This began an era of precision measurements of time.

Paris

Having been elected as the first foreign resident and a charter member of France's Académie Royale des Sciences, Huygens moved to Paris to continue his work from 1666 to 1681. During this time, he studied many topics, including a description of the physical pendulum, a topic that was later to lead physicists to the concept of the moment of inertia. Extending his work on the pendulum, Huygens conducted research on rotational motion and centrifugal forces.

Huygens studied collisions, favoring the concept of elastic collisions. He also studied forces, following Descartes' ideas on the topic rather than those of Sir Isaac Newton. Huygens' basic philosophy of nature tended to be mechanistic, again after the ideas of Descartes. One of the major triumphs of Huygens' time in Paris was his development of a theory of optics. Throughout his stay in France, however, he was ill. In 1682, his poor health finally forced him to return to his homeland.

Light and Optics

One of Huygens' lasting achievements was the development of the wave theory of light. He supposed that light was created by oscillators of some type and that light propagated itself by triggering other oscillators. This concept seemed to require a medium through which light must pass. The existence of such a medium, called the

The Principle of Secondary Wave Fronts

Huygens postulated that light propagates as a succession of vibrations in oscillators. Each oscillator in a wave front thus acts as a source for further oscillations.

Waves propagate from a point oscillator as circular wave fronts. This is analogous to the ripples set up on the surface of a still pool of water by a dropped pebble.

Huygens' idea of nature was essentially mechanistic. He believed that light was produced by oscillations of some sort and that these oscillations would trigger other oscillators. These oscillators would then cause yet more distant oscillators to begin oscillating, thus propagating the light as a wave. Further wave fronts would be formed by the sum of the wave fronts of the many oscillators forming earlier wave fronts. The later wave fronts are called secondary wave fronts. The concept that each part of a wave front can be the center of new wave fronts is now called Huygens' principle.

Two major problems arose from Huygens' theory of the wave propagation of light. The first was that his ideas conflicted with Sir Isaac Newton's corpuscular theory of light. As a consequence, Huygens' ideas were for the most part discounted until 1865, when James Clerk Maxwell showed that light does indeed propagate as oscillating electric and magnetic fields.

A second difficulty with Huygens' model arose from his almost wholly mechanistic view of nature. His model supposed that space must be filled with oscillators that can be excited to produce and transmit light. This medium through which light was supposed to travel was called the ether (or aether). It was not until the early twentieth century that the concept of the ether was dismissed.

Light does propagate in waves, but not waves of me-

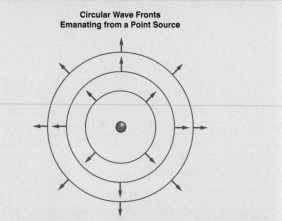

Circular Wave Fronts
Emanating from a Point Source

chanical oscillations, as supposed by Huygens. Light is instead made of time-varying electric and magnetic fields—concepts not yet realized in Huygens' day.

While Huygens was incorrect regarding a mechanistic method of light propagation through the ether, he was correct in the belief that light propagates as waves. Huygens' principle is still used today to describe the wave properties of light, such as diffraction, interference, and refraction. Many of these topics were unknown to Huygens, although he did study refraction. While the speed of light in a vacuum is constant, it varies from one medium to another. Huygens showed that as a wave front passes from one medium to another, the waves travel slower through one medium than through another, and so the wave front is bent.

Bibliography

Light, Magnetism, and Electricity. Isaac Asimov. Vol. 2 in Understanding Physics. New York: Walker, 1966.

Optics. Eugene Hecht and Alfred Zajac. Reading, Mass.: Addison-Wesley, 1974.

What Is Light? A. C. S. van Heel and C. H. F. Velzel. New York: McGraw-Hill, 1968.

ether, was rejected early in the twentieth century. The wave theory of light that Huygens proposed, however, was confirmed by James Clerk Maxwell in the nineteenth century.

Final Days

After returning to The Hague in 1682, Huygens published his *Treatise on Light*, written several years earlier. He also constructed telescopes and devised an eyepiece that minimized color distortions, now called a Huygian eyepiece.

Huygens studied philosophy and speculated about the cosmos. In a work published in 1698, after his death, he reflected on the planets of the solar system. With Earth having been shown to be merely one of six planets, Huygens speculated that the other planets might be worlds similar to Earth, complete with living beings. In 1695, Huygens' poor health finally resulted in his death.

Bibliography

By Huygens

De ratiociniis in ludo aleae, 1657 (Of the Laws of Chance, 1692).

Horologium, 1658.

Traité de la lumière, 1690 (Treatise on Light, 1912).

Cosmotheoros, sive de terris coelestibus, earumque ornatu, conjecturae, 1698 (The Celestial Worlds Discovered: Or, Conjectures Concerning the Inhabitants, Plants, and Productions of the Worlds of the Planets, 1698).

Oeuvres complètes de Christiaan Huygens, 1888-1950.

About Huygens

Bell, Arthur E. *Christiaan Huygens and the Development of Science in the Seventeenth Century.* New York: Longmans, Green, 1947.

Taton, René. *History of Science: The Beginnings of Modern Science.* New York: Basic Books, 1964.

(Raymond D. Benge, Jr.)

Jacobus Cornelius Kapteyn

Discipline: Astronomy

Contribution: Kapteyn helped organize the systematic collection and cataloging of basic stellar data, and investigated the distribution and motions of stars in the system today called the Milky Way.

Jan. 19, 1851	Born in Barneveld, the Netherlands
1868	Enters the University of Utrecht
1875	Accepts a position at Leiden Observatory
1878	Appointed a professor of astronomy at the University of Groningen
1896-1900	Publishes *Cape Photographic Durchmusterung*
1904	Announces his discovery of "star streaming" at the International Congress of Science in St. Louis
1905	Takes a trip to South Africa with the Astronomical Society of the Atlantic
1906	Publishes *Plan of Selected Areas*
1919	Named a Fellow of the Royal Society of London
1921	Retires from Groningen
1922	Publishes *Theory of the Arrangement and Motion of the Sidereal System*
June 18, 1922	Dies in Amsterdam, the Netherlands

Early Life

Jacobus Cornelius Kapteyn (pronounced "kahp-TINE") was born into a large family in 1851 in Barneveld, the Netherlands, where his parents ran a boarding school. Young Kapteyn showed considerable intellectual promise when he passed the entrance examination for the University of Utrecht at the age of sixteen. Thereafter, he studied physics and mathematics. He obtained his Ph.D. with a thesis on vibrating membranes.

In 1875, Kapteyn worked at Leiden Observatory, and three years later he was appointed to a professorship in astronomy and theoretical mechanics at the University of Groningen. He married Elise Kalshoven in 1879; they had a son and two daughters, one of whom married the famous Danish astronomer Ejnar Hertzsprung.

Cataloging Stars

Kapteyn's primary contributions were in stellar astronomy. He was a meticulous and critical researcher who excelled in the careful analysis of data and encouraged scientific cooperation. Among his first major accomplishments was the compilation, in collaboration with David Gill, of the *Cape Photographic Durchmusterung* (1896-1900). This was a catalog of photographic magnitudes and positions of more than 450,000 stars in the Southern Hemisphere, down to the tenth magnitude. An extremely valuable (and accurate) reference work, it complemented the earlier *Bonner Durchmusterung* for Northern Hemisphere stars.

At the time when this catalog was being compiled, Kapteyn recognized the need for vastly increasing the quantity of other stellar data, such as radial velocities, proper motions, and parallaxes. In order to promote an organized, systematic approach, in 1906 he proposed to the international astronomical community a plan to concentrate work on 206 specific selected areas. This plan was largely accepted by the world's observatories, and soon considerable quantities of data were being collected for these selected areas.

The Stellar System: Structure and Dynamics

Another major effort by Kapteyn was the attempt to ascertain, from statistical analysis, the space density of stars (the number of stars per unit volume of space) and their luminosity function (the distribution of absolute magnitudes). This problem is complicated by the fact that observable quantities such as apparent magnitude and proper motion (angular motion against the background sky) are functions of distance. The conclusion of Kapteyn and his coworkers was that the local stellar system was a somewhat flattened spheroidal system (lens-shaped) more or less centered on the sun—the so-called Kapteyn Universe. It is now known that interstellar absorption by dust grains, especially near the galactic plane, seriously affects apparent magnitudes; the solar system is far from the center of the galaxy.

Continuing his statistical analysis of the motions of stars, Kapteyn found that the stellar motions are not random but rather form two different groups that he called star streams. It was later pointed out by his student Jan Oort that Kapteyn had, in fact, discovered galactic rotation. Kapteyn continued his studies of stellar dynamics and discovered the star with the second largest proper motion, now called Kapteyn's star, with an annual motion of 8.73 seconds of arc. He died in 1922.

Bibliography

By Kapteyn

Cape Photographic Durchmusterung, 1896-1900 (with David Gill).

Plan of Selected Areas, 1906.

Contributions from the Mount Wilson Solar Observatory, 1920 (with P. J. van Rhijn).

"First Attempt at a Theory of the Arrangement and Motion of the Sidereal System," *Astro-physical Journal*, 1922.

Mount Wilson Catalogue of Photographic Magnitudes in Selected Areas 1-139, 1930 (with F. H. Seares and van Rhijn).

About Kapteyn

Eddington, Arthur S. "Jacobus Cornelius Kapteyn." *Observatory* 45 (1922).

de Sitter, Willem. *Kosmos*. Cambridge, Mass.: Harvard University Press, 1932.

(George W. Rainey)

Spectrum Analysis of Stars

The galaxy is a somewhat flattened, rotating system of stars. Stars closer to the galactic center than the sun have higher orbital velocities, while stars farther from the galactic center have lower orbital velocities.

A star's radial velocity, together with its proper motion and parallax, enables the star's space motion (with respect to the solar system) to be determined. Kapteyn carried out detailed statistical analysis of space velocities of stars in different directions. Such studies enabled him to determine that stellar motions are not random, but rather fall into groups, which he called streams.

It is now known that stars are in orbit about the center of the Milky Way. Stars generally in the direction of the galactic center (toward the constellation Sagittarius) have mean velocities somewhat different from those of stars generally in the opposite direction (toward the constellation Perseus). More recent studies have indicated that the differential rotation of the galactic disk is actually quite complicated. Nevertheless, stars in the galactic disk tend to move in more or less circular orbits about the galactic center as the galaxy rotates.

The situation is somewhat different for stars well above or below the galactic plane. These stars tend to move in much more eccentric orbits and at higher velocities.

Bibliography

Abell, George O., David Morrison, and Sidney C. Wolff. *Exploration of the Universe*. 6th ed. Philadelphia: W. B. Saunders, 1991.

Mihalas, Dimitri and James Binney. *Galactic Astronomy*. 2d ed. San Francisco: W. H. Freeman, 1981.

Zeilik, Michael, Stephen A. Gregory, and Elske V. P. Smith. *Introductory Astronomy and Astrophysics*. 3d ed. Philadelphia: W. B. Saunders, 1992.

Johannes Kepler

Disciplines: Astronomy, mathematics, and physics

Contribution: Kepler founded modern astronomy, supported and expanded the Copernican system, discovered the laws of elliptical orbits, and set the stage for Newtonian physics.

Dec. 27, 1571	Born in Weil, Swabia (now Stuttgart, Germany)
1584-1586	Attends the Lutheran seminary at Adelberg
1588	Graduated from the college at Maulbronn
1588-1594	Attends the University of Tübingen
1594	Teaches at the Lutheran school of Graz in Styria
1596	Publishes a paper that results in correspondence with Tycho Brahe and Galileo
1600	Accepts a position under Brahe at the observatory near Prague
1601	Appointed by Emperor Rudolph II to succeed Brahe
1609	Publishes a paper stating two laws of planetary motion
1612	Moves to Linz, becoming the mathematician to Upper Austria
1619	Publishes *Harmonices mundi,* containing a third law of motion
1618-1621	Publishes *Epitome astronomiae Copernicanae* (Epitome of Copernican Astronomy, 1939)
Nov. 15, 1630	Dies in Ratisbon, Bavaria (now Regensburg, Bavaria, Germany)

Early Life

Johannes Kepler was born to Lutheran parents in 1571 in Weil, near present-day Stuttgart, Germany. His home life was unstable, fraught with financial problems. Nevertheless, his parents showed him the Great Comet of 1577 and took him out to see an eclipse of the moon. Johannes did well in his studies at one of the Latin elementary schools established in Lutheran communities to educate promising boys. He was frail, sensitive, devoutly religious, and fascinated by nature. His parents and teachers agreed that he should study for the ministry.

An outstanding examination for his bachelor's degree at Maulbronn earned Kepler acceptance as a student at the University of Tübingen, which stood alongside Wittenberg as an outstanding center of German learning. There, Michael Mästlin taught Kepler the controversial theory of Nicolaus Copernicus, which held that Earth moved and circled the sun.

Completing his master's degree in divinity, Kepler was surprised to be recommended for a position teaching mathematics and astronomy at the Lutheran school at Graz. He had hoped to continue in theology. Apparently, the faculty had no reservations about Kepler's orthodoxy for the pulpit, but they saw him as clearly standing out among his classmates in mathematics. Financially, Kepler was obligated to accept.

Philosophy of Science

Kepler did not attract students at Graz but in a short time, he published his work. He was taken with finding God's underlying design for the solar system. There were six known planets at the time. Kepler asked "Why six?" and "Why are they not equally spaced?" Believing that geometry preceded creation in the mind of God, Kepler was struck with the idea that God had used the five perfect Pythagorean solids, one inside the other, to locate the planets in their orbits around the sun. In 1596, he published *Mysteriium cosmographicum*, which contained these ideas and at the same time openly supported the Copernican system. While his interesting design theory has been discarded, at the time Kepler gained fame and correspondence with noted astronomers Galileo and Tycho Brahe. The friendly contact with Tycho was critical to Kepler's future.

Flight to Brahe's Observatory

In 1598, all Lutheran teachers and preachers were banned from Graz by the Catholic archduke. Kepler was given some latitude by friendly Jesuits and could have stayed by converting to Catholicism, but he refused. By 1600, he welcomed Brahe's offer to work in his observatory near Prague. Brahe put Kepler to work on a major problem: the seemingly eratic orbit of Mars.

Within a year, Brahe died and Kepler was appointed head of the observatory and inherited all of Brahe's data on the movements of the planets. Kepler was in an ideal position to contribute to a greater understanding of the solar system.

The Discovery of Elliptical Orbits

In 1604, still working on the problem of the orbit of Mars using Brahe's records, Kepler reached his basic and paradigm-shattering conclusion: the data fit better if the speed of Mars varied and its path was an ellipse. In the process, Kepler had applied Copernican theory and overthrown the 2,000-year-old belief that heavenly bodies traveled in circles. In *Astronomia nova, seu physicsa coelestis, tradita commentariis de motibus stellae Martis* (1609), he stated his first two laws of elliptical orbits.

Later Life

In 1611, Kepler's wife died of fever, and his three children were lost to smallpox. Emperor Rudolph II died, and Prague became a battlefield. In 1612 Kepler, still retaining his position, moved to Linz to become the mathematician to Upper Austria. There, he remarried and resumed his studies.

Still driven to seek out God's underlying designs, Kepler published *Harmonices mundi* in 1619, which described the spheres of the planets as producing musical tones. The pitch of each sphere varied with the speed of the planet. Mercury had the highest average pitch and Saturn was given the lowest. These ideas sound strange today, but Kepler found a mystical beauty and truth in this type of thinking. This book also contains his third law of elliptical motion.

Next, he produced a popular work in parts from 1618 to 1621 called *Epitome astronomiae Copernicanae*, which clearly generalized his laws of motion to all planets. In 1627, Kepler completed *Tabulae Rudolphinae*, based on the ideas of Copernicus, which predicted planetary motion more accurately than any previous tables.

In 1630, Kepler died while on a trip to Ratisbon, Bavaria, to plead for his overdue wages.

Kepler's Three Laws of Planetary Motion

Kepler showed that each planet follows an ovalshaped path, called an ellipse, around the sun and that the planets do not travel at uniform speeds in circular orbits or combinations of circles.

What is now called Kepler's second law was discovered first. His analysis of the elliptical motion of Mars revealed that it moved faster when it was closer to the sun and slower when it was farther away. This led to his statement that when a line is connected from a planet to the sun, the line will sweep over an equal area in an equal amount of time, no matter where the planet happens to be in its orbit (see figure).

It then followed that every planet must travel in an ellipse around the sun. An ellipse is a closed curve defined by a fixed total distance from two points called foci. The sun is located at one of the foci. This is the first law of planetary motion.

The third law is that the cubes of the average distance of any planets from the sun are proportional to the squares of their periods (the time that it takes a planet to revolve around the sun). In other words, if Earth is by definition 1.000 astronomical units (AU) from the sun and its period is one Earth year, then Mars is 1.524 AU from the sun and its period is 1.881 Earth years. If the distance from the sun is cubed and the period is squared, they should be equal. For Mars, $(1.524)^3$ should equal $(1.881)^2$. The results are 3.540 and 3.538, which is close enough in celestial physics and allows for the smaller effects of one planet's gravitational effect on another, which becomes more evident with the outer planets.

Kepler's discoveries were impressive for two reasons. First, he dispensed with Earth-centered hypotheses and successfully applied the Copernican theory. Second, in the process he overthrew the ancient assumption that heavenly bodies travel in circles or in complicated circles within circles called epicycles. In *Astronomia nova, seu physicsa coelestis, tra-*

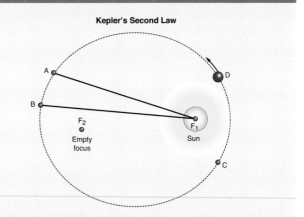

Kepler's Second Law

Kepler concluded that planets traveling in an ellipse move faster when they are closer to the sun. In this exaggerated drawing of an elliptical orbit, assume that the time for the planet to travel from A to B is equal to the time for its travel from C to D. If so, Kepler's second law states that the areas of ABF1 and CDF1 will also be equal. This relationship requires the planet to vary its speed depending on its distance from the sun.

dita commentariis de motibus stellae Martis (1609), he stated his first two laws of elliptical orbits. These two laws, and later a third, showed that the nature of a satellite's path is mechanistic. Kepler had set the stage for Sir Isaac Newton to formulate his laws of universal gravitation and motion to explain the forces that control movement.

Bibliography

Mitton, Simon ed. "The Solar System."
    The Cambridge Encyclopaedia of Astronomy.
    New York: Crown, 1977.
Glasstone, Samuel. "Space Orbits and Trajectories."
    Sourcebook on the Space Sciences. Princeton,
    N.J.: Princeton University Press, 1965.
Feynman, Richard P. "The Theory of Gravitation."
    In *Six Easy Pieces: Essentials of Physics
    Explained by Its Most Brilliant Teacher.* Reading,
    Mass.: Addison-Wesley, 1995.

Bibliography

By Kepler

Mysteriium cosmographicum, 1596 (partial trans. in The Physicist's Conception of Nature, 1958).

Astronomiae pars optica, 1604 (also known as Ad Vitellionem Paralipomena).

Astronomia nova, seu physicsa coelestis, tradita commentariis de motibus stellae Martis, 1609.

Epitome astronomiae Copernicanae, 1618–1621 (3 parts; Epitome of Copernican Astronomy, 1939).

Tabulae Rudolphinae, 1627.

About Kepler

Knight, David C. *Johannes Kepler and Planetary Motion*. New York: Franklin Watts, 1962.

Baumgardt, Carola. *Johannes Kepler: Life and Letters*. New York: Philosophical Library, 1951.

Armitage, Angus. *John Kepler*. New York: Roy, 1966.

Koestler, Arthur. *The Watershed: A Biography of Johannes Kepler*. Garden City, N.Y: Doubleday, 1960.

(Paul R. Boehlke)

Gerard Peter Kuiper

Discipline: Astronomy

Contribution: Kuiper contributed to the theoretical understanding of the solar system. He discovered moons of Uranus and Neptune, proposed a model of how the solar system formed, and predicted a disk of comets, called the Kuiper belt, outside Neptune's orbit.

Dec. 7, 1905	Born in Harenkarspel, the Netherlands
1927	Earns a B.S. from the University of Leiden
1933	Awarded a Ph.D. in astronomy from Leiden
1933	Fellow at the Lick Observatory, University of California
1936	Appointed a lecturer in astronomy at Harvard University
1937	Becomes an assistant professor of astronomy at the Yerkes Observatory, University of Chicago
1947-1949	Serves as director of the Yerkes Observatory
1948	Discovers Miranda, a moon of Uranus
1949	Discovers Nereid, a moon of Neptune
1951	Proposes that comets originate in a disk outside the orbit of Neptune
1960-1973	Serves as director of the Lunar and Planetary Laboratory at the University of Arizona
Dec. 23, 1973	Dies in Mexico City, Mexico

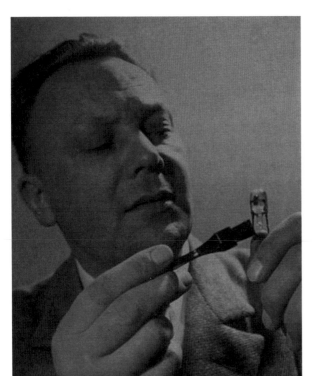

Early Life

Gerard Peter Kuiper (pronounced "KOY-pur") was born on December 7, 1905, to Gerard and Anna Kuiper in Harenkarspel, the Netherlands.

Kuiper enrolled at the University of Leiden, where he studied physics and astronomy, and received a B.S. in 1927. He then began a research project on binary stars (a pair of stars that orbits around each other). Kuiper received a Ph.D. in astronomy at Leiden in 1933 and moved to the United States, where he became a fellow at the Lick Observatory of the University of California.

In 1936, Kuiper was appointed a lecturer in astronomy at Harvard University. The next year, he accepted a position as an assistant professor of astronomy at the Yerkes Observatory of the University of Chicago. There, he continued his research on binary stars, studying systems in which the two stars are so close to each other that they complete an orbit in only a few hours.

Research in Planetary Science

Kuiper's interest shifted from the study of the stars to the study of the planets and moons of Earth's solar system. In 1944, he obtained the first evidence for an atmosphere surrounding a moon, detecting methane surrounding Titan. In 1948, he discovered Miranda, a moon of Uranus, and, in 1949 he discovered Nereid, a moon of Neptune.

Kuiper and several colleagues proposed that the solar system formed from a rotating disk of gas and dust, much greater in mass than the current mass of the planets. In 1951, he suggested that remnants of the disk of matter from which the planets formed might still exist beyond the orbit of Neptune. The first object in this disk, now called the Kuiper belt, was discovered in 1992.

Astronomical Observatories

In 1960, Kuiper was named director of the Lunar and Planetary Laboratory at the University of Arizona. In 1964, he persuaded the governor of Hawaii to build a road to the summit of Mauna Kea and the University of Hawaii to construct an observatory on that site.

Kuiper was among the first astronomers to recognize that jet aircraft could carry telescopes high enough to minimize interference from the atmosphere. He made infrared observations of Venus, which detected water vapor in its atmosphere, from a jet. In January, 1974, the National Aeronautics and Space Administration (NASA) named its C-141 aircraft, which carries a 35-inch telescope, the Kuiper Airborne Observatory.

Kuiper died on December 23, 1973, while in Mexico, looking for sites for a new observatory.

Bibliography

By Kuiper

The Atmospheres of the Earth and Planets: Papers Presented at the Fiftieth Anniversary Symposium of the Yerkes Observatory, September, 1947.

Hynek, J. A ed."On the Origin of the Solar System" in *Astrophysics*, 1951.

The Solar System, 1953 (vol. 1, The Sun, 1953, as editor; vol. 2, The Earth as a Planet, 1954, as editor; vol. 3, Planets and Satellites, 1961, as editor, with Barbara M. Middlehurst; vol. 4, The Moon, Meteorites, and Comets, 1963, as editor, with Middlehurst).

About Kuiper

Cruikshank, Dale P. *Gerard Peter Kuiper*. Washington, D.C.: National Academy Press, 1993.

Whipple, Fred. *Orbiting the Sun.* Cambridge, Mass.: Harvard University Press, 1981.

Ley, Willy. *Watchers of the Skies.* New York: Viking Press, 1963.

(George J. Flynn)

The Origin of the Solar System

Kuiper offered a model of the development of the solar system from a disk of matter.

At the end of World War II, the models for the origin of stars suggested that stars formed by condensation of interstellar gas clouds. A contradiction arose, however, because the known rocky planets—Earth, Mars, Venus, and Mercury—are larger than the lower size limit for the products of such condensation implied by these models.

Kuiper became interested in the origin of the planets. In October, 1949, he proposed a different scenario for how the solar system formed. In his model, the mass of the gas and dust was much greater, about seventy times greater than the current mass of the planets. Under these conditions, smaller "protoplanets," moon-sized objects out of which planets could grow, were capable of forming.

An outgrowth of this model was Kuiper's suggestion that in the outer region of the solar system, beyond the orbit of Neptune, many of these protoplanets, never having grown to the size of planets, might remain intact. He suggested that, occasionally, one of these objects would be disturbed from its nearly circular orbit and thrown into the inner solar system as a comet. The first of these objects was discovered in 1992, and this remnant of the original solar disk is now called the Kuiper belt.

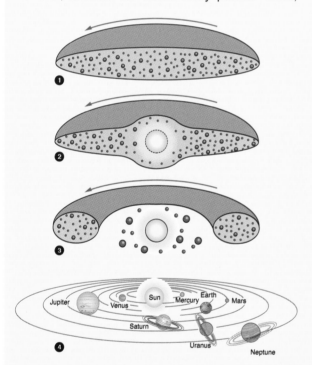

Kuiper was one of several scientists who proposed that the solar system has formed from a rotating cloud of gas and dust.

Bibliography

Alfvén, Hannes and Gustaf Arrhenius. *Evolution of the Solar System.* Washington, D.C.: NASA U.S. Government Printing Office, 1976.

Kuiper, Gerard P. "On the Origin of the Solar System." *Astrophysics*, 1951.

Henrietta Swan Leavitt

Discipline: Astronomy

Contribution: A pioneer in the photographic measurements of the brightness of stars, Leavitt discovered 2,400 variable stars and established the period-luminosity law for measuring the distances to galaxies.

Jul. 4, 1868	Born in Lancaster, MA
1885-1888	Studies at the Oberlin College Conservatory of Music
1892	Earns an A.B. at the Society for the Collegiate Instruction of Women (now Radcliffe College)
1895	Volunteers as a research assistant at the Harvard College Observatory
1902	Appointed to the staff of the Harvard College Observatory
1904	Begins observing the galaxies called the Magellanic Clouds
1907	Begins a survey of stars as chief of the photographic photometry department
1908	Publishes her study of 1,777 variables in the Magellanic Clouds
1912	Proposes the period-luminosity law for Cepheid variable stars
1917	Publishes "The North Polar Sequence," offering a brightness standard for stars in the Milky Way
1920	Provides the basis for Harlow Shapley's determination of the size of the universe
Dec. 12, 1921	Dies in Cambridge, MA

Early Life

Henrietta Swan Leavitt, one of seven children, was the daughter of a prominent Congregationalist minister with a parish in Cambridge, Massachusetts. Both parents instilled stern Puritan virtues in their daughter. She attended public schools in Cambridge but entered Oberlin College in 1885 after her family moved to Cleveland, Ohio. She enrolled in the Conservatory of Music there, even though her hearing was seriously impaired.

In 1892, Leavitt completed her undergraduate education at the Society for the Collegiate Instruction of Women, nicknamed the "Harvard Annex" and now known as Radcliffe College. Her interest in astronomy began with a course during her senior year; following her graduation, she took an advanced astronomy course. After a period of traveling and further graduate work, she became a volunteer research assistant at the Harvard College Observatory. In 1902, she received a permanent position there, measuring the brightness of variable stars on photographic plates.

The Harvard College Observatory

Edward C. Pickering, the director of the Harvard College Observatory at the end of the nineteenth century, was a pioneer in the hiring of women, assigning them to analyze the increasing volume of telescopic data collected on photographic plates. Leavitt advanced rapidly to become chief of the photographic photometry department with several young women working for her, some with only minimal training in astronomy. She devoted the rest of her life to the accurate measurements of the brightness of stars. In 1907, Leavitt began a survey of stars near the north celestial pole to establish a standard photographic sequence, comparing 299 plates from thirteen telescopes. In 1913 Leavitt's "north polar sequence" became the standard for brightness measurements of stars in the Milky Way and was adopted in 1913 by the International Committee on Photographic Magnitudes for its projected astrographic map of the sky. It was eventually published in the Annals of the Harvard College Observatory in 1917.

Magellanic Cloud Studies

In 1890, the Harvard College Observatory set up a 24-inch telescope above the city of Arequipa, Peru. Two particular areas of study were the Great and Small Magellanic Clouds, which are the faint patches of light first observed by explorer Ferdinand Magellan's crew in 1521. A series of sixteen long-exposure photographic plates, sent from Arequipa to Cambridge, revealed very faint stars within the Magellanic Clouds, now known as small satellite galaxies of the Milky Way.

Leavitt's first conclusion from her analysis of the Magellanic Cloud photographs was that a large number of its stars had a variable brightness.

The Period-Luminosity Law for Cepheid Variable Stars

The average luminosity of Cepheid variable stars increases with the period (time) of their pulsations.

Using photographic photometry, Leavitt discovered 2,400 variable stars, about half of those known at the time. In her 1908 paper "1,777 Variables in the Magellanic Clouds," she derived periods for seventeen variables and noted that the brighter variables have longer periods. Such variable stars had been observed earlier in the constellation Cepheus and were called Cepheid variables.

Extending her analysis in 1912 to twenty-five stars in the Small Magellanic Cloud, Leavitt took advantage of the fact that they were all at nearly the same distance from Earth. Thus, she could move beyond the apparent magnitude (brightness) of stars to their absolute magnitude (luminosity), since any apparent differences could be attributed not to relative distances but rather to their actual emission of light as determined by their size and surface brightness. In this way, she showed that the intrinsic luminosity of Cepheid variables increases in a simple way with their period. Once the luminosity of a star is known, its measured brightness can be used to estimate its distance from Earth. By 1920, Harlow Shapley had calibrated the luminosities of the Cepheid variables and used the period-luminosity law to ascertain the size of the Milky Way. In 1924, Edwin Hubble used the law to find the distance to other galaxies.

Bibliography

Percy, John R. "Pulsating Stars." *Scientific American* 232. June, 1975.

Shapley, Harlow ed. *Source Book in Astronomy*. Cambridge, Mass.: Harvard University Press, 1960.

Spradley, Joseph L. "Women and the Stars." *The Physics Teacher*. September, 1990.

In 1908, she published her discovery of 1,777 variables in the Magellanic Clouds in the *Annals of the Harvard College Observatory*. By 1912, she had established the period-luminosity law for a special category of these variables.

Unfortunately, Leavitt's career was cut short when she died of cancer in Cambridge, Massachusetts at the age of fifty-three.

Bibliography

By Leavitt

"1,777 Variables in the Magellanic Clouds," *Annals of the Harvard College Observatory*, 1908.

"Ten Variable Stars of the Algol Type," *Annals of the Harvard College Observatory*, 1908.

"Periods of Twenty-Five Variable Stars in the Small Magellanic Cloud," *Harvard College Observatory Circular*, 1912.

"The North Polar Sequence," *Annals of the Harvard College Observatory*, 1917.

About Leavitt

Hoffleit, Dorrit. "Henrietta Swan Leavitt." *Notable American Women*. Cambridge, Mass.: The Belknap Press of Harvard University Press, 1971.

Mitchell, Helen Buss. "Henrietta Swan Leavitt and Cepheid Variables." *The Physics Teacher* (March, 1976).

Bailey, Solon I. *History and Work of the Harvard College Observatory*. New York: McGraw-Hill, 1931.

(Joseph L. Spradley)

Georges Lemaître

Disciplines: Cosmology and mathematics
Contribution: Lemaître proposed the primeval atom theory of the origin of the universe, which later came to be known as the "big bang."

Jul. 17, 1894	Born in Charleroi, Belgium
1914	Joins the Fifth Corps of Volunteers during World War I
1920	Completes a dissertation at the University of Louvain
1920	Enters the Maison Saint Rombaut to study for the priesthood
1923	Ordained into the priesthood
1923-1924	Studies at the University of Cambridge
1924-1925	Studies at the Massachusetts Institute of Technology (MIT)
1927	Becomes professor of astrophysics at Louvain
1933	Publishes *Discussion sur l'évolution de l'Univers*
Oct. 28, 1936	Becomes a member of the Pontifical Academy of Science
1946	Publishes *L'Hypothèse de l'atome primitif* (The Primeval Atom, 1950)
1950	Publishes *L'Univers*
1960	Becomes president of the Pontifical Academy of Science
June 20, 1966	Dies in Louvain, Belgium

Early Life

Georges Henri Lemaître (pronounced "luh-MEHTR"), the son of a Belgian lawyer, attended a parish grade school and a Jesuit high school. His father moved the family to Brussels in 1910, where Georges attended a Jesuit school, studying mathematics in preparation for a career as a research scientist. He graduated from the College of Engineering in 1913 and took a job as a mining engineer. Just days after Germany invaded Belgium, Lemaître joined the Fifth Corps of Volunteers.

Early in World War I, he dug trenches in preparation for battle. He was later transferred to an artillery unit, where he fought in the trenches. He reached the rank of master sergeant and was cited for bravery.

After the war, Lemaître devoted himself to finishing an advanced degree in the sciences and to studying for the priesthood. He took a degree in mathematics in 1920 and was ordained in 1923.

Cosmological Theory

Lemaître studied for a year at the University of Cambridge, England, under Sir Arthur Stanley Eddington, and for a year at the Massachusetts Institute of Technology (MIT), where he worked closely with Harlow Shapley of Harvard University. His career was marked by an ability to apply higher mathematics to problems in astrophysics and celestial mechanics.

His work under Eddington and Shapley drew Lemaître to problems in astrophysics. After working on the problem of the motion of galaxies, he turned to the work for which he is most famous. Lemaître proposed the first theory that brought together relativity theory and observational astronomy into a model for the origin of the universe. This model, which he called the primeval atom, is the basis for modern big bang cosmology.

Science and Religion

Lemaître's priesthood was a source of some interest for many of his colleagues in the sciences—he was often referred to by his Catholic title, "The Abbé Lemaître," to reinforce his connection with the Catholic Church.

Lemaître was reticent, however, to bring the world of science and the world of religion together. He admonished Pope Pius XII not to associate his primeval atom with the creation account in Genesis, and he often spoke of the different ways of thinking that for him divided questions of science and questions of religion.

Numerical Calculations

Throughout his career, Lemaître continued his work in pure mathematics, and he is also known for having brought the first computer to Belgium. He was an active participant in all facets of the computer's operation—its programming, application to mathematical problems, and administration.

The Primeval Atom

The primeval atom is Lemaître's term for the super-dense state of matter at the beginning of the universe.

Lemaître combined the work of Alexander Friedmann, a Russian mathematician who developed a mathematical model for an expanding universe, with the work of Edwin Hubble, the U.S. astronomer who discovered the expansion of the universe.

Before Lemaître, Friedmann's work was considered to be a form of theoretical physics that was merely a mathematical exercise. Lemaître developed the theory into an account for the physical origin of the universe. He claimed that the universe was once a "primeval atom," an atom that contained all the matter of the universe. Just as the elements of atomic number 92 (uranium) and higher are radioactive, he proposed that this primeval atom, with an atomic number equal to the number of all the protons and neutrons in the universe, would be "super-radioactive."

The fission of this cosmic egg into smaller and smaller parts and the force of the decay would result in the outward expansion of the universe that Hubble observed. Later, Lemaître claimed, some of this matter would condense to form stars and galaxies.

His was the first modern cosmology to combine relativistic mathematics and observational evidence from astronomy to describe the creation of the universe. Later theories that built on Lemaître's theory were first dubbed "big bang" theories by Sir Fred Hoyle in a British radio broadcast in 1950.

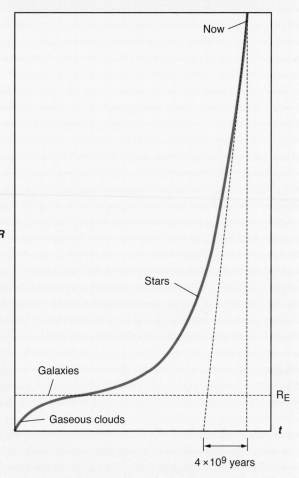

The history of the universe as Lemaître envisioned it, from the superdense primeval atom at the far left of the curve to the present at the far right. R is the size of the universe, 1 is the age, and the upward slope of the curve represents the expansion of the universe. (from *Cosmology of Lemaître*, by O. Godart and M. Heller, 1985).

Bibliography

North, John. *Astronomy and Cosmology*. New York: W. W. Norton, 1995.

Silk, Joseph. *The Big Bang*. 2d ed. New York: W. H. Freeman, 1989.

Gribbin, John. *In Search of the Big Bang*. New York: Bantam Books, 1986.

He removed himself from cosmological work as the steady state model of Fred Hoyle, Herman Bondi, and Thomas Gold gained popularity, but he lived long enough to see his concept of the primeval atom, by then called the big bang theory, vindicated by the observation of cosmic background radiation in 1965. He died in Louvain on June 20, 1966.

Bibliography

By Lemaître

"Un Univers homogene de masse constante et de rayon croissant rendant compte de la vitesse radiale des nebuleuses extragalactiques," *Annales de la Société Scientifique de Bruxelles,* 1927 ("A Homogeneous Universe of Constant Mass and Increasing Radius Accounting for the Radial Velocity of Extra-Galactic Nebulae," *Monthly Notices of the Royal Astronomical Society,* 1931).

"The Expanding Universe," *Monthly Notices of the Royal Astronomical Society,* 1931.

Discussion sur l'évolution de l'Univers, 1933.

L'Hypothèse de l'atome primitif: Essai de cosmogonie, 1946 (The Primeval Atom: An Essay on Cosmogony, 1950).

L'Univers, 1950.

Heller, M. and O. Godart, eds.*The Expanding Universe: Lemaître's Unknown Manuscript,* 1985.

About Lemaître

Berger, A. ed. *The Big Bang and Georges Lemaître.* Boston: D. Reidel, 1984.

Godart, O. and M. Heller. *Cosmology of Lemaître.* Tucson, Ariz.: Pachart, 1985.

Ferris, Timothy. *The Red Limit.* New York: William Morrow, 1977.

(Craig Sean McConnell)

Jane X. Luu

Disciplines: Astronomy and physics
Contribution: Luu discovered and studied objects in the region of the outer solar system known as the Kuiper belt, leading to a greater understanding of the origin of comets.

Jul. 15, 1963	Born in Saigon, South Vietnam
1975	Immigrates to the United States
1984	Earns a bachelor's degree in physics from Stanford
1984	Works at the Jet Propulsion Laboratory at California insititue of Technology (Caltech)
1986-1990	Graduate student at the Massachusetts Institute of Technology (MIT)
1990	Earns a Ph.D. in planetary astronomy from MIT
1991	Awarded the Annie Jump Cannon Prize
1990-1992	Postdoctorate fellowship to the Harvard-Smithsonian Center for Astrophysics
1992	Discovers the first known object in the Kuiper belt
1992-1993	Receives a Hubble Fellowship to Stanford
1993-1994	Receives Hubble Fellowship to the University of California, Berkeley
1994-1998	Becomes an assistant professor at Harvard University
1998-2001	Takes tenured position at Leiden University in the Netherlands
2001	Joins MIT's Lincoln Laboratory
2012	Receives the Kavli Prize with David C. Jewitt

Early Life

Jane X. Luu was born Luu Le Hang in Saigon, South Vietnam, on July 15, 1963. Luu and her family fled to the United States when the North Vietnamese army entered Saigon on April 30, 1975. After living in a refugee camp in Paducah, Kentucky, in 1975 and 1976 Luu's family settled in Southern California.

Her name was changed to Jane Luu at this time. The "X" in Luu's name does not stand for a middle name. Instead, she selected it as a middle initial for convenience.

After her graduation from high school as valedictorian in 1980, Luu attended Stanford University in Palo Alto, California. She graduated in 1984 with a bachelor's degree in physics.

During the summer of 1984, she was employed as a computer operator at the Jet Propulsion Laboratory (JPL) at the California Institute of Technology (Caltech) in Pasadena, California. Her experience

at JPL, where the studies of the Voyager space probes were conducted, inspired Luu to focus on astronomy.

Luu began graduate studies in astronomy at the Massachusetts Institute of Technology (MIT) in Cambridge, Massachusetts, in 1986. Her thesis adviser was astronomer David C. Jewitt, with whom Luu began a long and productive collaboration. They continued to work together when Jewitt transferred to the University of Hawaii in 1988. Luu earned a Ph.D. in planetary astronomy from MIT in 1990.

The Discovery of 1992 QB1

In 1987, Luu and Jewitt began searching for objects in the region of the outer solar system known as the Kuiper belt. Most of this work was done using a 7.2-foot telescope on the peak of Mauna Kea on the island of Hawaii. Electronic detectors known as charge-coupled devices (CCDs) were used to search for small, distant objects too dim to be detected by photographic plates.

The search continued while Luu completed her doctorate studies. She received a postdoctorate fellowship to the Harvard-Smithsonian Center for Astrophysics in Cambridge, Massachusetts, from 1990 to 1992.

In 1991, she was awarded the Annie Jump Cannon Prize from the American Astronomical Society. Luu and Jewitt discovered the first known object in the Kuiper belt on August 30, 1992. The object, officially known as 1992 QB1, was nicknamed "Smiley" after a character in the novels of John Le Carré. 1992 QB1 was seen to be a reddish object with a diameter of about 174 miles orbiting the sun at a distance of about 4.1 billion miles.

More Fellowships, More Discoveries

Luu received Hubble Fellowships to Stanford from 1992 to 1993 and to the University of California, Berkeley, from 1993 to 1994.

The Kuiper Belt

The Kuiper belt is a region of the outer solar system containing numerous small objects believed to be the source of certain comets.

In 1951, the Dutch-American astronomer Gerard Peter Kuiper suggested that there exists a region of space beyond the orbit of Neptune that contains material left over from the formation of the solar system. The small objects found there could be drawn closer to the sun by the gravitational pull of the large planets, transforming them into comets.

The existence of the Kuiper belt was confirmed in the 1990s when Luu and other astronomers discovered several small objects in this region. The Kuiper belt is believed to be the source of a group of objects known as Centaurs that cross the orbits of the planets of the outer solar system. The Centaurs are thought to have been pulled away from the Kuiper belt by the gravitational force of the planets. Their orbits are unstable and astronomers believe that they may be pulled into the inner solar system to become comets.

Luu has suggested that the dwarf planet Pluto, its moon Charon, and Triton, one of the moons of Neptune, may be large Kuiper-belt objects that were pulled into their present orbits by the gravity of Neptune. These three objects are all much denser than the other planets and moons of the outer solar system and have unusual orbits that suggest such an origin.

Bibliography

Beatty, J. Kelly and Andrew Chaikin, eds. *The New Solar System.* Cambridge, Mass.: Sky, 1990.

Levy, David H. *The Quest for Comets: An Explosive Trail of Beauty and Danger.* New York: Plenum Press, 1994.

Lang, Kenneth R. and Charles A. Whitney. *Wanderers in Space: Exploration and Discovery in the Solar System.* Cambridge, England: Cambridge University Press, 1991.

The Kuiper Belt

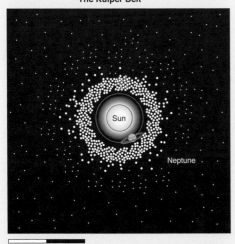

100 Astronomical units

Objects that could be detected by the observatory on Mauna Kea in Hawaii are shown clustered near the inner border of the Kuiper belt, according to this computer simulation (from Peter Samek's illustration for Luu and David C. Jewitt's "The Kuiper Belt," Scientific American, May, 1998).

The Orbit of 1992 QB$_1$

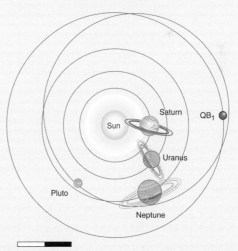

20 Astronomical units

In 1992, Luu and David C. Jewitt identified QB1, an object in the Kuiper belt, and they were able to determine its orbit (from Peter Sarnek's illustration for Luu and Jewitt's "The Kuiper Belt," Scientific American, May, 1996).

She became an assistant professor at Harvard University in Cambridge, Massachusetts, in 1994.

Meanwhile, Luu and other astronomers discovered new objects in the Kuiper belt. Five objects were found in 1993, and about a dozen objects were identified each year from 1994 to 1996. Luu was directly involved in the majority of these discoveries.

Despite Luu's success, her position as an assistant professor at Harvard meant that she could not expect to be considered for a tenured position and she decided to take a position at Leiden University in the Netherlands. She lectured in English while her students would ask her questions in Dutch. There Luu met her husband, astronomer Ronnie Hoogerwerf. Unfortunately, because of the international politics, her time with large telescopes was limited at Leiden. She missed her friends and family and decided to return to the United States.

A New Direction

When Luu returned to the United States she avoided the grueling process of tenure, and decided to go in another direction entirely. She joined MIT's technical staff at Lincoln Lab as an engineer working on defense projects. Luu now builds laser-based radar systems.

Even though Luu has left academia, her work with the Kuiper belt is still being acknowledged as a great advancement. In 2012 she was awarded both the Shaw and the Kavli Prize.

Bibliography

By Luu

"The Kuiper Belt" in *Asteroids, Comets, and Meteors,* 1993, 1994.

"The Solar System Beyond Neptune," *Astronomical Journal,* 1995 (with David C. Jewitt).

"The Kuiper Belt," *Scientific American,* 1996 (with Jewitt).

About Luu

"An Interview With . . . Jane Luu," Imagiverse, http://imagiverse.org/interviews/janeluu/jane_luu_21_03_03.htm.

"The Authors." *Scientific American* 274, May, 1996.

Bartusiak, Marcia. "The Remarkable Odyssey of Jane Luu." *Astronomy* 24, February, 1996.

Venkatraman, Vjaysree, "No Starry-Eyed Astronomer," *Science*, October 19, 2012, http://sciencecareers.sciencemag.org/career_magazine/previous_issues/articles/2012_10_19/caredit.a1200116

Who's Who in Science and Engineering. New Providence, N.J.: Marquis, 1996.

(Rose Secrest)

Antonia Maury

Disciplines: Astronomy and physics

Contribution: Maury created an improved method of classifying stellar spectra and studied the spectrum of Beta Lyrae.

Mar. 21, 1866	Born in Cold Spring, New York
1887	Earns a bachelor's degree from Vassar College
1888-1896	Works as research assistant at Harvard Observatory
1889	Discovers the second known spectroscopic binary star
1891-1894	Employed as teacher at the Gilman School
1896-1918	Teaches and lectures at various locales
1897	Publishes the results of her studies of stellar spectra
1918-1935	Returns to Harvard Observatory as a research assistant
1919-1920	Receives the Pickering Fellowship
1933	Publishes the results of her studies of Beta Lyrae
1935-1938	Serves as curator of the Draper Park Observatory Museum
1938-1948	Makes annual visits to Harvard Observatory
1943	Awarded the Annie Jump Cannon Prize
Jan. 8, 1952	Dies in Dobbs Ferry, New York

Early Life

Antonia Caetana De Paiva Pereira Maury was born in Cold Spring, New York, on March 21, 1866. Her father, Mytton Maury, was a clergyman and amateur naturalist. Her mother, Virginia Draper Maury, was the sister of Henry Draper, a physician and noted amateur astronomer. Antonia Maury earned a bachelor's degree from Vassar College in Poughkeepsie, New York, in 1887, with honors in astronomy, physics, and philosophy.

First Years at Harvard

In 1888, Maury began working for Edward C. Pickering, the director of the Harvard College Observatory in Cambridge, Massachusetts. Her work was part of a large project of studying stellar spectra known as the Henry Draper Memorial. Maury's task was to investigate the spectra of bright northern stars. Based on these studies, she decided that the system used to classify stellar spectra was inadequate, and she created her own.

Maury classified stellar spectra while working at the Harvard Observatory.

During this time, Maury also studied the spectra of spectroscopic binary stars. These stars appear to be single stars when viewed through a telescope, but they have spectra that reveal them to be double stars. Pickering discovered the first such star, Zeta Ursae Majoris, in 1889. Maury discovered the second, Beta Aurigae, later the same year.

Although Pickering respected Maury's ability, he grew impatient with the slowness of her detailed studies and thought her new classification system unnecessary. Maury was unhappy with Pickering's close supervision of her work. She began teaching science at the Gilman School in Cambridge in 1891 and worked only intermittently at Harvard until 1896. The results of her studies were published in 1897.

Return to Harvard

Maury worked as a teacher and lecturer at various institutions from 1896 to 1918. She returned to Harvard Observatory in 1918, where she received a Pickering Fellowship from 1919 to 1920. Maury investigated the spectra of binary stars, particularly the complex, variable spectrum of Beta Lyrae. Her studies of this star were published in 1933.

Maury left Harvard in 1935 and served as curator of the Draper Park Observatory Museum in Hastings, New York, until 1938. From 1938 to 1948, she visited the Harvard Observatory annually to check the accuracy of her predictions of the behavior of the spectrum of Beta Lyrae. Maury received the Annie Jump Cannon Prize from the American Astronomical Society in 1943.

She died in Dobbs Ferry, New York, on January 8, 1952.

Classification of Stellar Spectra

The spectra of stars can be organized in ways that reveal patterns of stellar evolution.

Light from a star forms a spectrum when it passes through a prism, just as sunlight forms a rainbow. Soon after Henry Draper made the first photograph of a steller spectrum in 1872, astronomers began classifying spectra based on patterns of bright and dark lines.

The system used by Harvard Observatory divided spectra into groups labeled with the letters of the alphabet. Maury realized that this system did not organize the spectra into a logical sequence. She created her own system using groups labeled with Roman numerals. Spectra within each group were labeled "a" (wide, sharp lines), "b" (wide, blurred lines), or "c" (narrow, sharp lines). The Danish astronomer Ejnar Hertzsprung discovered that all "c" stars were giant stars.

Influenced by Maury's system, the Harvard system was simplified and rearranged into a sequence based on temperature, from hottest to coolest: O, B, A, F, G, K, M. Hertzsprung and the American astronomer Henry Norris Russell independently charted stars on a chart comparing temperature and brightness. These charts, known as Hertzsprung-Russell (H-R) diagrams, reveal four major groups of stars: the main sequence (medium-sized stars ranging from hot and bright to cool and dim), white dwarves (small, hot, dim stars), and red giants (large, cool, bright stars), and even supergiant stars. As a main sequence star ages, it expands into a red giant, then loses its outer layers to become a white dwarf.

Bibliography

Jaschek, Carlos. *The Classification of Stars*. Cambridge, England: Cambridge University Press, 1987.

Kaler, James B. *Stars*. New York: Scientific American Library, 1992.

Kaler, James B. *Stars and Their Spectra: An Introduction to the Spectral Sequence*. Cambridge, England: Cambridge University Press, 1989.

Bibliography

By Maury

"Spectra of Bright Stars Photographed with the 11-inch Draper Telescope as a Part of the Henry Draper Memorial and Discussed by Antonia C. Maury Under the Direction of Edward C. Pickering," *Annals of the Astronomical Observatory of Harvard College*, 1897.

"The Spectral Changes of ß Lyrae," *Annals of the Astronomical Observatory of Harvard College*, 1933.

About Maury

Abbott, David ed. *The Biographical Dictionary of Scientists: Astronomers*. New York: Peter Bedrick Books, 1984.

Zaban Jones, Bessie and Lyle Gifford Boyd. *The Harvard College Observatory: The First Four Directorships*, 1839-1919. Cambridge, Mass.: Harvard University Press, 1971.

Ogilvie, Marilyn Bailey. *Women in Science: Antiquity Through the Nineteenth Century*. Cambridge, Mass.: MIT Press, 1986.

Albert Abraham Michelson

Disciplines: Astronomy and physics

Contribution: Michelson invented the interferometer, performed a classic experiment trying to measure Earth's motion through the "ether," devised an exact means of determining the speed of light, and measured the diameter of stars.

Dec. 19, 1852	Born in Strelno, Prussia (now Strzelno, Poland)
1875	Appointed an instructor of physics at the U.S. Naval Academy
1882	Appointed an instructor of physics at the Case School of Applied Science in Cleveland, Ohio
1885	Becomes a Fellow of American Academy of Arts and Sciences
1887	With Edward W. Morley, performs ether-drift experiment
1889	Named Chair of Physics at Clark University in Massachusetts
1894	Appointed Chair of Physics at the University of Chicago
1899	Elected president of the American Physical Society
1907	Awarded the Nobel Prize in Physics and the Copley Medal of Royal Society of London
1922	Measures the diameter of Betelgeuse
1925-1927	Conducts velocity of light experiments
May 9, 1931	Dies in Pasadena, California

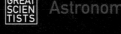

Early Life

Albert Abraham Michelson was born in the Prussian town of Strelno (now Strzelno, Poland) in 1852. Within a few years, his parents imigrated to the United States, settling first in California and then in Nevada. They sent him to San Francisco to attend high school, where he lived with the principal and earned three dollars a month keeping the instruments in the science laboratory in order.

As his family could not afford tuition at a private college or university, Michelson applied for appointment to the U.S. Naval Academy in Annapolis. Nevada was allowed a single appointment and it went to the son of a Civil War veteran. Undeterred, Michelson applied directly to President Ulysses S. Grant, who eventually gave him the appointment. He graduated from Annapolis in 1873 and spent the next two years on naval duty.

A Scientific Career

The navy recognized Michelson's scientific talent by appointing him as an instructor of physics at the academy in September, 1877. That same autumn, as he prepared a lecture on the topic, Michelson became interested in previous methods used to measure the velocity of light. With characteristic experimental insight, he modified the techniques used by earlier European scientists and reported the results of his measurements to the *American Journal of Science* in the spring of 1878. His continuing work on measuring the velocity of light brought him, at the age of only twenty-six, a growing reputation in the United States and abroad as a talented and brilliant physicist.

Sensing the need to enhance his knowledge of physics, especially optics, Michelson took leave of the naval academy to study in Europe from 1880 to 1882. In Berlin and Paris, he studied with such renowned scientists as Hermann von Helmholtz and first devised his famous interferometer, which he used throughout his life to perform precise measurements of a variety of items. With financial backing from inventor Alexander Graham Bell, he tried to measure the relative velocity of Earth and the surrounding "ether" (a light-carrying medium believed to fill space) with his newly created instrument. In 1881, he reported in the *American Journal of Science* that he had not found the so-called ether drift.

Studies of Light

While in Europe, Michelson realized that his interest in experimental physics, especially his studies of light, needed a supportive research environment, which he did not find at Annapolis. He gladly accepted a position as an instructor in physics at the newly formed Case School of Applied Science in Cleveland, Ohio.

While there, Michelson teamed with Edward W. Morley, a professor of chemistry at Western

Reserve University, adjacent to Case. In 1887 they repeated, with more precision and refinement, Michelson's earlier interferometer experiment, seeking to measure the effect of the ether on the movement of light. As a strong advocate of the ether theory as the mechanism for electromagnetic transmission, Michelson hoped that this carefully crafted experiment would produce evidence of the existence of ether. Once again, the results indicated that the ether had no effect on the movement of light. This null result compounded the confusion of nineteenth century physicists in their attempts to explain electromagnetic radiation. More importantly, it eventually led scientists to use the Michelson-Morley outcome as experimental evidence supporting Einstein's theory of relativity.

The Michelson-Morley Experiment

Between 1886 and 1887, Michelson, joined by Edward W. Morley, improved his experimental efforts to measure the ether's effect on the movement of light. Using his ingenious interferometer, they found no evidence of this effect.

Michelson used his interferometer to measure various aspects of light precisely. In the historically famous experiment of 1887, Michelson and Morley used this apparatus, which split a beam of light in two at *b* so that it could travel in perpendicular paths *d* to *e* and *d'* to *e'*, be reflected by mirrors at each corner of the apparatus (*d*, *e*, *d'*, and *e'*), and return to central observation point f after the two beams were combined at *b* (see figure). They mounted the apparatus on a stone floating in mercury, rotating it through a full circle to account for any possible effect of position on Earth's surface.

Michelson and Morley made several observations for four days and found no interference pattern attributable to a slowing the speed of light by the ether, the imagined medium in space through which Earth was thought to move. Although they hoped to find such an effect to demonstrate experimentally the existence of the ether, they were unable to do so. Scientists later used this null result to support Albert Einstein's notion in his special theory of relativity that the speed of light is constant; the interferometer experiment would only measure a constant speed of light, not a varying one. Physicists eventually abandoned the ether theory.

The Path of Light Beams in the Interferometer

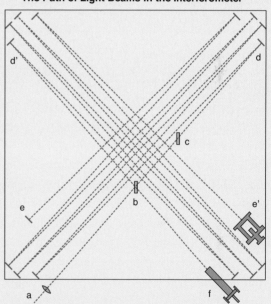

(From Michelson and Morely's "On the Relative Motion of the Earth and the Luminferous Ether" in *American Journal of Science*, 1887.)

Bibliography

Swenson, Loyd S. *The Ethereal Aether: A History of the Michelson-Morley-Miller Aether-Drift Experiments, 1880-1930*. Austin: University of Texas Press, 1972.

Shankland, Robert S. "Michelson-Morley Experiment." *American Journal of Physics* 32, 1964.

Einstein's theories eliminated the need for an ether. However, Einstein never claimed any direct connection between his formulation of the relativity theory and this classic experiment.

Scientific Legacy

Michelson's superb experimental measurements gained him growing acclaim in the scientific community. In 1889 he moved from Case to the new Clark University in Worcester, Massachusetts, and, in 1894 he accepted an appointment as chair of the physics department at the University of Chicago. In each of these academic positions, he continued his research work using the interferometer, which gave him a precise means to determine the speed of light, to establish the length of the standard meter using the light waves of cadmium, and to measure the diameter of stars. These well-regarded achievements earned for him the 1907 Nobel Prize in Physics; Michelson was the first American so honored.

When he died on May 9, 1931, in Pasadena, California, Michelson was still involved in measuring the speed of light. The figures that he reported from his work between 1925 and 1927 remained definitive for a generation. This pioneering U.S. physicist left a legacy of precise, accurate experimentation and ingenious techniques that gave the world of science an experimental foundation for relativity and accurate measurements of light and length.

Bibliography

By Michelson
"On a Method of Measuring the Velocity of Light," *American Journal of Science*, 1878.
"On the Relative Motion of the Earth and the Luminiferous Ether," *American Journal of Science*, 1887 (with Edward W. Morley).
Light Waves and Their Uses, 1903.
Studies in Optics, 1927.

"Measurement of the Velocity of Light Between Mount Wilson and Mount San Antonio," *Astrophysical Journal*, 1927.

About Michelson
Millikan, Robert A. "Biographical Memoir of Albert Abraham Michelson, 1852-1931," *National Academy of Sciences Biographical Memoirs* 19, 1938.
Michelson Livingston, Dorothy. *The Master of Light: A Biography of Albert A. Michelson.* New York: Charles Scribner's Sons, 1973.
Jaffe, Bernard. *Michelson and the Speed of Light.* New York: Doubleday, 1960.
Goldberg, Stanley and Roger H. Stuewer, eds. *The Michelson Era in American Science*, 1870-1930 New York: American Institute of Physics, 1988.

(H. J. Eisenman)

Maria Mitchell

Disciplines: Astronomy and mathematics

Contribution: Mitchell became the United States' first well-known female astronomer by discovering a comet. She spent her life teaching, traveling, and advancing the causes of women's education and women in science.

Aug. 1, 1818	Born on Nantucket Island, MA
1835-1836	Opens a school that accepts the children of immigrants and slaves
1836	Assists her father with astronomical observations
1847	Observes a new comet
1848	Receives the Frederic VI Gold Medal from the King of Denmark
1848	Voted the first female member of the American Academy of Arts and Sciences
1849	Hired by the U.S. Nautical Almanac Office
1850	Voted the first female member of the Association for the Advancement of Science
1857	Receives a telescope from a group of prominent U.S. women
1865	Becomes a professor of astronomy at Vassar College
1869	Elected a member of the American Philosophical Society
1873	Founds the American Association for the Advancement of Women
1876	Presides over the fourth session of the Women's Congress, Philadelphia
June 28, 1889	Dies in Lynn, MA

Early Life

Maria Mitchell grew up on Nantucket Island in a large Quaker family. From her early childhood, she tirelessly investigated her many interests using what books were available on the small whaling island. Her father, William, adhered to the Quaker belief that a girl's education should be comparable to that given boys. Not only did Maria attend the Quaker school on the island, but William made her a part of the astronomical and other scientific work that he did. Her father always praised her willingness to work carefully for long hours and her will not to be repressed by the conventional views of women and girls.

Mitchell had more strong female role models than most girls in the United States. Men would leave on whaling voyages for months, even years, leaving women to run the town.

Commitment to the Education of Girls

By the time that she was sixteen, Mitchell's accomplished study of science and literature was renowned on the island, and so she became the assistant to the master of the Quaker school.

The following year, she opened her own girls' school and accepted the daughters of slaves and immigrants, as well as Quaker girls. The school closed after its first year because most of the pupils were poor, but Mitchell continued to believe in the necessity of education for girls.

Librarian by Day, Astronomer by Night

When her school closed, Mitchell was appointed to the post of island librarian, a position that she held for many years. It was the ideal job for her because she could teach and help visitors while having access to most of the books on the island.

What the Stars Reveal

Through nightly surveillance of the sky, Mitchell was the first in the world to detect a new comet visiting Earth in 1847. Her lifelong, patient study of the stars helped both navigators and astronomers developing the new field of cosmology, the structure and evolution of the universe.

Humankind has studied the stars since prehistoric times out of wonder and awe of their beauty. Many believed that stories were recorded in the heavenly bodies, and others thought that the stars could foretell destiny. Humankind has also studied the stars in order to know their positions for navigational purposes and to understand them.

On the open sea, there are no landmarks. Early sailors realized that they could navigate by the stars. Accurate maps of the heavens were made for use by sailors working with sextants, compasses, and clocks. Sextants are used for measuring a star or planet's angle above the horizon. Knowing when a particular star would rise at a given time of year at a given position on Earth helped a navigator determine the ship's position on the ocean. Today, air and sea navigation are performed with the aid of satellites, but a good navigator still knows the constellations.

Another reason to observe the stars is to determine their chemical makeup. Starlight contains important information about the chemical elements present. Stars are mostly hydrogen and helium, but they contain other elements as well. Stars are the birthplace of the elements. Young stars are almost completely hydrogen. The older a star is, the more elements that it will contain.

When light from one star is focused through a telescope and broken down using a prism, one finds the same rainbow effect obtained from sunlight through a prism. Careful analysis of the spectrum formed, however, shows narrow black lines in some places where color has been removed from the spectrum by a chemical element present in the star.

Each chemical element is capable of absorbing certain known wavelengths of light. If that element is present in the outer regions of a star, it will absorb the appropriate wavelength of light being produced by the interior of the star. This is seen as a black line at a characteristic place in the star's spectrum.

Thanks to the work of the early modern astronomers, scientists now have a thorough understanding of many of the processes occurring in stars. These theories have helped in determining how the universe has progressed from the big bang to the present.

Bibliography

Reeves, H. *Atoms of Silence: An Explanation of Cosmic Evolution.* Cambridge, Mass.: MIT Press, 1984.

Clark, D. H. and F. R. Stephenson. *The Historical Supernovae.* Oxford, England: Pergamon Press, 1977.

Shklovskii, I. S. *Stars: Their Birth, Life, and Death.* San Francisco: W. H. Freeman, 1978.

At about the same time, her father was appointed cashier of the island bank. This position came with a house attached to the bank. Fortunately for Mitchell and her father, because of the importance of whaling to their community, a telescope for locating ships was built on the roof of the bank. The stars themselves are also important to navigation at sea, and for this purpose Mitchell and her father spent thousands of nights in the observatory.

Routine Observation

Mitchell and her father were hired by the U.S. Coast Guard to make precise maps of the stars for the purposes of navigation at sea. Using their telescope in the night sky, they patiently recorded positions of even the faintest stars.

Over the years, Mitchell came to know the exact locations of the stars and other heavenly bodies. One night, she spotted a star in an unaccustomed place. She recorded her observation and returned the next night to find that the star had moved considerably with respect to the other stars. This was no star—it must have been a new comet. She wrote immediately to an astronomer at Harvard University about her discovery.

Fame for the Lady Astronomer

The comet that Mitchell sighted was observed by other astronomers around the world but, after some confusion the authorities decided that Mitchell had seen the comet first. Much disbelief was generated in the public about a woman making such an impressive discovery—and before men had done so. She received a gold medal from the king of Denmark and was elected to many scientific societies that had previously excluded women.

Mitchell traveled to Europe and around the United States in the years following her discovery, and she met several prominent male scientists, but not many female ones. She began to use her own prominence to publicize the issues of education for women and the lack of support for female scientists.

A Return to the Education of Women

In the early 1860s, Matthew Vassar was organizing a college for women and was recruiting professors. He tempted Mitchell to join the Vassar College faculty by giving her charge of the new college observatory, which featured the third-largest telescope in the United States at that time. Mitchell was also attracted by the chance to educate women.

For the next twenty-five years, Mitchell divided her time between teaching her adoring students and speaking about the importance of women's education. In 1873, she helped to found the American Association for the Advancement of Women. She died in 1889.

Bibliography

By Mitchell

"On Jupiter and Its Satellites," *American Journal of Science and Arts*, 1871.

"Astronomical Notes," *Scientific American*, 1876.

"The Need of Women in Science" *Association for the Advancement of Women: Papers Read at the Fourth Congress of Women*, 1876.

Mitchell Kendall, Phebe ed. *Maria Mitchell: Life, Letters, and Journals*, 1896.

About Mitchell

Henderson, Janet K. *Four Nineteenth Century Professional Women*. New Brunswick, N.J.: Rutgers University Press, 1982.

Kohlstedt, Sally Gregory. "Maria Mitchell: The Advancement of Women in Science." *New England Quarterly* 51, no. 1, 1978.

Wright, Helen. *Sweeper in the Sky: The Life of Maria Mitchell, First Woman Astronomer in America*. New York: Macmillan, 1949.

(Wendy Halpin Hallows)

Wilhelm Olbers

Disciplines: Astronomy and medicine
Contribution: An ophthalmologist by profession, Olbers contributed much to modern astronomy notably the discovery of numerous comets and asteroids, a streamlined method for calculating cometary orbits, and an explanation as to why the night sky is dark and not fully illuminated by the myriad stars in space.

Oct. 11, 1758	Born in Arbergen, near Bremen, Germany
1777	Begins his medical studies at the University of Göttingen
1779	Observes Bode's comet and calculates its orbit
1780	Discovers a comet
1781	Visits Vienna and uses the observatory there to study the newly discovered planet Uranus
1797	Publishes a book on a new method for calculating cometary orbits
1802	Confirms the existence of Ceres, the first of several asteroids to be discovered between Mars and Jupiter
1815	Discovers a comet similar to Halley's comet
1820	Retires from his medical practice to pursue astronomy exclusively
1823	Publishes an article explaining the paradox of darkness at night
Mar. 2, 1840	Dies in Bremen, Germany

Early Life

Heinrich Wilhelm Matthäus Olbers was born into a large family, the eighth child of a Protestant clergyman who fathered a total of sixteen children. He was given a humanistic education in Bremen but became interested in the field of astronomy and taught himself mathematics so as to pursue the subject.

At the age of sixteen, Olbers attempted to compute the course of the solar eclipse that occurred in that year, 1774. In 1777, he entered the University of Gottingen to study medicine and graduated in 1780 with a dissertation on involuntary changes in the shape of the eye, *De oculi mutationibus internis*.

After something akin to a hospital residency in Vienna in 1781, during which he also visited the university's observatory at night, Olbers returned to Bremen to practice medicine. He was interested in what would now be called public health policy, and he was largely responsible for the introduction of the practice of inoculation in Germany.

Astronomy as an Avocation

Olbers made his astronomical observations in his spare time from an observatory in his house. As is sometimes the case, the enthusiasm of the amateur is more intense even than that of the professional, and Olbers was soon in active correspondence with many of the foremost German astronomers of the day, including J. H. Schröter, F. X. von Zach, and the famous mathematician Carl Friedrich Gauss.

On von Zach's recommendation, in 1797 Olbers published his treatise on the best way to calculate the parabolic orbits of comets, a work that met with much professional acclaim and established his reputation.

Personal Life

Olbers was married twice. His first wife, Dorothea Köhne, died during a difficult childbirth in 1786, after a marriage of only a year. Their daughter would be reared by Olbers' second wife, Anna Adelheid Lurson, whom he married in 1789. The couple had one son. Beginning with the death of his daughter in 1818, a tragedy that was followed by his second wife's death two years later, Olbers withdrew from practical affairs to a large extent.

Still, public life would not allow him to remain inactive, and he continued to be consulted by physicians seeking his help with difficult cases and astronomers seeking his scientific counsel.

Comets and a Paradox

Olbers' observations of comets and his explanation for the darkness of the night sky helped pave the way for modern astronomy.

Olbers is known for his modern view that a comet's cloud is composed of matter that is repelled by the sun, creating a "tail" directed away from the solar radiation as the body approaches and moves around the center of the solar system. He formed this theory in 1811.

His observations confirmed the orbit, proposed by Carl Friedrich Gauss, of an asteroid once presumed to be a new planet. Olbers thought that the second asteroid discovered by him, Pallas (the first was Vesta), might be the remnant, along with Juno, of an earlier, larger planet. It is now believed, however, that most asteroids were formed the same way that the planets were, by the aggregation of "dust." Olbers rejected the contemporaneous idea that meteorites might be stones expelled from the volcanoes of the moon, citing their extreme speed on impact with Earth. The comet that bears his name was discovered by Olbers in 1815.

While Olbers was not the first to propose a modern solution to the paradox of the darkness of the night sky, his explanation of 1823 is surely the most famous. The paradox confronts the problem that, if one considers the universe to be uniform and infinite and space to be transparent, then billions of suns burning in space should fill the night sky with light.

That this is not the case can be explained by positing sufficient interstellar, non-transparent matter to absorb a portion of the light of distant stars. Modern observations have gone beyond Olbers' paradox to confirm the existence of vast areas of so-called dark matter in outer space.

Bibliography

Sagan, Carl and Ann Druyan. *Comet*. New York: Random House, 1985.

Jaki, Stanley L. *The Paradox of Olbers' Paradox: A Case History of Scientific Thought*. New York: Herder and Herder, 1969.

On two occasions during the French occupation under Napoleon, Olbers was sent to Paris as an official representative of the government of the city-state of Bremen.

Most of his life, Olbers enjoyed robust health and was known to have slept only four hours nightly, allowing his extensive astronomical observations. Not only his untiring efforts in the field of astronomy but also his generosity and collegiality set him apart. It may be seen as another of his many permanent contributions to science that he recognized and encouraged the young Friedrich Wilhelm Bessel, who would go on to become one of the great astronomers of the nineteenth century. Olbers died on March 2, 1840, at the age of eighty-one.

Bibliography

By Olbers

Abhandlung über die leichteste und bequemste Methode, die Bahn eines Cometen Zu einigen Beobachtungen zu berechnen, 1797.

"Über die Durchsichtigkeit des Weltraums" *Berliner astronomisches Jahrbuch für das Jahr 1826,* 1823.

About Olbers

Gillispie, Charles Coulston ed. "Heinrich Wilhelm Matthias Olbers." Lettie S. Multhauf. *The Dictionary of Scientific Biography,* Vol. 10. New York: Charles Scribner's Sons, 1974.

Asimov, Isaac. "Olbers, Heinrich Wilhelm Matthäus." *Isaac Asimov's Biographical Encyclopedia of Science and Technology.* New York: Avon Books, 1976.

(Mark R. McCulloh)

Jan Hendrik Oort

Discipline: Astronomy

Contribution: Oort's theoretical and observational work established the structure, size, mass, and motion of the Milky Way. He also postulated the existence of the Oort cloud, which is widely accepted as the source of most comets.

Apr. 28, 1900	Born in Franeker, Friesland, the Netherlands
1924	Appointed an astronomer at Leiden Observatory
1926	Receives a doctorate from the University of Groningen
1927	Calculates the mass and size of the Milky Way
1935	Made a professor of astronomy at Leiden University
1935	Elected the general secretary of the International Astronomical Union
1942	Receives the Bruce Medal for his achievements in astronomy
1945	Made the director of Leiden Observatory
1950	Proposes the existence of the Oort cloud
1951	With Hendrik Van de Hulst, discovers 21-centimeter radiation from neutral hydrogen in space
1956	With Theodore Walraven, discovers synchrotron radiation from the Crab Nebula
1958	Elected president of the International Astronomical Union
1970	Retires as director of Leiden Observatory
Nov. 5, 1992	Dies in Leiden, the Netherlands

Early Life

The son of a doctor, Jan Hendrik Oort (pronounced "ahrt") was born in the Netherlands on April 28, 1900, in the town of Franeker, Friesland. He completed his education at the University of Groningen, where he studied under Jacobus Cornelius Kapteyn, from whom he acquired an interest in galactic structure and motion.

After completing his doctorate in 1926, Oort worked briefly at Yale University before returning to the Netherlands and the University of Leiden, where he remained for the rest of his career.

The Shape of the Galaxy

In 1927, Oort was able to confirm and modify the theories of Bertil Lindblad concerning the structure of the Milky Way. Two years earlier, Lindblad had advanced the theory that the Galaxy rotates in its own plane about its center.

The Structure of the Galaxy

The solar system to which Earth belongs is part of a rotating spiral galaxy approximately 30 kiloparsecs across, with a mass 150 billion times that of the sun.

Around the beginning of the twentieth century, it became apparent that the structure of the Milky Way must be similar to that of the spiral nebulas and that these nebulas themselves must be galaxies composed of many stars.

Oort measured the motions of stars relative to Earth to confirm Bertil Lindblad's theory that the Galaxy must rotate. Oort and other researchers continued to refine their observations, using optical and then radio astronomy to penetrate deeper into the galactic disk. The following overall structure has now emerged. The Galaxy rotates faster near the center than toward the edge. Earth's solar system, which is 8.7 kiloparsecs—about 28,000 light-years—from the center, completes a rotation about that center every 200 million years.

Increasingly precise observations and dynamic analyses of this and other spiral galaxies have made it clear that the masses of the stars and other objects visible cannot account for the rotational speeds observed. Much additional mass must exist outside the visible disks of the galaxies. In addition, most current theories about the origin, structure, and evolution of the universe require the existence of more mass than can be directly observed. These anomalies of galactic motion provide evidence that at least some of this mass must exist, but its nature is undetermined.

Bibliography

Jones, B. J. T. and J. E. Jones. *The Origin and Evolution of Galaxies*. Dordrecht, the Netherlands: D. Reidel, 1983.

J. Lequeux. *Structure and Evolution of Galaxies*. New York: Gordon and Breach, 1969.

Oort, by measuring the velocities of a number of stars in the Milky Way relative to Earth's solar system, was able to verify this theory and to produce estimates for the size and mass of the Galaxy. Eventually he was able to estimate its rate of rotation and the direction and the distance of the galactic core from the solar system.

Much of this work was made possible by Oort's pioneering research in radio astronomy. Because radio waves pass through the dust particles that obscure the inner parts of the Galaxy from optical observation, they can be used to study the galactic core directly.

After World War II, new radio and microwave technologies produced a rapid expansion in radio astronomy, and Oort is credited with establishing the radio observatories at Dwingeloo and Wester-bork. These facilities brought the Netherlands to the forefront of this exciting and productive new research area.

In 1951, Oort and his student Hendrik Van de Hulst discovered 8-inch microwave radiation emitted by neutral hydrogen in space. This radiation travels freely through dust clouds and is emitted from regions near stars, which made it possible for Oort and Van de Hulst to produce the first maps of the Galaxy, showing the sizes and positions of the spiral arms with respect to Earth.

A Cloud of Comets

As a second area of research, Oort took up the study of comets. In 1950, he proposed what has become known as the Oort cloud.

He suggested that the solar system is surrounded by a cloud of perhaps as many as 10 trillion small icy bodies, at a distance extending to about 1.5 light-years from the sun. Gravitational forces from passing stars occasionally change the orbits of some of these bodies, sending them toward the inner solar system to become comets. This hypothesis accounts for the observed trajectories of comets and has come to be widely accepted.

A Distinguished Senior Scientist

Oort's later career was marked by many honors as a renowned and well-liked researcher. From 1958 to 1961, he served as president of the International Astronomical Union. He retired in 1970 and died in Leiden on November 5, 1992.

Bibliography

By Oort

"Radio Astronomical Studies of the Galactic System," *Proceedings of the Vetlesen Symposium*, 1966.

About Oort

Streomgren, B. "An Appreciation of Jan Hendrik Oort." *Galaxies and the Universe*. New York: Columbia University Press, 1968.

van Woerden, H, W. N. Brouw, and H. Van de Hulst, eds. *Oort and the Universe: A Sketch of Oort's Research and Person—Liber Amicorum Presented to Jan Hendrik Oort on the Occasion of His Eightieth Birthday, 28 April 1980*. Boston: D. Reidel, 1980.

(Firman D. King)

Cecilia Payne-Gaposchkin

Discipline: Astronomy

Contribution: A leader in stellar astrophysics, Payne-Gaposchkin made numerous contributions to the study of stars and their structure. In her 1925 doctoral dissertation, she was the first to propose that stars are composed mainly of hydrogen and helium.

May 10, 1900	Born in Wendover, England
1919	Enters Newnhan College, the University of Cambridge
1919	Attends an astronomy lecture by Sir Arthur Eddington
1923	Enters Radcliffe College and conducts research at Harvard Observatory
1925	Receives a Ph.D. from Radcliffe with a groundbreaking dissertation on the composition of stars
1936	Nominated to the National Academy of Sciences
1938	Receives an appointment to the Harvard Corporation and becomes a faculty member at the university
1956	Becomes the first woman to be made a full professor at Harvard and is appointed head of the astronomy department
1977	Awarded the Henry Norris Russell Prize from the American Astronomical Society
Dec. 6, 1979	Dies in Cambridge, Massachusetts

Early Life

Cecilia Payne-Gaposchkin (pronounced "PAYN gah-PEHSH-kyihn") was born Cecilia Helena Payne in rural Wendover, England, in 1900. Her father died when she was four and she was reared by her mother, who ensured that her daughter received an education.

As a young girl, Cecilia became fascinated with the sciences and was determined to pursue a career as a scientist. Schools in England at the time did not educate girls in the sciences, however, so her early science instruction was mainly self-taught, using whatever few textbooks she could locate.

Payne also had to overcome the stated opposition of many of her teachers. The principal at one school, a churchwoman, told Payne that she was wasting her gifts by going into science. She overcame these difficulties, however, and entered Newnhan College at the University of Cambridge in 1919.

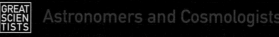
Astronomy

In 1919, Payne attended a lecture by noted astronomer Sir Arthur Eddington. She later wrote that she was able to recall the entire speech. It was as a result of this lecture that she decided to pursue a career in astronomy and enrolled in as many astronomy courses as she could.

While at Newnhan, she met Harlow Shapley, the director of the Harvard Observatory. Shapley told Payne to seek him out when she graduated, but he did not expect to hear from her again. After finishing her degree at Newnhan, however, she contacted Shapley and went to America.

Harvard Observatory

Payne did her graduate work in astronomy at Radcliffe College. She became the first person to receive a doctorate in astronomy from either Radcliffe or Harvard and the first person to re-ceive a Ph.D. for work performed at Harvard Observatory. In her dissertation, she argued that stars are made primarily of hydrogen and helium. This theory was counter to the beliefs of the day and was quickly rejected by leading astronomers. Within a few years, however, these same astronomers would acknowledge that Payne was correct. Her dissertation has been called "the most brilliant Ph.D. thesis ever written in astronomy."

Harvard University

Payne continued on at Harvard Observatory and began to teach at the university. The president of Harvard was opposed to allowing women to be faculty members, and she was paid as a technical assistant to one of the male faculty members. She finally received an appointment to the Harvard Corporation in 1938 and became a faculty member. However, her courses were not listed in

The Composition of Stars

Payne-Gaposchkin argued that the apparent variation in the composition of stars was attributable to differing temperatures, not a differing abundance of elements. She correctly deduced that stars are made of mostly hydrogen and helium, with all other elements present only in small amounts.

Breaking sunlight into its individual colors with a prism produces a rainbow of colors called a spectrum. The emission of light from an individual element creates not a rainbow but a set of colored lines that is unique to that element and acts like a fingerprint. Differing stars have different spectra.

Prior to Payne-Gaposchkin's work, it was believed that all stars had the same surface temperature and that any differences among them resulted from the presence of different elements. Payne-Gaposchkin, through her intensive study of spectra, deduced that these differences exist because some stars have dif-ferent surface temperatures. She claimed that the relative abundance of heavy elements in the sun, such as nitrogen and oxygen, are the same as on Earth but that the light elements hydrogen and helium are more than a million times more abundant. This conclusion was initially rejected as being impossible, but it was accepted as fact only a few years later.

Payne-Gaposchkin's ideas quickly led to major advances in the understanding of stars, including the understanding of the power source of stars, fusion. Today, her work is the cornerstone of much work in astronomy.

Bibliography
Astronomy: Journey to the Cosmic Frontier. John D. Fix. St. Louis: C. V. Mosby, 1995.

Astronomy Today. Eric Chaisson and Steve McMillan. Englewood Cliffs, N.J.: Prentice Hall, 1996.

the school catalog until 1945. Another obstacle to Payne's advancement was her marriage in 1943 to Sergei Gaposchkin, a fellow scientist. Women at this time were expected to sacrifice their careers for their husbands. Payne-Gaposchkin continued to pursue her career as a scientist, often working with her husband, while also pursuing a life as a wife and mother.

Finally, in 1956, she was appointed a full professor and made the head of the astronomy department at Harvard University, becoming the first female full faculty member.

In 1977, Payne-Gaposchkin received the prestigious Henry Norris Russell Prize from the American Astronomical Society. During her career, she wrote or co-wrote nearly 350 scientific papers and several books. She died on December 6, 1979, of lung cancer and donated her body to science.

Bibliography

By Payne-Gaposchkin

Stellar Atmospheres: A Contribution to the Observational Study of High Temperature in the Reversing Layers of Stars, 1925.

Variable Stars and Galactic Structure, 1954.

Introduction to Astronomy, 1954 (with Katherine Haramundanis).

Stars and Clusters, 1979.

Cecilia Payne-Gaposchkin: An Autobiography and Other Recollections, 1984.

About Payne-Gaposchkin

Greenstein, George. "The Ladies of Observatory Hill." *The American Scholar*, Summer, 1993.

McMurray, Emily J. ed. *Notable Twentieth-Century Scientists*. New York: Gale Research, 1995.

(Christopher Keating)

Ptolemy

Disciplines: Astronomy, cosmology, earth science, mathematics, and general science

Contribution: Ptolemy developed a mathematical model to explain the motion of the sun, moon, and the planets revolving around an Earth-centered universe. Although his explanation was wrong, it influenced astronomical and religious teaching for more than fifteen centuries.

c. 100	Born
c. 178	Dies

Life

History records very little about the life of Ptolemy (pronounced "TAHL-uh-mee"), also known as Claudius Ptolemaeus. No records of his birth or death exist. What little is known of him comes from legends and his few surviving scientific works.

Ptolemy's life is generally placed around the time period 100 to 178. He was probably born to Greek parents who lived as colonists in Egypt. Some scholars suggest that his name may be a clue to his place of birth. At that time, there was a town known as Ptolemais Hermii situated on the banks of the Nile. It was often the custom to name children after the place where they were born. Other historians think that Ptolemy may have been born in Greece and later moved to Egypt. No one knows for certain where he was born.

Ptolemy flourished when Rome was at the height of its power and influence over the Mediterrean world. He lived and studied in Alexandria, Egypt, which was the center of learning in the second century. His interests were in mathematics, science, and philosophy. Astronomy was particularly interesting to him.

It is said that he established an observatory on the top floor of a temple in order to give himself a better view of the heavens.

Alexandria would be Ptolemy's home during the period of his greatest writings and discoveries. His proximity to the great library there and to the many scholars who used it provided him with a creative environment. He was greatly influenced by the writings of the Greek philosophers Plato and Hipparchus.

Four Major Works

The four major works of Ptolemy that have survived the ages are commonly known as the *Almagest,* the *Geography,* the *Tetrabiblos,* and the *Optics.* The principle work for which history remembers Ptolemy is the *Almagest,* or *Mathematike syntaxis,* as it was known in Greek. Later Arabic scholars named it the *Almagest* (literally "the great"), which clearly indicates how revered the work was to astronomers up to the time of Nicolaus Copernicus and Galileo.

In the *Almagest,* Ptolemy would be best remembered for his explanation of motion in the heavens. In his vision, he pictured Earth as the center of the universe. Around Earth moved the sun, the moon, and the planets. Surrounding everything else was a sphere of stars. To explain motion, Ptolemy introduced a complicated geometric system based on circular motion around a central and stationary Earth. Many of his ideas came from the earlier works of Plato, Aristotle, and Hipparchus. He used a concept called spherical trigonometry to calculate the motion of the five known planets. The accuracy of his calculations convinced many of his fellow scientists that his view of an Earth-centered universe must be correct.

In the *Geography,* Ptolemy introduced the concept of latitude and longitude as a means of determining positions on the surface of Earth. He accepted Earth as a perfect sphere and based the system on the 360-degree geometry of a circle. On land, he reduced actual distances to degrees of a circle. Over water, he simply guessed at distances.

Latitude positions could be accurately measured by observing the sun or certain stars, but longitude could not be measured. Consequently, Ptolemy's maps were considerably off, making the world smaller than it actually was. In 1492, Christopher Columbus relied on maps based on Ptolemy's calculations. Had he realized Ptolemy's mistake, Columbus may have never attempted to sail over a much-larger Earth.

The work *Tetrabiblos* describes Ptolemy's views on astrology. In his day, astrology and astronomy were closely related. Most natural phenomena were explained by supernatural causes. Ptolemy believed that some form of physical energy radiated down from heaven and influenced human lives, which represented his attempt to understand astrological concepts.

Ptolemy's Epicycles: A Model for Planetary Motion

Despite its failure, Ptolemy's epicycle model remained the best explanation for motion in the heavens for more than 1,500 years; there was no other until Nicolaus Copernicus and Johannes Kepler.

In the *Almagest*, Ptolemy begins with the belief that Earth is a perfect sphere. Since all things on Earth fall toward it, he naturally assumed that all heavenly bodies must be influenced by the force of Earth as well. If that were true, then Earth had to be the center of the universe.

The universe that Ptolemy envisioned had the moon, Mercury, Venus, the sun, Mars, Jupiter, and Saturn all moving about a stationary Earth in circular orbits. The stars would occupy an outer sphere that enclosed the entire universe.

Ptolemy's model of the universe was by no means flawless. Most of the time, his observations of the planets did not agree with what his explanations suggested. He believed that all the planets moved in perfectly circular motion around Earth, and at uniform speeds. This was certainly not the case, as evident in the motion of Mercury, Venus, and Mars.

In order to make his model work, Ptolemy invented complicated mathematical concepts to correct for his apparent errors. The use of "epicycles," "eccentrics," and "equants" seemed to provide the solution to planetary motion. They worked well for each planet, but when combined as a unit the entire model fell apart.

The basis of the motion that Ptolemy was trying to explain was founded in Aristotle's Earth-centered universe. Aristotle's logic stated that all objects in heaven must be perfect and that their motion should be perfect as well. In order for this to be true, the planet's motion had to be uniform and follow a circular path. This is what Ptolemy hoped to see in the movement of the planets, but motion centered on Earth presented a different picture. At various times, the planets changed speed and even moved backward. This created a difficult problem for Ptolemy if he were to keep Earth at the center of the universe.

Ptolemy's solution was to create a series of wheels within wheels. A planet would move within a smaller circle called an epicycle. The center of the epicycle in turn would move in its own circular path or deferent around Earth. In a final attempt to duplicate planetary motion, Ptolemy added an equant. To do so, he had to place Earth off-center in the deferent circle. The equant was the exact point opposite Earth from the deferent's center. When viewed from this point, all planets appeared to move at a constant speed. Moving all the different wheels seemed to reproduce the motion of the planets. Right or wrong, Ptolemy had created a mathematical explanation for the movement of the planets.

As convincing as it was to scholars in the second century however, his model was wrong. Planets do not orbit Earth; they orbit the sun. Yet, even today, it is still not easy to believe that Earth is in motion because human senses simply cannot feel the direct motion of Earth. It is trust in basic scientific principles and observations of other planets and star systems that makes the movement of Earth believable.

Bibliography

Neugebauer, O. *The Exact Sciences in Antiquity.*
New York: Barnes & Noble Books, 1993.

Seeds, Michael A. *Horizons: Exploring the Universe.*
Belmont, Calif.: Wadsworth, 1995.

Hodges, Henry. *Technology in the Ancient World.*
New York: Alfred A. Knopf, 1970.

Tetrabiblos still serves as the basic argument for the validity of modern-day astrology. The last work of Ptolemy was *Optics*, the most scientific and accurate of the four. In it, he followed a basic scientific approach to problem solving and demonstrated a few of the basic principles of optics. The concepts of reflection and refraction were discussed, and he demonstrated a certain awareness of the behavior of light.

Bibliography

By Ptolemy

Mathematike syntaxis, c. 150 (commonly known as the Almagest; English trans. as Almagest, 1948).
Geographike hyphegesis (commonly known as the Geography; The Geography of Ptolemy. 1732).
Apoteles matika (commonly known as the Tetrabiblos; Ptolemy's Quadripartite: Or, Four Books Concerning the Influences of the Stars, 1701).
Opticae thesaurus, 1572 (incomplete, lost in Greek and Arabic; commonly known as the Optics; Ptolemy's Theory of Visual Perception, 1996).

About Ptolemy

Gingerich. Owen *The Eye of Heaven: Ptolemy, Copernicus, Kepler*. New York: American Institute of Physics, 1993.
Magill, Frank N. ed. "Ptolemy." *Great Lives from History: Ancient and Medieval Series* Pasadena, Calif.: Salem Press, 1988.

(Paul P. Sipiera)

Vera C. Rubin

Disciplines: Astronomy and physics
Contribution: Rubin's study of the movement and rotation of galaxies provided evidence for the existence of the Local Supercluster, the Great Attractor, and dark matter.

Jul. 23, 1928	Born in Philadelphia, PA
1950	Presents paper to the American Astronomical Society
1951	Earns a master's degree from Cornell University
1954	Awarded a Ph.D. from Georgetown University
1962	Promoted to assistant professor
1963-1964	Conducts research with Margaret and Geoffrey Burbidge at the University of California, San Diego
1965	Begins work at the Department of Terrestrial Magnetism
1972-1982	Serves as associate editor of the *Astronomical Journal* and then of the *Astrophysical Journal Letters*
1979-1987	Serves on the editorial board of *Science* magazine
1981	Elected to the National Academy of Sciences
1990-1992	Serves on the visiting committee of the Space Telescope Scientific Institute
1993	Awarded the National Medal of Science
1996	First Woman to receive the Royal Astronomical Society's Gold Medal since 1828
2003	Receives the Catherine W. Bruce Medal from the Astronomical Society of the Pacific

Early Life

Vera C. Rubin was born Vera Cooper in Philadelphia, Pennsylvania, on July 23, 1928. Her parents were Philip Cooper, an electrical engineer, and Rose Applebaum Cooper. In 1938, the family moved to Washington, D.C.

Vera developed an interest in astronomy at an early age. She attended Vassar College in Poughkeepsie, New York, earning her bachelor's degree in 1948. She was encouraged by the example of Maria Mitchell, the first American woman to become a noted astronomer, who had been a professor at Vassar in the late nineteenth century. In 1948 Cooper married Robert Rubin, a graduate student in physical chemistry at Cornell University in Ithaca, New York. She attended Cornell with her husband, earning her master's degree in 1951.

Vera Rubin presented her first paper, "Rotation of the Universe," to the American Astronomical Society in December, 1950. In it, she offered findings that supported the idea that galaxies in different regions of the universe were moving away from Earth at different speeds that could not be explained fully by the general expansion of the universe. Her paper was soundly rejected by most astronomers, but she was vindicated in 1956 when French astronomer Gérard de Vaucouleurs used her work to support his concept of the Local Supercluster, a vast conglomerate of many clusters of galaxies, including the Milky Way.

The Georgetown Years

Rubin obtained her Ph.D. from Georgetown University in Washington, D.C., in 1954. Her doctoral thesis on the uneven distribution of galaxies in the universe anticipated the work of other astronomers by about fifteen years. After teaching mathematics and physics for a year at Montgomery Junior College in Takoma Park, Maryland, she returned to Georgetown as a research associate in 1955. She was promoted to lecturer in 1959 and assistant professor in 1962.

While still employed by Georgetown, Rubin spent a year at the University of California, San Diego from 1963 to 1964, where she worked with astronomers Margaret and Geoffrey Burbidge on determining the rotation of the Andromeda galaxy. She also spent time making observations at Kitt Peak National Observatory, near Tucson, Arizona, and other large observatories. She was the first woman officially allowed to make observations at Mount Palomar Observatory near San Diego.

The Great Attractor and Dark Matter

In 1965, Rubin left Georgetown to work at the Department of Terrestrial Magnetism at the Carnegie Institute in Washington, D.C. The department was originally founded in the early twentieth century to promote the study of Earth's magnetic field, but its goals expanded to include research on a variety of astronomical topics. Rubin began a collaboration with physicist W. Kent Ford that led to her most important discoveries. At first, Rubin worked on quasars, newly discovered objects that are extremely distant but very bright. She soon tired of the intense competition among astronomers over this new topic, however, and returned her attention to the movement of galaxies. Rubin found evidence that local galaxies are moving in a way that cannot be explained by simple expansion. Her observation, known as the Rubin-Ford effect, led later astronomers to theorize the existence of a distant massive concentration of galaxies known as the Great Attractor that pulls local galaxies in its direction with gravitational force.

Disappointed by the initial skeptical reaction to the Rubin-Ford effect, Rubin turned to the rotation of galaxies. She repeated the studies that she had

Dark Matter

Rubin's measurements of the rotation of galaxies provided evidence that they contain large amounts of unseen mass known as dark matter.

Galaxies are made up of billions of stars held together by gravity. These stars rotate around the center of the galaxy, just as the planets in the solar system rotate around the sun. Astronomers can measure the speed at which these stars rotate by making use of the Doppler effect.

The Doppler effect, named for the nineteenth century Austrian physicist Christian Doppler, causes light from objects that are approaching the observer to appear more blue and light from objects receding from the observer to appear more red. When a galaxy rotates, in most cases part of it will be moving in such a way that it is approaching Earth, while another part of it will be receding from Earth. By measuring how far the light from these parts of the galaxy are shifted toward the blue and red ends of the light spectrum, astronomers can tell how fast the galaxy is rotating.

Before astronomers made careful measurements of the rotation speeds of galaxies, they assumed that they would follow a simple relationship known as Kepler's third law, first announced by German astronomer Johannes Kepler in 1618. This law states that the further an object is from the center of mass around which it rotates, the more slowly it will move. For example, the dwarf planet Pluto, which is distant from the sun, moves much more slowly than Mercury, which is near the sun. In a galaxy, Kepler's third law would mean that stars far from the bright center of the galaxy should move more slowly than those near to it.

When Rubin made her observations, she discovered that the expected results did not occur. Instead, the stars at the edge of the galaxy moved as quickly or even slightly more quickly than those nearer the center. This result implies that the majority of mass is not located at the bright center, but that there must be some unseen mass surrounding the galaxy. Measurements revealed that this unseen mass, called dark matter, makes up as much as 95 percent of the mass of a galaxy.

Rubin's work implied that astronomers had ignored most of the matter in the universe. The exact nature of dark matter became one of the most active areas of research. Some possibilities suggested to explain this unseen mass include small, dim stars; large, planetlike bodies; black holes; neutrinos, assuming that these subatomic particles are shown to possess mass; and hypothetical gravity particles or magnetic particles.

Bibliography

The Fifth Essence: The Search for Dark Matter in the Universe. Lawrence Maxwell Krauss. New York: Basic Books, 1989.

Modern Cosmology and the Dark Matter Problem. D. W. Sciama. Cambridge, England: Cambridge University Press, 1993.

Through a Universe Darkly: A Cosmic Tale of Ancient Ethers, Dark Matter, and the Fate of the Universe. Marcia Bartusiak. New York: HarperCollins, 1993.

made of the Andromeda galaxy with the Burbidges, this time using more sensitive equipment. She then studied the rotation of several other galaxies. Her results indicated that these galaxies contain large amounts of unseen material. Perhaps as much as 95 percent of a galaxy might be made up of this invisible mass, known to astronomers as dark matter.

Rubin currently is a Senior Fellow of the Department of Terrestrial Magnetism where she continues to observe galaxies and their relationship to dark matter.

Editing and Awards

Rubin was also active in editing scientific journals. She served as associate editor of the *Astronomical Journal* from 1972 to 1977, then as associate editor of the *Astrophysical Journal Letters* from 1977 to 1982. From 1979 to 1987, she served on the editorial board of the prestigious journal *Science.*

Among her many awards were several hononary degrees from major universities. She was also awarded the National Medal of Science in 1993.

Bibliography

By Rubin

"Dark Matter in Spiral Galaxies," *Scientific American*, 1983.

"Women's Work," *Science*, 1986.

Large-Scale Motions in the Universe: A Vatican Study Week, 1988 (as editor, with George V. Coyne).

About Rubin

Fort, Deborah C., ed. *A Hand Up: Women Mentoring Women in Science*. Washington, D.C.: Association for Women in Science, 1993.

Overbye, Dennis. *Lonely Hearts of the Cosmos: The Scientific Quest for the Secret of the Universe*. New York: HarperCollins, 1991.

(Rose Secrest)

Henry Norris Russell

Disciplines: Astronomy and physics

Contribution: Russell studied the composition, structure, and dynamics of stars, discovering a fundamental relationship among their size, temperature, and intrinsic brightness that clarifies the process of stellar evolution.

Oct. 25, 1877	Born in Oyster Bay, New York
1897	Graduates insigne cum laude from Princeton University
1899	Earns a Ph.D. in astronomy from Princeton
1902-1905	Studies at the University of Cambridge
1905	Appointed an instructor of astronomy at Princeton
1911	Becomes professor of astronomy
1911	Publishes *Determination of Stellar Parallax*
1912	Becomes the director of Princeton's observatory
1914	Publishes "Relations Between the Spectra and Other Characteristics of the Stars" *Nature*
1918-1919	Works as an engineer for the Army Aviation Service
1927	Appointed C. A. Young Research Professor at Princeton
1933	Elected president of the American Association for the Advancement of Science
1934-1937	Serves as president of the American Astronomical Association
Feb. 18, 1957	Dies in Princeton, New Jersey

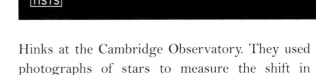

Early Life

Born in Oyster Bay, New York, in 1877, Henry Norris Russell grew up in a well-educated, cultured family of Scottish descent. Alexander G. Russell, his father, was a Presbyterian minister; Eliza Norris, his mother, was a gifted amateur mathematician, as was her mother. They taught Henry at home until he was twelve years old, developing his considerable mathematical talent.

In 1889, the family moved to Princeton, New Jersey. Russell later studied at Princeton University, graduating with the highest possible honor, insigne cum laude, in 1897. In 1899, he earned a doctorate from Princeton as well, having already published articles on what was to become a major focus of his scientific career: binary stars.

Stellar Parallax

Russell went to the University of Cambridge in England for postgraduate studies in 1901. There, he became the research assistant of Arthur R. Hinks at the Cambridge Observatory. They used photographs of stars to measure the shift in position of nearby stars as seen from different vantage points in Earth's orbit, a technique called stellar parallax.

In 1908, Russell married Lucy May Cole, with whom he had three daughters and a son. In 1908, he also became an assistant professor of astronomy at Princeton, where he had served as an instructor since 1905. In 1911, he became a full professor, and he was named director of the university's observatory the next year.

Measuring Stars

Russell devoted much of his career to studying binary star systems in which the stars eclipse each other. He analyzed the varying light intensity from these eclipsing binaries and the shapes of their orbits. His findings supplied methods for determining the density of stars and for calculating their mass.

Russell is best known, however, for discovering the relation between a star's absolute magnitude and its spectral type, which he announced in a 1913 lecture. The relation contradicted the prevailing theory describing the evolution of stars and inspired him to publish his own theory. He proposed that stars change in appearance, shrinking when they heat up or expanding when they cool down. Although briefly influential, the theory was later discarded.

Spectra and Atomic Structure

Russell also studied the spectra of stars extensively to infer their chemical composition. Turning his attention to the sun, he astonished his colleagues by claiming, correctly, that hydrogen is the most common solar element. He also used detailed spectral analyses of elements to infer how electrons absorb and emit light.

Throughout his long career, Russell wrote popular articles on astronomy for *Scientific*

American, as well as one for the *Encyclopaedia Britannica.* By the time that he retired in 1947, Russell was popularly regarded as the dean of American astronomy. He served as president of the American Association for the Advancement of Science and was a member of the National Academy of Sciences. Russell died in 1957.

Bibliography

By Russell

Determination of Stellar Parallax, 1911.
"On the Determination of the Orbital Elements of Eclipsing Variable Stars," *Astrophysical Journal,* 1912.
"Relations Between the Spectra and Other Characteristics of the Stars," *Nature,* 1914.
The Solar System and Its Origin, 1935.
The Masses of the Stars, with a General Catalog of Dynamical Parallaxes, 1940 (with C. E. Moore)

About Russell

Herrmann, Dieter B. *The History of Astronomy from Herschel to Hertzsprung.* Cambridge, England: Cambridge University Press, 1984.
North, John. *The Norton History of Astronomy and Cosmology.* New York: W. W. Norton, 1995.

(Roger Smith)

The Hertzsprung-Russell Diagram

This diagram plots the relation between a star's temperature and its intrinsic brightness, providing information about its size and stage in stellar evolution.

The Hertzsprung-Russell diagram, derived independently by Russell and Danish astronomer Ejnar Hertzsprung, classifies stars by size, brightness, and temperature. It is a graph whose vertical axis gives the absolute magnitudes of stars and the horizontal axis gives their surface temperatures.

Absolute magnitude measures how bright stars would look if they were all at the same distance from Earth. The graph places the dimmest stars at the bottom and the brightest stars at the top. Since large stars have more surface area from which to broadcast light, they are at the top of the graph, and smaller stars are found at the bottom. Astronomers can deduce surface temperature from a star's spectrum—its light separated into its colors, like a rainbow. The horizontal axis orders the temperatures from the hottest at the right to the coolest at the left.

About 90 percent of stars fall on a gentle, elongated S-curve from the top left of the graph to the bottom right. This curve is known as the main sequence of stars. Three groups of stars are found away from the

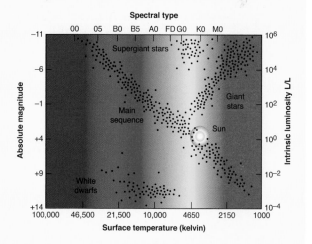

main sequence: cool supergiant and giant stars are above it, and hot dwarfs are beneath it.

Bibliography

Cooke, Donald A. *The Life and Death of Stars.* New York: Crown, 1985.
Kippenhahn, Rudolf. *One Hundred Billion Suns: The Birth, Life, and Death of Stars.* New York: Basic Books, 1983.
Kaler, James B. *Stars.* New York: *Scientific American* Books, 1992.

Carl Sagan

Disciplines: Astronomy, biology, cosmology, and physics

Contribution: Sagan's greatest contribution to science came from his ability to communicate astronomical concepts to the general public. He participated in many space missions as a consultant.

Nov. 9, 1934	Born in Brooklyn, New York
1959	Becomes involved with the U.S. space program
1960	Awarded a doctorate in astronomy and astrophysics from the University of Chicago
1960-1962	Named Miller Resident Fellow in Astronomy at the University of California, Berkeley
1962-1968	Assistant professor of astronomy at Harvard University
1968	Named an associate professor of astronomy at Cornell University
1969	Wins NASA's Apollo Achievement Award
1972	Given NASA's Exceptional Scientific Achievement Award
1977	Becomes David Duncan Professor of Astronomy and Space Sciences at Cornell
1978	Wins a Pulitzer Prize for *The Dragons of Eden*
1980	Publishes the book *Cosmos*, based on his popular television series
1991	Receives the Mazursky Award from the American Astronomical Association
Dec. 20, 1996	Dies in Seattle, Washington

Early Life

Carl Edward Sagan was born in Brooklyn, New York, on November 9, 1934, to Samuel and Rachel Sagan. At the age of five, Carl boldly announced that he hoped to be an astronomer some day. This wish developed from his early fascination with the stars and later from reading science fiction. Among his favorite books was a series of novels that described various heroic adventures that took place on Mars written by Edgar Rice Burroughs, the creator of Tarzan. The images of Mars that Burroughs created would stay with Sagan forever.

Sagan's childhood took place during World War II. It was a time of rapid technological change. The war demanded new technology, and scientists produced faster airplanes and more powerful rockets.

After the war, many of those who had created the weapons of war turned their attention to the heavens. The first rockets were reaching the edge of space, and a huge astronomical telescope had been built in California. The universe was opening itself up to human exploration, and Sagan was ready to join in.

A Life of Science

In the early 1950s, many notable scientists either taught at or were associated with the University of Chicago. Among the more famous scientists there were Hermann Joseph Muller, Joshua Lederberg, and Harold C. Urey, all Nobel Prize winners. It proved to be an irresistible environment for Sagan, and he went on to complete all of his academic degrees at the University of Chicago.

He achieved an A.B. degree in 1954, a B.S. in 1955, an M.S. in physics in 1956, and a doctorate in astronomy and astrophysics in 1960. His doctoral dissertation was entitled "Physical Studies of the Planets." His adviser was the astronomer Gerard Peter Kuiper. No doubt it was Kuiper who galvanized Sagan's interest in the planets, and it was Lederberg who encouraged him to become involved in the United States' growing space program.

A Rising Star

Sagan's professional career began after his 1960 graduation from the University of Chicago. He accepted a position as a resident fellow in astronomy at the University of California, Berkeley (UCB), that would last from 1960 to 1962. From UCB, it was on to Harvard University, where he accepted an assistant professorship. He would remain at Harvard from 1962 to 1968.

After Harvard, it was on to Ithaca, New York, to become an associate professor of astronomy at Cornell University. Later, he was promoted to professor and made associate director of the Center for Radiophysics and Space Research. In 1977, he was named the David Duncan Professor of Astronomy and Space Science.

An Award-Winning Career

It was the extremely successful Mariner 9 mission to Mars that propelled Sagan into prominence. Up to this time, he had been involved in the planning stages of several planetary probes and had worked with the results of those missions for the National Aeronautics and Space Administration (NASA). He had established himself as a respected scientist. The photographs of volcanoes and huge canyons on Mars caught the public's attention.

People wanted to know more about the planets, and science needed a spokesperson. Sagan was chosen to appear in several educational films that described the Mars discoveries. His mannerism and delivery worked well and led to many appearances on television talk shows. Sagan quickly became the public's expert on astronomy and space issues. In 1973, Sagan's book *The Cosmic Connection* was published. In this book, he conveyed his philosophy about the universe and humanity's place in it. It was an instant success, and several other books would follow. His book *The Dragons of Eden* (1977) won a Pulitzer Prize in 1978. Perhaps Sagan's most influential work was the television series *Cosmos*, which ran on public television in 1979. Millions of people heard about everything from the origin of life to the detection of black holes in space. In each episode, Sagan's personality captivated the audience. It is estimated that, by the mid-1990s, more than 600 million people had viewed the *Cosmos* series.

Throughout his career, Sagan received numerous awards for his work in both science and literature. He promoted science for the average person and made it enjoyable. Although many of his colleagues argued that he presented scientific speculation as fact, he certainly inspired people's imaginations. Without a scientist such as Sagan, millions of people would never have experienced the wonders of astronomy.

Sagan died in 1996 at the age of sixty-two.

Exploration of the Planet Mars

Prior to 1965, the planet Mars was believed to be like Earth, and then the Mariner 4 spacecraft showed it to be similar to the moon in appearance. All that changed when the Mariner 9 probe revealed huge canyons, giant volcanoes, and a system of river channels. Scientists such as Sagan quickly realized that Mars was a unique world unto itself.

For centuries, Earth-based astronomers studied the planet Mars and observed dramatic color variations that were believed to represent changing seasons. The reddish surface would apparently turn green as the polar ice caps melted during the Martian summer. It was believed that melted water from the ice caps would nourish plant life. Some astronomers such as Percival Lowell imagined a system of canals conveying water from the polar regions to the dry equatorial zones. All of this fired the imagination of Earth-bound astronomers and science-fiction writers alike.

The first three spacecraft to Mars—Mariners 4, 6, and 7—all showed a surface terrain very similar to the moon. The planet appeared to be covered by craters of all sizes, and there was no evidence of the rivers, forests, or large bodies of water for which scientists had hoped. For all practical purposes, Mars could have been just another moon. The unfortunate thing about these three Mariner missions was that they were designed to take a series of pictures as they flew by the planet. As luck would have it, they each flew over some of the least interesting terrain on Mars. It would be left up to Mariner 9 to show the real Mars.

Mariner 9 reached Mars in 1971 and photographed the surface from orbit. During its operational lifetime, it discovered a volcanic region populated by four huge volcanoes. The largest, Olympus Mons, is thought to be the largest volcano in the solar system. It is a basaltic volcano similar to the Hawaiian Island volcanoes on Earth, but twice their size. Nearby, an enormous canyon system named Valles Marineris stretched across the equatorial region. In length, Valles Marineris is ap-proximately ten times the size of the Grand Canyon, in Arizona.

Perhaps the most significant discovery made by the Mariner 9 was the presence of long river channels resembling those of the largest river systems on Earth. The only difference was that they were totally dry. Apparently, water has not flowed across the surface of Mars for millions of years.

Following the successful Mariner 9 mission, Project Viking landed two robot spacecraft on Mars in 1976. Their primary mission was to answer one of the fundamental questions about Mars: Is life present? Throughout his life, Sagan had asked this question, and he hoped that Viking would provide the answer. Unfortunately, the Viking experiments provided no conclusive evidence for life, but they did not rule it out either.

Mars was Sagan's best hope for finding evidence of extraterrestrial life during his lifetime. His search for life did not end with Mars; he looked to the moons of Jupiter and Saturn for possible evidence. As for intelligent life, Sagan joined with fellow Cornell scientist Frank Drake to develop the Search for Extra Terrestrial Intelligence (SETI) Project, a radio search. At the time of Sagan's death in 1996, scientists thought that they had found evidence of a fossil life form in a meteorite believed to have come from Mars. It may not have been conclusive proof, but it certainly fired the imagination of Carl Sagan.

Bibliography

Hamblin, W. Kenneth and Eric H. Christiansen. *Exploring the Planets*. New York: Macmillan, 1990.

Cattermole, Peter. *Mars: The Story of the Red Planet*. London: Chapman & Hall, 1992.

Henbest, Nigel. *The Planets: A Guided Tour of Our Solar System Through the Eyes of America's Space Probes*. London: Viking Press, 1992.

In July, 1997, after the Mars Pathfinder mission successfully reached the surface of that planet, the lander for the Sojourner rover was officially christened the Sagan Memorial Station in his honor.

Bibliography

By Sagan

Intelligent Life in the Universe, 1966 (with I. S. Shklovskii).

The Dragons of Eden, 1977.

Cosmos, 1980.

A Path Where No Man Thought: Nuclear Winter and the End of the Arms Race, 1990 (with Richard Turco).

Pale Blue Dot: A Vision of the Human Future in Space, 1994.

About Sagan

"Carl Edward Sagan: Astronomer and Popularizer of Science." A. R. Hogan. *Ad Astra* 3 (1991).

"In the Valley of the Shadow." Carl Sagan. *Parade Magazine*. March 10, 1996.

"A Man Whose Time Has Come." Rian Ridpath. *New Scientist* 63 (July 4, 1974).

"Shadows of Forgotten Ancestors." Roger Lewin. *New Scientist* 137 (January 16, 1993).

*The Visible Scientist*s. Rae Goodell. Boston: Little, Brown, 1975.

(Paul P. Sipiera)

Allan Rex Sandage

Disciplines: Astronomy and cosmology

Contribution: Sandage continued Edwin Hubble's work mapping the distances to galaxies, in order to determine the rate of expansion of the universe and the decrease in that rate over time. He did important work in theoretical cosmology, putting it into a form that could be verified by observations.

June 18, 1926	Born in Iowa City, Iowa
1944	Enters Miami University, Ohio, in physics
1945	Drafted into the U.S. Navy
1948	Receives an A.B. degree in physics from the University of Illinois
1952	Joins the staff of Mount Wilson Observatory
1953	Receives a Ph.D. in astronomy from the California Institute of Technology (Caltech)
1958	Given the Helen Warner Prize from the American Astronomical Society
1960	Becomes the first person to identify a quasar
1961	Publishes a paper suggesting that the universe began from a "big bang"
1963	Awarded the Eddington Medal of the Royal Astronomical Society
1973	Wins the Russell Prize of the American Astronomical Society
1991	Awarded the Crafoord Prize, astronomy's equivalent to the Nobel Prize
2000	Receives the Gruber Prize in Cosmology
Nov. 13, 2010	Dies in San Gabriel, California

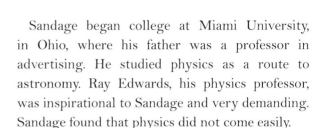

Early Life

Allan Rex Sandage was born in Iowa City, Iowa, on June 18, 1926. His father was the son of a farmer and was the first in his family to go to high school; from there, he went on to college and then to the University of Iowa for a Ph.D. Sandage's mother was born in the Philippines, where her father was the commissioner of education. Upon their return to the United States, Sandage's grandfather became president of Graceland College, the church school of the Reorganized Church of Latter-day Saints.

Neither of Sandage's parents were particularly interested in science. Sandage first became interested in the subject when he was in the fourth grade, living in Philadelphia. His friend had a telescope, and Sandage soon was spending his weekends at the Franklin Institute and the planetarium. James Stokely, then head of the Fels Planetarium, became his hero. From that time, Sandage felt compelled to be an astronomer, reading astronomy texts and teaching himself.

Sandage, center of photo, getting the Hale telescope ready for a viewing.

Sandage began college at Miami University, in Ohio, where his father was a professor in advertising. He studied physics as a route to astronomy. Ray Edwards, his physics professor, was inspirational to Sandage and very demanding. Sandage found that physics did not come easily.

In 1944, he was drafted by the U.S. Navy and served for two years repairing electronic equipment. Afterward, Sandage attended the University of Illinois, where he received his bachelor's degree in physics in 1948. For his junior and senior theses, he worked for Robert Baker, the only astronomer at Illinois at that time. Baker taught him observational techniques that would later prove invaluable to Sandage.

Sandage entered the California Institute of Technology (Caltech), in Pasadena, California. That year, an astronomy program was begun, and he became one of the first class of astronomy graduate students, receiving his Ph.D. in 1953. In the summer of 1950, he worked for Edwin Powell Hubble observing a bright, variable star. When Hubble suffered his first heart attack, in 1952, Sandage took a position at the Mount Wilson Observatory, overlooking Pasadena, as a research assistant to Hubble.

Mount Wilson

Although his dissertation had been in the area of stellar evolution, Sandage felt compelled to carry on the work of Hubble. He undertook the measurement of the speeds and distances to galaxies. This information is necessary to determine the rate of expansion of the universe and the rate of deceleration of that expansion. Although an observational astronomer by training and inclination, Sandage taught himself cosmology (the study of the structure and origin of the universe) in order to carry on this work.

In 1960, Sandage, along with radioastronomer Thomas Matthews, optically identified a distant,

The Big Bang

Sandage's work supported the theory that the universe began with a "big bang," in which all the matter now existing exploded outward from a single point to create galaxies.

Cosmology is the study of the structure and evolution of the universe. The foundation of this field is based on two assumptions: the universe is homogeneous, having the same composition everywhere, and the universe is isotropic, appearing the same in any direction. These two assumptions form the cosmological principle.

It was assumed until the twentieth century that the universe was also infinite in extent and unchanging in time. If this is true, and assuming the cosmological principle holds, then the universe should be uniformly populated with galaxies filled with stars. No matter where one looks, one should see a star. The night sky should be as bright as the surface of the sun. That it is not, a situation known as Olbers' paradox, implies that either the universe is finite or it changes over time.

In 1912, Vesto Melvin Slipher discovered that almost every spiral galaxy has a redshifted spectrum. This shift of the spectra toward lower frequencies indicates that the galaxies are moving away from Earth, just as the sound of a siren shifts to a lower pitch as the source moves past the observer. In the 1920s, Edwin Powell Hubble began plotting the recessional velocities of the galaxies versus their distances from Earth and noticed a relationship. Called Hubble's law, it states that velocity is directly proportional to distance, where the constant of proportionality is called Hubble's constant:

velocity = Hubble's constant x distance

Considerable work has been done to determine Hubble's constant accurately, since it is a fundamental quantity. Using the simple definition of velocity, the time taken for the galaxies to reach their present distances from Earth is as follows:

time = distance/velocity = 1/Hubble's constant

Using the accepted value for Hubble's constant, this time is about 13 billion years. The implication of Hubble's law is important: The universe is expanding. The fact that the time of expansion is the same for all galaxies implies that at some time, all the galaxies were at the same place. It is believed that about 13 billion years ago, everything—matter and radiation—was confined to a single point that exploded, flying apart at high speeds in all directions. This gigantic explosion is called the "big bang."

The big bang theory helps resolve Olbers' paradox. Whether the universe is infinite or finite does not matter since it is finite in age. One can only see a finite part of the night sky, since the light from any object more than 13 billion light-years away has not reached Earth yet. The idea that everything seems to expand from a single point seems to violate homogeneity. The only explanation is that the big bang is an expansion of the universe itself, much like a balloon inflating.

To understand the idea of the entire universe shrinking to a point requires general relativity, the idea that the presence of matter causes a curvature of space. This curvature of space implies that there are three possible futures for the universe: It can continue to expand forever at a constant rate, it can expand for a while and then start to deflate, or it can expand forever but at a decreasing rate. The correct alternative depends on the density of the universe, which determines the gravitational attraction between objects. Unfortunately, the determination of the universe's density is not an easy task.

Will the universe end as a small, dense point as it began, or will it expand forever? The task of present-day astronomers is to determine the answer to this question.

Bibliography

Chaisson, Eric and Steve McMillan. *Astronomy Today*. Englewood Cliffs, N.J.: Prentice Hall, 1993.

Barrow, John D. and Joseph Silk. *The Left Hand of Creation: The Origin and Evolution of the Expanding Universe*. New York: Basic Books, 1983.

Jastrow, Robert. *Red Giants and White Dwarfs*. New York: W. W. Norton, 1990.

starlike object as the source of the radio waves being emitted from that part of the sky—the first identification of an individual object that was a radio source. This very unusual object, which was not identifiable as a star or a galaxy, became known as a quasi-stellar object, or quasar.

In 1961, Sandage presented a paper that summarized his and Hubble's work into a theoretical cosmology that could be verified by observations. He described the universe as made of dynamic galaxies that are moving away from Earth at velocities proportional to their distances. This motion, he claimed, was most likely caused by some primordial "big bang."

Honors

Sandage's contributions have been widely recognized. He received numerous awards from astronomical societies around the world. His greatest award came from the Royal Swedish Academy when it bestowed on him the Crafoord Prize. Astronomy is not a science honored with a Nobel Prize; the Crafoord Prize is considered to be astronomy's equivalent.

Although Sandage spent his entire career at Mount Wilson and Palomar Observatories, visiting lectureships and fellowships took him around the world. A dedicated Christian, Sandage maintained that "life is not a dreary accident." His childlike awe of the universe was replaced by "the awe of the enormous complication and order of the world of physics."

Sandage died in 2010 in California.

Bibliography

By Sandage

"The Ability of the 200-inch Telescope to Discriminate Between Selected World Models," *Astrophysical Journal*, 1961.

"The Light Travel Times and the Evolutionary Correction to Magnitudes of Distant Galaxies," *Astrophysical Journal*, 1961.

"The Change of Redshift and Apparent Luminosity of Galaxies Due to the Deceleration of Selected Expanding Universes," *Astrophysical Journal*, 1962.

"Evidence from the Motions of Old Stars that the Galaxy Collapsed," Astrophysical Journal, 1962 (with O. J. Eggen and D. Lynden-Bell).

Atlas of Galaxies: Useful for Measuring the Cosmological Distance Scale, 1988 (with John Bedke).

About Sandage

"2000 Cosmology Prize," Gruber Foundation, http://gruber.yale.edu/cosmology/2000/allan-r-sandage.

Overbye, Dennis. *Lonely Hearts of the Cosmos: The Story of the Scientific Quest for the Secret of the Universe.* New York: HarperCollins, 1991.

Rowan-Robinson, Micheal, "Allan Rex Sandage," *Physics Today*, June 2011.

Lightman, Alan and Roberta Brawer. *Origins: The Lives and Worlds of Modern Cosmologists.* Cambridge, Mass.: Harvard University Press, 1990.

(Linda L. McDonald)

Maarten Schmidt

Disciplines: Astronomy and cosmology

Contribution: Schmidt conducted research on the structure, dynamics, and evolution of the galaxy. He is best known for his discovery of quasars, which are highly energetic quasi-stellar objects at great distances from the Milky Way.

Dec. 28, 1929	Born in Groningen, the Netherlands
1949	Receives a B.A. degree from the University of Groningen
1956	Receives a Ph.D. in astronomy from the University of Leiden
1956	Begins working at the Leiden Observatory
1956	Becomes a Carnegie Fellow in Pasadena, California, at Mount Wilson Observatory
1959	Joins the astronomy department of the California Institute of Technology (Caltech)
1960	Takes up the work of Rudolph Minkowski upon his retirement from Mount Wilson Observatory
1964	Wins the Warner Prize of the American Astronomical Society
1968	Awarded the Rumford Award of the American Academy of Arts and Sciences
1972-1975	Head of Astronomy at California Institute of Technology
1978-1980	Director of Hale Observatories
1992	Receives the Bruce Medal from the Astronomical Society of the Pacific
2008	Awarded the Kavli Prize in Astrophysics

Early Life

Maarten Schmidt was born on December 28, 1929, in Groningen, the Netherlands. It was Schmidt's uncle, an amateur astronomer, who introduced him to the joys of observing the skies. One summer at his grandfather's house in the country, Schmidt found a large lens, which he then combined with an eyepiece, using a toilet-paper roll as a spacer, to make a telescope. His uncle told him to try to resolve a double star to test his telescope. Schmidt had to get a book on astronomy to look up the location of the star and became interested in what the book had to say.

Although concerned about his prospects in this field, Schmidt's parents were always supportive and encouraged his interest in astronomy. Schmidt became an avid stargazer; the blackout conditions of World War II were perfect for making observations. As a result of this early experience, Schmidt later became known to his colleagues as a "good eye,"—a talent that would later pay off.

Research on the Galaxy

When Schmidt entered the University of Groningen in 1946, he knew that he wanted to study astronomy. His interest at first lay in the study of the Milky Way. His initial area of study was an observation of one of the spiral arms. For his thesis, he prepared a mass model of the Galaxy. In 1956, he accepted a Carnegie Fellowship at Mount Wilson Observatory in Pasadena, California. Schmidt published a mass model of the galaxy M31, which was an extension of the work that he had done on the Milky Way. He also became interested in the consequences of the change of gas density in the Galaxy as a consequence of star formation.

Quasars

In 1959 Schmidt returned to Mount Wilson in a permanent position. In 1960, he investigated the helium abundance in the center of M31. He found that the abundance of helium did not follow the distribution of a metal as expected. This was later explained by the idea that the helium had been produced primordially in the big bang.

Rudolph Minkowski and Walter Baade had been using the 200-inch telescope at Mount Wilson Observatory for the past decade in an attempt to identify radio sources optically. When Minkowski retired in 1960, Schmidt took up this work, since there seemed to be no one else to do it. Two interesting objects, 3C48 and 3C273, were starlike objects that could not be identified as either a galaxy or a star. The most baffling part of the problem was their spectra; they were totally different from those of any star.

In 1963, Schmidt noticed in the spectrum of 3C273 the distinctive spacing of four hydrogen lines that had been highly redshifted. This large

Quasars

In 1963, Schmidt observed spectral (light) readings from two stellar objects unlike any seen before. These objects were later identified as quasars.

In the 1950s, radioastronomers, who observe emissions in the radio region of the electromagnetic spectrum, began locating new objects. They needed visual analysis of the objects' light in order to tell if they were stars or galaxies. Increasingly powerful telescopes were able to look farther out than ever before. At the edges of the observable universe, they found very different objects. They are rather faint and starlike, are extragalactic, emit radiation (which is usually polarized) at all frequencies, show a large redshift, and are usually largely variable over short time periods. These objects became known as quasi-stellar objects, or quasars.

These characteristics paint a strange picture. The variation in their brightness over short periods indicates that quasars are quite small, no more than twice the diameter of the solar system. Their great distances and small size mean that in order to be seen at all, they must be at least a hundred times brighter than anything else previously observed. The extreme redshift of the quasars indicates that they are moving away from Earth at very high speeds and are very far away.

No completely satisfactory model for a quasar yet exists. They exhibit all of the properties of active galaxies, which has led to a theory that quasars lie at the center of galaxies. Their energy source, however, is still unknown. The most commonly accepted theory is that quasars have a black hole at their cores. As the black hole exhausts its fuel, it begins to feed on passing galaxies, a concept that has been observed.

Bibliography

Chaisson, Eric and Steve McMillan. *Astronomy Today*. Englewood Cliffs, N.J.: Prentice Hall, 1993.

Lerner, Rita G. and George L. Trigg, eds. *Encyclopedia of Physics*. New York: VCH, 1990.

shift in the spectral lines toward the red end of the spectrum indicated that 3C273 was receding from the Galaxy at a high rate of speed and was a huge distance away. Given its distance and small size, this meant that 3C273 had to be about a hundred times brighter than any other luminous radio source identified thus far. A similar analysis was possible for 3C48. Both objects seemed to be too far, too small, and too powerful for anything previously observed. They were named quasi-stellar radio sources, or quasars.

Schmidt became the executive officer for the astronomy department at Caltech in 1972, and chaired the Caltech Division of Physics, Mathematics, and Astronomy from 1976-1979. Though he has now retired, Schmidt has continued his work, researching the phenomena of redshift.

Bibliography

By Schmidt

"A Model of the Distribution of Mass in the Galactic System," *Bulletin of the Astronomical Institutes of the Netherlands*, 1956.

"The Distribution of Mass in M31," *Bulletin of the Astronomical Institutes of the Netherlands*, 1957.

"The Rate of Star Formation," *Astrophysical Journal*, 1959.

"Space Distribution and Luminosity Functions of Quasi Stellar Radio Sources," *Astrophysical Journal*, 1968.

About Schmidt

"Faculty File," *Engineering & Science*, Fall 2008. http://calteches.library.caltech.edu/711/2/Faculty.pdf

Lightman, Alan and Roberta Brawer. *Origins: The Lives and Worlds of Modern Cosmologists.* Cambridge, Mass.: Harvard University Press, 1990.

(*Linda L. McDonald*)

Harlow Shapley

Discipline: Astronomy

Contribution: Shapley developed a means of determining distances within the solar system that enabled him to locate its center and to establish Earth's position within it.

Nov. 2, 1885	Born in Nashville, Missouri
1910	Receives an A.B. from the University of Missouri
1911	Receives an A.M. in astronomy from Missouri
1913	Receives a Ph.D. from Princeton
1914	Joins the staff at Mount Wilson Observatory in California
1918	Measures the Milky Way's dimensions and locates its center
1921	Becomes the director of Harvard Observatory
1926	Given the Draper Medal by the National Academy of Sciences
1927	Given an honorary LL.D. by the University of Missouri
1933	Granted honorary degrees form both Harvard and Princeton
1939	Made president of the American Academy of Arts and Sciences
1946	Helps found the United Nations Educational, Scientific, and Cultural Organization (UNESCO)
1947	Elected president of the American Association for the Advancement of Science
1956	Retires as director of Harvard Observatory
Oct. 20, 1972	Dies in Boulder, Colorado

Early Life

Harlow Shapley and his twin brother were born November 2, 1885, on the family hay farm in Missouri. Harlow had a pleasant childhood, but his early education was limited to a few years in a rural schoolhouse. At sixteen, he tried his luck as a crime reporter for a newspaper in Chanute, Kansas. While in Chanute, Shapley began to read history and poetry in the public library and decided to continue his education. He and a younger brother tried to enter high school but were not qualified to enroll.

Shapley did manage to attend a very small Presbyterian school and then to enroll at the University of Missouri. Because of his newspaper experience, he wanted to study journalism. A journalism major was not offered at the time, however, and he chose astronomy instead. One of his professors recommended him for a fellowship to attend graduate school at Princeton, and he enrolled there in 1911.

Finding the Size of the Milky Way

Shapley used the properties of Cepheid variable stars to establish a distance scale for the Milky Way.

Astronomers have long known that some stars change in brightness over fairly short periods of time. For some of these, called Cepheid variables, the longer it takes to brighten and then dim, the more luminous the star is. This characteristic was key to Shapley's discovery.

To an observer on Earth, a star's brightness depends on its luminosity and the distance to it. By measuring the time required for a Cepheid's brightening cycle, its luminosity can be determined using the relationship between period and luminosity. Then by comparing this luminosity to the observed brightness, the distance to the star can be computed. Shapley used this principle to locate globular clusters of stars within the Milky Way by determining the distance to Cepheids contained within them. Assuming these clusters to be uniformly distributed in the Galaxy, he was able to locate the center of the Milky Way and the position of Earth relative to it. The outcome established a distance scale for the Galaxy and showed that the sun is not near its center. The distances that he computed were far greater than previous estimates and forever changed the way that astronomers thought about the Milky Way.

Bibliography

Abell, George O., David Morrison, and Sidney C. Wolff. *Exploration of the Universe.* 5th ed. New York: Saunders College Publishing, 1987.

Bok, Bart J. and Priscilla F. Bok. *The Milky Way.* 4th ed. Cambridge, Mass.: Harvard University Press, 1974.

After receiving his Ph.D. in astronomy in 1914, Shapley was hired to work at the Mount Wilson Observatory in California. On his way to Mount Wilson, he stopped in Kansas City to marry Martha Betz, a college classmate whom he had met while at the University of Missouri.

Astronomical Research

At Mount Wilson, Shapley worked with Frederick Seares measuring the brightness and colors of stars and also made his own observations of stars whose brightness varied. He became interested in Cepheid variable stars and globular clusters.

This work formed the basis for his primary achievement: finding a way to determine the size of the Milky Way and the location of its center. He was also able to locate the sun within it. His estimates of distances within the Galaxy were distrusted at first by many astronomers but were eventually accepted.

Later Career

In 1921, Shapley was appointed director of the Harvard Observatory where he presided over a dramatic growth in the programs that soon attracted large numbers of top students. He also participated in the establishment of the National Science Foundation and the United Nations Educational, Scientific, and Cultural Organization (UNESCO). Shapley wrote numerous articles and books, many of which helped stimulate popular interest in astronomy. He became widely known and was awarded a total of seventeen honorary degrees.

Ants

Throughout his life, he pursued a curious side interest: He was fascinated by ants. He studied their behavior, collected specimens all over the world, and occasionally wrote articles describing his observations. Shapley died on October 20, 1972.

Bibliography

By Shapley

"The Scale of the Universe, Part I," *Bulletin of the National Research Council,* 1921.

Starlight, 1926.

Flights from Chaos: A Survey of Material Systems from Atoms to Galaxies, 1930.

Of Stars and Men, 1958.

The View from a Distant Star, 1963.

About Shapley

Camp, Carole Ann. *American Astronomers.* Springfield, N.J.: Enslow, 1996.

"Dr. Harlow Shapley." *Nature* 240 (1972).

Shapley, Harlow. *Through Rugged Ways to the Stars.* New York: Charles Scribner 's Sons, 1969.

(Cecil O. Huey, Jr.)

Vesto Melvin Slipher

Discipline: Astronomy

Contribution: Slipher's discovery that spiral nebulas are receding into space at extremely high speeds helped convince astronomers that these nebulas are independent galaxies and that the universe is expanding.

Nov. 11, 1875	Born in Mulberry, Indiana
1902	Starts spectrographic work at Lowell Observatory
1903	Measures the rotational speed of Venus
1904	Marries Emma Rosalie Munger
1906	Begins to study the spectra of spiral nebulas
1908	Finds calcium gas in space
1909	Receives a doctorate from Indiana University
1912	Identifies the Pleiades Nebula as dust reflecting local starlight
1912-1913	Discovers that the Andromeda Nebula is rapidly moving toward the sun
1915	Becomes an assistant director of Lowell Observatory
1919	Receives the Lalande Prize of the Académie des Sciences
1922	Wins the National Academy of Science's Draper Gold Medal
1926	Becomes the director of Lowell Observatory
1930	Supervises Clyde Tombaugh's discovery of Pluto
1933	Wins the Gold Medal of the Royal Astronomical Society
Nov. 8, 1969	Dies in Flagstaff, Arizona

Early Life

An Indiana farm boy, Vesto Melvin Slipher (pronounced "SLI-fur") was one of eleven children. He entered Indiana University at Bloomington, where he received a degree in mechanics and astronomy. After graduation, he found work at Lowell Observatory in Flagstaff, Arizona.

At that time, the observatory was highly controversial. Its director, Percival Lowell, incorrectly believed that Mars was covered with long, thin lines or "canals" built by Martians. Lowell also thought that he saw similar puzzling features on the surface of Venus and, by observing their motion, tried to time the Venusian rotation speed. To support his timing estimate, Lowell ordered Slipher to study Venus with a spectrograph— specifically, to measure its Doppler shift. In that way, Slipher found that Venus rotates much more slowly than generally thought.

Later, Slipher measured the rotation speeds of the planets Jupiter, Saturn, Uranus, and Mars. In

Slipher discovered that the Andromeda Nebula is moving toward the sun.

1908, while examining the spectrum of a binary star, he noticed a puzzling spectral line associated with calcium gas. He correctly concluded that the space between planets and stars is not empty. Rather, it contains vast clouds of gas. He also detected dust clouds in the Orion Nebula.

Spiral Nebulas

In 1913, using the spectrograph, Slipher made his greatest discovery. He observed that the spiral-shaped Andromeda Nebula is approaching the sun at hundreds of miles a second. Over the next decade, he found that most spiral nebulas are receding from the sun, some at much faster speeds. Astronomers later realized that the universe is expanding and that spiral nebulas are actually distant galaxies.

After Lowell's death, Slipher ran the observatory until 1952. Under his supervision, observatory staff member Clyde Tombaugh discovered the planet Pluto in 1930.

The Doppler Shift of the Andromeda Nebula

The large Doppler shift in its spectrum indicates that the Andromeda Nebula is moving at about 190 miles per second.

With a spectrograph attached to a telescope, an astronomer can measure the chemical composition and velocity of a star as it moves through space. The spectrograph breaks light from the star into a rainbow-like spectrum, which contains thin lines that represent chemicals in the stellar atmosphere. If the star is moving, then the lines shift position—the bigger the shift, the faster the star.

In the early twentieth century, many astronomers believed that spiral nebulas were clouds of dust and gas within the only known galaxy, the Milky Way. Perhaps the spiral nebulas were condensing into new planetary systems, they thought.

In late 1912 and early 1913, however, Slipher showed that the spiral nebula Andromeda had a remarkably high Doppler shift of about 190 miles per second. It was moving in the general direction of Earth's solar system. Later, he found other spiral nebulas moving faster than 1,000 kilometers per second. Unlike Andromeda, however, most spiral nebulas are moving away from the sun, as if fleeing into the outer universe.

Astronomers interpreted their high speeds to mean that spiral nebulas are, in fact, separate galaxies far from the Milky Way. As a typical galaxy contains billions of stars and is millions or billions of light-years away, the cosmos had to be far larger than previously thought.

In the 1920s, Edwin Hubble relied heavily on Slipher's work to show that the fastest spiral nebulas are also the most distant. This observation is best explained by assuming that the universe as a whole is expanding, like an inflating balloon. By the 1970s, most cosmologists attributed the expansion to the "big bang," a primordial explosion that spawned space, time, and matter billions of years ago.

Bibliography

Kragh, Helge. *Cosmology and Controversy: The Historical Development of Two Theories of the Universe.* Princeton, N.J.: Princeton University Press, 1996.

Hubble, Edwin. *The Realm of the Nebulae.* Reprint. New Haven, Conn.: Yale University Press, 1982.

Ferris, Yimothy. *The Red Limit: The Search for the Edge of the Universe.* New York: William Morrow, 1977.

Awards

Although little known to the general public, Slipher was highly esteemed by other astronomers. He received major international awards and also held high posts in the International Astronomical Union, the American Astronomical Society, and the American Association for the Advancement of Science. A savvy investor in local businesses and properties, he died a rich man a few days before his ninety-fourth birthday.

Bibliography

By Slipher

"A Spectrographic Investigation on the Rotational Velocity of Venus," *Lowell Observatory Bulletin*, 1903.

"Peculiar Star Spectra Suggestive of Selective Absorption of Light in Space," *Lowell Observatory Bulletin*, 1909.

"The Radial Velocity of the Andromeda Nebula," *Lowell Observatory Bulletin*, 1913.

"Spectrographic Observations of Nebulae," *Popular Astronomy*, 1915.

About Slipher

Putnam, William Lovell et al. *The Explorers of Mars Hill: A Centennial History of Lowell Observatory*, 1894–1994. West Kennebunk, Maine: Phoenix, 1994.

Graves Hoyt, William. *Lowell and Mars*. Tucson: University of Arizona Press, 1976.

Hall, J. S. "V M. Slipher's Trailblazing Career." *Sky and Telescope* 39 (February, 1970).

(Keay Davidson)

Fritz Zwicky

Disciplines: Astronomy and physics
Contribution: An original thinker in physics and astronomy, Zwicky helped discover neutron stars. His insights led indirectly to the theory of black holes, extremely dense material from which no light or gravitation can escape.

Feb. 14, 1898	Born in Varna, Bulgaria
1922	Earns a Ph.D. in theoretical physics from the Eidgenössiche Technische Hochschule in Zurich, Switzerland
1925	Travels to the United States and begins working at the California Institute of Technology (Caltech)
1931-1933	Becomes a colleague of Albert Einstein, a visiting professor at Caltech
1934	Along with astronomer Walter Baade, presents his theory of neutron stars
mid-1930s	Finds the first evidence of dark matter in the universe
1942	Becomes professor of astrophysics at Caltech
1943-1949	Serves as the scientific director of Aerojet General Corporation, one of the first companies to manufacture rocket engines
1945-1946	Travels to Germany and Japan to interview pioneers in jet propulsion research
1949	Receives a Presidential Medal of Freedom from Harry S. Truman
1957	Publishes his book *Morphological Astronomy*
Feb. 8, 1974	Dies in Pasadena, California

Early Life

Fritz Zwicky, born in Varna, Bulgaria, just before the turn of the twentieth century, lived in his native land only until he was six. At this young age, his Swiss father, Fridolin, and his Czechoslovakian mother, Franziscka, sent him to Switzerland for schooling. Zwicky excelled in the sciences and mathematics and gravitated toward engineering while still a teenager.

During World War I, Zwicky matriculated in the Eidgenössiche Technische Hochschule, a well-known technical institute in Zurich whose teachers included physicist Hermann Weyl. He passed his qualifying examinations in 1920 and gained his Ph.D. in theoretical physics two years later, in 1922, writing his thesis on the theory of ionic crystals. Coincidentally, this was seventeen years after Albert Einstein had received his doctorate from the University of Zurich. Zwicky was at one time Einstein's student; he later became the great German physicist's colleague while Einstein

was a visiting professor at the California Institute of Technology (Caltech) from 1931 to 1933.

Zwicky remained in Switzerland until 1925, when he became a postgraduate student at Caltech. There, he conducted research alongside the institute's Nobel Prize-winning president, Robert Millikan. Caltech appointed Zwicky assistant professor of theoretical physics in 1927. Two years later, he became associate professor, and finally, in 1942, professor of astrophysics.

Zwicky worked on several different problems within the realm of physics, ranging from rocket propulsion to the dynamics of colliding galaxies to the philosophy of science. By the late 1930s, he had published several papers on astronomy. These papers gradually uncovered the secrets of supernovas and neutron stars.

Work in Rocketry

Zwicky was among those twentieth century scientists who chose to work in rocketry while it was still new and experimental. In the 1940s, Zwicky helped design and test rocket boosters known as JATO's for the U.S. Army and Navy. The JATO, which stands for "jet-assisted takeoff," could be stored under a range of temperature conditions, would not explode upon ignition, and could boost aircraft into the air from short runways at a dramatically steep angle. The JATO was unusual not only because it was a reliable solid fuel rocket but also because its propellant was not a powder but rather a mixture of oxidizer and common asphalt.

Before Zwicky became involved in the JATO project in 1940, he actually failed to understand the potential importance of rocket development. In 1937, when Frank Malina, a young Caltech graduate student, tried to tell Zwicky some of the problems that he was having with his doctoral dissertation on liquid-propellant rockets, Zwicky angrily dismissed him with the opinion that he was wasting his time on an impossible subject. Zwicky

Neutron Stars and Dark Matter

In 1934, Zwicky, working alongside astronomer Walter Baade at the Mount Wilson Observatory, sketched out his vision of neutron stars. Nearly thirty-four years were to elapse before physicists began to accept the theory of neutron stars.

In the 1930s, when Zwicky first began writing about neutron stars, the theory was controversial. At the theory's heart lies the idea that electrons might be forced into the nuclei of stellar atoms and that stars could then become a mass composed only of neutrons. Zwicky and Baade, observing supernova explosions through the Mount Wilson Observatory telescope, believed that supernovas might form neutron stars. If, reasoned the two astronomers, a white dwarf were near the supernova, remnants of material from the exploding star might be absorbed by the white dwarf, which would then contract into an extremely dense core of material. (A white dwarf is a compact star near the end of its existence.)

Zwicky's work on neutron stars led to the possibility that other dense matter might exist in the universe, including black holes. Zwicky also pioneered in the study of the morphology of galaxies. He wondered how galaxies that collide avoid mutual destruction, since their individual stars move by each other so rapidly that it seems the galaxies would tend to fly apart. Yet, many do not. Could some nonluminous form of matter keep these large clustered galaxies together? Zwicky and fellow physicist Sinclair Smith had found the first evidence of dark matter in the universe.

Bibliography

Penrose, Roger. "Black Holes." *The World of Physics: A Small Library of the Literature of Physics from Antiquity to the Present*. Vol 3. New York: Simon and Schuster, 1987.

Hodge, Paul W. "Dark Matter in Spiral Galaxies." *The Universe of Galaxies*, New York: W. H. Freeman, 1984.

Riordan, Michael and David N. Schramm. *The Shadows of Creation: Dark Matter and the Structure of the Universe*. New York: W. H. Freeman, 1991.

insisted that a rocket could not operate in space, as it required the atmosphere to push against in order to provide thrust. By 1940, Zwicky had realized his mistake and worked alongside Malina. Even in the mid-twentieth century, it was difficult for some physicists to conceive of action in a vacuum.

It is ironic that Zwicky was not well known outside the field of astronomy and rocketry. When he died in 1974, his name became a footnote to the history of physics, and he has been remembered only slightly in the literature of physics. He did not gain recognition as one of the giants of astrophysics, as have Subrahmanyan Chandrasekar, Roger Penrose, and Stephen Hawking. Yet, Zwicky's writings were voluminous (559 publications) and his insights paved the way for the modern conception of the universe's past and its structure. His work formed a cornerstone of twentieth century astrophysical theory.

Bibliography

By Zwicky

"On the Thermodynamic Equilibrium in the Universe," *Proceedings of the National Academy of Sciences*, 1928.

"Types of Novae," *Reviews of Modern Physics*, 1940 *Catalogue of Selected Compact Galaxies and of Post-Eruptive Galaxies*, 1971 (with Margit A. Zwicky).

Morphological Astronomy, 1957.

About Zwicky

Payne-Gaposchkin, Cecelia. "A Special Kind of Astronomer." *Sky and Telescope* (1974).

Hoyle, Fred. "Presidential Addresses on the Society's Awards." *Quarterly Journal of the Royal Astronomical Society* 13 (1972).

(Benjamin Zibit)

Glossary

Atmosphere: The gaseous matter surrounding a celestial body that is held by that body's gravitational field.

Big bang theory: A theory that holds that the universe was produced at a single instant in time and at a single point in space and has been rapidly expanding and cooling ever since.

Binary stars: A pair of stars that orbits around each other.

Black hole: A collapsed star so dense that its gravitational field is strong enough to prevent the escape of any form of radiation, including light.

Blackbody: An ideal body that absorbs all radiation striking it and emits no radiation.

Celestial sphere: An imaginary sphere of infinite radius against which celestial objects such as the sun, moon, and stars seem to be projected, as viewed from Earth.

Comet: A celestial object that has either an elliptical orbit with high eccentricity or a parabolic path.

Cosmic rays: Ionizing radiation originating outside Earth's atmosphere and producing secondary radiation within the atmosphere through collisions or decay.

Dark matter: Invisible matter in the universe.

Diffraction: The modification of a wave by a barrier placed in its path.

Eccentricity: The degree of an orbit's deviation from a circle.

Eclipse: The partial or total obscuring of one celestial object by another, as viewed from a relative position on Earth.

Electromagnetism: The magnetism that arises from electrical charges in motion.

Element: A substance composed of atoms which all have the same number of protons in their nuclei.

Ellipse: An oval-shaped, closed curve defined by a fixed total distance from two points.

Equilibrium: The state of any system in which the net result of all acting forces is zero.

Ether: The all-pervasive, massless medium through which electromagnetic waves were once thought to propagate.

Fission: The breaking apart of a single entity into two pieces. In physics, large atoms break up into smaller fragments with the creation of energy. *Compare* **Fusion**.

Frequency: For periodic motions, the number of cycles occurring per unit of time.

Fusion: The joining of two pieces into a single whole. In physics, the joining of two light nuclei to form a heavier one with the release large amounts of energy. *Compare* **Fission**.

Galaxy: One of many large-scale aggregations of stars, dust, and gases in the universe that have some discernible structure.

Gravity: The force exerted by every body on every other body.

Heavy elements: Elements with atomic numbers greater than 150. Heavy elements will undergo fission into smaller fragments if sufficient excitation energy is provided. *Compare* **Light elements**.

Heliometer: A telescope in which the objective lens is cut along the diameter.

Inertia: The tendency of a body to remain either at rest or in motion.

Infrared light: Electromagnetic radiation with a wavelength just longer than the red portion of the visible spectrum.

Light elements: Elements with an atomic number less than about 50. These elements have a low binding energy and may undergo fusion to produce heavier elements if sufficient excitation energy is provided. *Compare* **Heavy elements.**

Light-year: The distance traveled by light in a vacuum in one year.

Magnitude: A measure of the apparent brightness of a star, from 1 (for the brightest stars) to 6 (for the dimmest visible stars).

Nebula: A cloud of interstellar dust and gas.

Neutron star: A star consisting of an extremely dense mass composed almost entirely of neutrons from which only neutrinos and very-high-energy photons can escape, making the star invisible.

Optics: The study of electromagnetic radiation in or near the visible portion of the spectrum.

Photon: A massless particle that carries electromagnetic force; often used to describe a packet of light.

Planet: A celestial object that orbits around a star and is not luminous.

Polarity: A property of a physical system that has two points or regions with different (usually opposite) characteristics.

Propagation: In physics, the traveling of light, sound, or radio waves through space or a material.

Pulsar: A rapidly spinning neutron star that emits periodic bursts of radio frequency radiation.

Quasar: A distant, starlike, and intense object that emits electromagnetic radiation.

Radiation: The process of emitting energy in any form. Also, electromagnetic energy in the form of waves with a characteristic frequency, amplitude, and phase.

Radioactivity: The emission of subatomic particles from unstable nuclei.

Reflection: The return of particles or waves from a surface that they strike.

Refraction: The change of direction of a wave as it moves out of one medium and into another medium with a different velocity of propagation. In astronomy, the change in the apparent position of a celestial object as the light coming from that object bends passing through the atmosphere.

Relativity: The theory that recognizes the universality of the speed of light and the dependence of measurements of space, time, and mechanical properties; also, the theory that attributes gravitational forces to fluctuations in the properties of space-time.

Space-time: The system of four coordinates—time and the three dimensions of space—in which a physical object or event can be located.

Spectroscopy: The branch of physics concerned with electromagnetic spectra.

Spectrum (pl. spectra): A plot of the intensity of radiation as a function of a given quantity, usually wavelength or frequency.

Steady state theory: A cosmological theory, no longer in favor, that proposes the continuous creation of interstellar matter at a rate which allows the universe to expand at the observed pace, while the mean density of matter remains constant.

White dwarf: Star of low mass that is reaching the end of its life. Typically, it has exhausted its thermonuclear fuel and has contracted to roughly the size of Earth.

A

Alhazen, 8–10
Anaximander, 11–12
Andromeda galaxy, 147, 149, 165
Arago, Francois, 58
Aristarchus of Samos, 13–14
asteroids, 89, 137
astronomical units (AUs), 39
astronomy
   rocket astronomy, 62–63
   satellite astronomy, 62
   sidereal astronomy, 88–89
   stellar astronomy, 110
atmospheric refraction, 40
AU (astronomical units), 39

B

Baade, Walter, 15–17
Babbage, Charles, 85
Bacon, Roger, 10
Barnard, Edward Emerson, 18–20
Barnard's Star, 19
Bessel, Friedrich Wilhelm, 23–25
Beta Aurigae, 128
big bang theory, first use of term, 97
birefringent prism, 60
black holes, 81, 83
Bondi, Hermann, 98
Brahe, Tycho. *See* Tycho
Burbridge, E. Margaret, 28–31
Burnell, Dame Jocelyn Bell, 20–22

C

Cannon, Annie Jump, 32–34
Carruthers, George R., 34–36
Cassini, Gian Domenico, 37–40
Cavalieri, Bonaventura, 38
CCDs (charge-coupled devices), 124
Centaurs, 125
Cepheid variable stars, 49, 102, 103, 162
C-field, 98
Chandrasekhar, Subrahmanyan, 41–43
Chandrasekhar limit, 42
collisions, 107
Columbus, Christopher, 144
comets

   Halley, Edmond, 79
   Mitchell, Maria, 134
   Oort cloud, 140
   tail, 137
   Tycho, 27
compass, 65
composition of stars, 142
conics, 9
Copernicus, Nicolaus, 44–46
   heliocentric universe, 14, 27
corpuscular theory of light, 108
cosmology
   Earth-centered, 8–9
   observational, 88
Crab Nebula, 16, 94
Cygnus A, 16
Cygnus X-1, 81, 83

D

dark matter, 29, 52, 147–148, 168
distribution of galaxies, 70
Doppler, Christian, 56, 102, 148
Doppler effect, 148
Doppler shift, Andromeda Nebula, 165
Doppler-Fizeau effect, 56

E

Earth
   distance to sun, 14
   rotation, 58–59
   shape, 40
Earth-centric universe, 27, 45, 144–145
eclipses, 49
Eddington, Arthur Stanley, 47–50, 142
Einstein, Albert, 48–49, 82
elliptical orbits, 113
Eta Carinae Nebula, 86
event horizon, 83
evolution, 12
expansion of the universe, 49, 157

F

Faber, Sandra, 51–53
Faber-Jackson relation, 53
falling objects, 65, 66
far-ultraviolet spectroscopy, 35, 36

Fizeau, Hippolyte, 54–56
flatness problem, 73
Foucault, Lèon, 57–60
Fowler, William A., 29
Friedman, Herbert, 61–64
Friedmann, Alexander, 122

G
galaxies
    classifications, 103
    dark matter, 148
    distribution, 147
    The Great Wall, 70–71
    large-scale distribution, 70
    Local Supercluster, 147
    photographing, 16
    redshift, 71
    rotation, 29, 139–140, 148
    structure, 139–140
Galileo, 64–68
Geller, Margaret, 69–71
geocentrism, 11
German V-2 rockets, 62–63
Goddard, Robert H., 62
Gold, Thomas, 94, 98
gravity
    Einstein's theory of gravitation, 49
    latitudes and, 40
    pendulum and, 40, 59
Great Attractor, 53, 147–148
Great Wall, 70–71
Grote, Harriet, 101
Guth, Alan H., 72–74
gyroscope, 58

H
Hale, George Ellery, 75–77
Hale Telescope, 77
Halley, Edmond, 78–80
Hawking, Stephen, 80–84
heliocentric universe, 13–14, 27, 46
heliography, 54
heliometer, 24
Herschel, Caroline, 85
Herschel, Sir John, 84–86
Herschel, Sir William, 85, 87–90

Herschel effect, 85
Hertzsprung, Ejnar, 90–93
Hertzsprung-Russell diagram, 151
Hewish, Antony, 21, 93–96
horizon problem, 73
Hoyle, Sir Fred, 29, 96–99
Hubble, Edwin Powell, 49, 100–103, 122, 157
Hubble's Constant, 102
Hubble's Law, 102
Huggins, Sir William, 104–106
Humason, Milton, 103
Huygens, Christiaan, 106–109

I
inertia, 66
inflationary universe, 73, 74
interferometer, 56, 131
intergalactic distance, 91–92
interstellar matter, 19
IPS (interplanetary scintillation), 94

J
Jackson, Robert, 53
JATO (jet-assisted takeoff), 167–168
Jupiter, 38, 67

K
Kapteyn, Jacobus Cornelius, 109–111
Kepler, Johannes, 28, 66, 112–114
Kuiper, Gerard Peter, 115-117, 125, 153
Kuiper belt, 117, 124–126

L
Lamaître, Georges, 120–123
latitude, 144
laws of motion, 66, 114
Leavitt, Henrietta Swan, 91–92, 118–120
LGM (Little Green Men), 94
light, 9
    speed, 55
    velocity, 58–59, 130
    wave theory, 55, 108
Lindblad, Bertil, 139
Local Supercluster, 147
longitude, 144
Luu, Jane X., 123–126

M
Mach, Ernst, 98
Magellanic Clouds, 86, 119–120
magnetic charts, 80
magnetic fields, sun, 76
magnetosphere, 95
mapmaking
  Anaximander, 11
  Ptolemy, 144
Mariner 9 mission to Mars, 153, 154
Mars
  Barnard, Edward Emerson, 19
  Mariner 9 mission, 153, 154
  rotational period, 107
mass-luminosity relation of stars, 49, 50
Matthews, Thomas, 156
Maury, Antonia, 127–129
Maxwell, James Clerk, 108, 109
measurements
  atmospheric refraction, 40
  Herschel effect, 85, 86
  intergalactic distance, 91–92
  parallax, 39
  precision, 27
  scale of solar system, 39
  sextants, 134
  speed of light, 55
  star brightness, 119
  triangulation, 24, 39
  Tycho, 27
Michelson, Albert Abraham, 129–132
Michelson-Morley experiment, 131
Milky Way
  Baade, Walter, and, 16
  Barnard, Edward Emerson, 19
  gas density changes, 160
  Local Supercluster, 147
  size, 162
  structure, 139–140
mirrors
  Foucault, Lèon, 60
  optics and, 9
Mitchell, Maria, 133–135
moon, 67, 68, 80
motion (Galileo), 66

N
nebulas
  Crab Nebula, 16
  Eta Carinae Nebula, 86
  Herschel, Sir John, 86
  Herschel, Sir William, 88
  Hubble, Edwin Powell, 101
  spiral, 165
Neptune, 67
neutron stars, 94, 95, 168
Newcomb, Simon, 18
Newton, Isaac
  corpuscular theory of light, 108
  Earth's rotation, 59
  Halley, Edmond, and, 79
No-Boundary theory, 81, 82
north polar sequence, 119
novas, 106
nucleosynthesis, 29, 30, 99

O
observational cosmology, 88
Olbers, Wilhelm, 136–138
Olbers' paradox, 157
Oort, Jan Hendrik, 138–140
Oort cloud, 140
optics, 8, 9–10
orbits, 113, 137
oscillators, wave theory of light and, 108

P
parabolic mirrors, 9
parallax measurement, 39, 92, 150–151
parallax of stars, 24
Pauli exclusion force, star collapse and, 95
Payne-Gaposchkin, Cecilia, 141–143
Peacock, George, 85
pendulums, 40, 58–59
Perfect Cosmological Principle, 98
period-luminosity law, 119
photometer, 60
photometry, 35
physics, theoretical, 82
Picard, Jean, 38
Pickering, Edward, 33

planetary motion, 145

planetary rotation, 38

Pluto, Kuiper belt and, 125

primeval atom, 121, 122

Ptolemy, 8–9, 27, 45, 46, 143–146

pulsars, 22

 Burnell, Jocelyn Bell, 21

 causes, 95

 LGM (Little Green Men), 94

Q

QB1 (Smiley), 124

quasars, 31, 158–161

Quasi Steady State theory, 98, 99

quasi-stellar objects. See quasars

R

Raman, Chandrasekhara Venkata, 41–43

Reber, Grote, 101

redshift, 71, 102

reflective telescope, 85

refracted starlight, 104–106

rocket astronomy, 62–63

rocketry, 167–168

Rubin, Vera C., 29, 146–149

Rubin-Ford effect, 148

Russell, Henry Norris, 149–151

Ryle, Martin, 21

S

Sagan, Carl, 152–155

Sandage, Allan Rex, 155–158

satellite astronomy, 62

Saturn, 40, 107

Schmidt, Bernhard Voldemar, 16

Schmidt, Maarten, 159–161

scintillation, 94

Shapley, Harlow, 161–163

sidereal astronomy, 88–89

Slipher, Vesto Melvin, 101, 102, 157, 164–166

smoothness problem, 73

sodium thiosulfate, 86

solar magnetic fields, 76

solar system

 development of, 117

 Galileo, 67

space density of stars, 110–111

spectral classification of stars, 32–33, 128

spectroheliograph, 76

spectroscope, 104–106

spectroscopic binary stars, 128

spectroscopy, 30

 far-ultraviolet, 35, 36

 Hertzsprung, Ejnar, 91

spectrum analysis of stars, 106, 111

speed of light, 55

spherical mirrors, 9

spiral nebulas, 165

starlight refracted by prism, 104–106

stars

 61 Cygni, 25

 absolute magnitude, 150–151

 Barnard's Star, 19

 brightness measurement, 119

 cataloging, 79, 110

 Cepheid variable, 49

 Chandrasekhar limit, 42

 classifications, 16, 91

 collapse, 95

 composition, 142

 Cygnus X-1, 81, 83

 density, 49

 distance calculation, 24

 Doppler-Fizeau effect, 56

 Herschel, Sir John, 86

 Hertzsprung-Russell diagram, 151

 light elements, 97

 luminosity, 88, 119

 mapping, 134–135

 mass-luminosity relation, 49, 50

 nucleosynthesis, 99

 observation benefits, 134

 parallax, 24

 pulsars, 22

 quasars, 31

 radiation from dust clouds, 140

 scintillation, 94

 space density, 110–111

 spectral classification, 32–33, 128, 150–151

 spectroscopic, 128

 spectrum analysis, 106, 111

 speed, 56

stellar structure, 49
Tycho, 27
X-rays, 81
steady state cosmological theory, 97–99
stellar astronomy, 110
stellar motion, 111
stellar parallax, 150–151
sun
magnetic fields, 76
photographs, 54, 58
position in sky, 40
size, 14
sundials, 13
sunspots, 76
supernova, 16, 17, 97
systematic errors, 24–25

T
telescopes
radio telescope, 21
reflective, 85
Thales, 11
theoretical physics, 82
thermometer (Galileo), 65
time-squared law (Galileo), 66
Tycho, 26–27, 28, 113

U
universe
evolution of, 82
expansion, 49, 157
inflationary, 73, 74
Uranus, 89

V
V-2 rockets (German), 62–63
Vaucouleurs, Gérard de, 147
velocity of light, 58–59, 130
Venus, rotation, 164–165

W
wave theory of light, 55, 108
women in science
Burnell, Jocelyn Bell, 22
Mitchell, Maria, 134
World War II, Baade, Walter, and, 16

X–Y–Z
X-ray
Friedman, Herbert, 63
stars, 81

Yerkes Observatory
Barnard, Edward Emerson, 19
Burbidge, E. Margaret, 29
Chandrasekhar, Subrahmanyan, 43
Hale, George Ellery, 76–77
Hubble, Edwin Powell, 101

Zeta Ursae Majoris, 128
Zwicky, Fritz, 16, 166–168